Globalization and Restructuring of African Commodity Flows

Edited by

Niels Fold and Marianne Nylandsted Larsen

NORDISKA AFRIKAINSTITUTET, UPPSALA 2008

Indexing terms:
Economic performance
International trade
Commodities
Commodity markets
Capital movements
Marginality
Globalization
Economic analysis
Case studies
Marginalization
Africa

Cover: Amigos Design
Language checking: Peter Colenbrander
Index: Rohan Bolton
ISBN 978-91-7106-616-9
© The authors and Nordiska Afrikainstitutet 2008
Printed in Sweden by 08 Tryck, Stockholm 2008

Contents

List of Tables

List of Figures

List of Abbreviations and Acronyms

A&R	Artists and Repertoire
AGOA	African Growth and Opportunity Act
ASEAN	Association of Southeast Asian Nations
ASSP	Agricultural Sector Support Programme
BMG	Bertelsmann Music Group
BRC	British Retail Consortium
BSE	Bovin Spongiform Encephalopati (mad cow disease)
CAD	Computer Aided Design
CAP	Common Agricultural Policy (of the European Union)
CBK	Coffee Board of Kenya
CBS	Citrus Black Spot
CD	Compact Disc
CFDT	Compagnie Française pour le Développement des Fibres Textiles
CIF	Cost, Insurance and Freight
CMB	Coffee Marketing Board
CMC	Cocoa Marketing Company
CMDT	Compagnie Malienne pour le Développement Textile
COCOBOD	Ghana Cocoa Board
CSCE	New York Coffee, Sugar and Cocoa Exchange
CSRP	Centrale de Sécurisation des Paiements et des Recouvrements
ECLA	Economic Commission for Latin America
EEC	European Economic Community
EMI	Electrical and Music Industries
EPZ	Export Processing Zone
EOI	Export Oriented Industrialization
EU	European Union
EUREPGAP	Euro-Retailer Produce Working Group Good Agricultural Practice
FAO	Food and Agriculture Organization
FDI	Foreign Direct Investment
FOB	Free On Board
FPEAK	Fresh Produce Exporters Association of Kenya
FPS	Full Package Supplier
GATT	General Agreement on Tariffs and Trade
GCC	Global Commodity Chain
GDP	Gross Domestic Product
GNP	Gross National Product
GMO	Genetically Modified Organism
GoM	Government of Mauritius

GVC	Global Value Chain
HACCP	Hazard Analysis Critical Control Point
HCDA	Horticultural Crop Development Authority
HVI	High Volume Instrument
ICA	International Coffee Agreement
ILO	International Labour Organization
ISI	Import Substitution Industrialization
ISO	International Organization for Standardization
ITMF	International Textiles Manufacturers Federation
LBC	Licensed Buyer Company
LIFFE	London International Financial Futures and Options Exchange
MERCOSUR	Mercado Común Sudamericano (Southern Common Market)
MFA	Multi Fibre Arrangement
MNC	Multi National Corporation
MRL	Maximum Residual Levels
NAFTA	North American Free Trade Agreement
NCB	Nigerian Cocoa Board
NIC	Newly Industrialized Countries
OBM	Own Brand Manufacture
ODM	Own Design Manufacture
OECD	Organisation for Economic Co-operation and Development
OEM	Own Equipment Manufacture
PPECB	Perishable Products Export Control Board
QC	Quality Control
SACCE	South African Cooperative Citrus Exchange
SAP	Structural Adjustment Program
SITC	Standard International Trade Classification
SPS	Sanitary and PhytoSanitary agreement
TEU	Twenty-Foot Equivalent Units (intermodal shipping container)
TNC	Trans National Corporation
UCDA	Uganda Coffee Development Authority
UGEA	Uganda Ginners and Exporters Association
UN	United Nations
UNCTAD	United Nations Conference on Trade and Development
URAA	Uruguay Round Agreement on Agriculture
USDA	United States Department of Agriculture
USSR	Union of Soviet Socialist Republics
WFP	World Food Programme
WTO	World Trade Organisation
WWI	First World War
WWII	Second World War

1. Globalization as Marginalization of African Economies?

Marianne Nylandsted Larsen and Niels Fold

Introduction

During the 1990s, the participation of developing countries in the global economy increased tremendously in terms of both world merchandise trade and private capital inflows. The decade's annual growth in trade and foreign investments involving developing countries surpassed by far their growth in production terms. At the same time, the deeper functional integration, on a global scale, of productive activities in these countries further accelerated economic globalization in those countries. However, the involvement of sub-Saharan African economies lagged far behind countries in other continents. Africa's share of world exports declined from 6 per cent to 2 per cent from the early 1980s to the late 1990s, and its annual growth in terms of world exports seriously trailed export growth in dynamic East and Southeast Asia. Moreover, apart from some oil- and mineral-rich countries, most economies in the continent failed to attract foreign direct investment. Whereas private inflows as a percentage of GNP averaged about 4 per cent for developing countries as a group, the figure for Africa was less than 2 per cent during the 1990s (UNCTAD 2000; UNCTAD 2003).

Several explanations have been put forward to account for sub-Saharan Africa's poor economic performance in ongoing processes of globalization, or what observers consider the progressive marginalization of most African national economies in the world economy. In broad terms, the causal factors can be located within two broad explanatory frameworks focusing primarily on domestic conditions and external constraints respectively. These explanatory frameworks are outlined in the following two sections. In the third and final section of this introduction we provide an overview of each of the chapters in this volume.

However, sweeping statements and general explanatory frameworks do little to uncover the variety of different processes actually taking place 'on the ground' in African economies during the present phase of globalization. This is because they are not operating at a level of analysis sufficiently detailed to add to our understanding of the real nature of economic linkages between African societies and global markets. This book seeks to identify and unveil some of the different ways in which African economic activities are incorporated into global dynamics by adopting a common analytical approach known as Global Value Chain (GVC) analysis. This approach does not lead to sets of comprehensive and general explanations, but rather to sensitive understandings of causality and the context of key globalization dynamics. In Chapter 2, we present the analytical dimensions of GVC analysis, followed by an outline of the debate related to external (public) regulation and global value chains. We also sketch the debates on two key concepts provided by the GVC approach, namely 'chain governance' and 'upgrading' in global value chains. Finally, we point out some methodological issues relevant to the analysis of concrete global value chains.

Domestic conditions

The explanations discussed in this section emphasize the role of domestic conditions and policy mistakes in impeding economic growth in sub-Saharan Africa. This view goes back to the so-called 'Berg Report' (World Bank 1981), which called for a move away from state intervention in economic activities and a 'freeing' of markets (Dorward et al. 1998:2). The early versions were followed up during the 1980s and early 1990s with more elaborate policies for the introduction of an efficient market system without price distortions through liberalization, deregulation and privatization. A third and more nuanced view during the late 1990s advocated a new and more active role for the state in the promotion of economic development by improving markets and facilitating the emergence of certain institutions. The last strand also includes causal factors that are traditionally referred to as geographical determinants.

According to these explanations, openness to foreign trade and investment has played an important facilitating role in accelerating growth and poverty reduction in a large group of developing countries over the last couple of decades. In contrast, lack of openness and integration with the world economy have increased inequality between countries, since closed developing economies have performed much more poorly than more open ones. Hence, some developing countries (including most countries in sub-Saharan Africa[1]) have become increasingly marginalized in the 'new wave of globalization', suffering declining incomes and rising poverty over the same

---

1. Hereafter 'Africa'.

period due to the inability of these countries to achieve greater integration (World Bank 2000).

Collier and Dollar (2002) argue that one of the main reasons several developing counties have become 'globalizers'[1] is that they have succeeded in harnessing their abundance of labour to give them a competitive advantage in labour-intensive manufacturing and services (e.g., China, Bangladesh, Sri Lanka, India and Indonesia). The successful diversification of the export base towards services and manufacturing has been accompanied by changing economic policies in both developed and developing countries. Tariffs on manufactured goods in developed countries continued to fall, and many developing countries undertook major liberalization of their trade and investment regimes. Subsequently, as the 'more globalized' developing countries reformed and became integrated into the world market, they started to grow rapidly and entered a virtuous circle of rising growth and rising penetration of world markets. In contrast, most of the 'less globalized' developing countries, including most countries in Africa, are still primarily dependent on the export of a narrow range of primary commodities, and they often suffered from deteriorating and volatile terms of trade in the markets for those commodities (Collier and Dollar 2002:31–6).

Although external barriers (for example, those caused by continued protectionism in key OECD markets) and the geographical disadvantages of many African countries[2] may be part of the explanation for the economic marginalization of the continent, this set of explanations considers significantly improved domestic conditions and economic policies to be absolutely necessary in order for developing countries to 'break out' of economic marginalization. This entails not only the further liberalization of trade: the entire investment climate must also be improved, from infrastructure through to the supporting institutions.

1. Collier and Dollar (2002) adopt a distinction between 'more globalized' and 'less globalized' developing countries, based on a classification of the extent to which a country increased trade relative to income between the 1970s and 1990s. The 'more globalized' developing countries constitute the top third of developing countries in terms of increased trade to GDP. These countries are Argentina, Bangladesh, Brazil, China, Colombia, Costa Rica, Côte d'Ivoire, the Dominican Republic, Haiti, Hungary, India, Jamaica, Jordan, Malaysia, Mali, Mexico, Nepal, Nicaragua, Paraguay, the Philippines, Rwanda, Thailand, Uruguay and Zimbabwe. The 'less globalized' group consists of all the other developing countries for which data are available (Collier and Dollar 2002:51).

2. Most countries in Africa are land-locked and the infrastructure is severely underdeveloped in many of them. Thus, according to Collier and Dollar (2002), transport costs to OECD markets are even more of a barrier to integration than the trade policies of developed countries (see below).

This view is supported by a number studies comparing the performance of Africa and other developing country regions (among others, see Collier and Gunning (1999), Akyüz and Gore (2001) and Rugumanu (2002)).

For instance, Collier and Gunning group different explanations for the poor economic performance of Africa (relative to other developing country regions) in a two-by-two matrix, differentiating between policy and exogenous 'destiny' on the one hand, and between domestic and external factors on the other (1999:6). Drawing on an assessment of these different explanations, they argue that, 'while the binding constraint upon Africa's growth may have been externally-oriented policies in the past, those policies have now been softened. Today, the chief problem is those policies which are ostensibly domestically-oriented, notably poor delivery of public services' (ibid. 20). Therefore, the authors suggest that domestic policies largely unrelated to trade may now be the main obstacles to growth in much of Africa (ibid. 18)

As for the general investment climate in African economies, most governments have until recently been unambiguously hostile to capital, altering public policy at will and threatening the security of property rights. This lack of policy consistency and security for private capital is the main reason Africa is marginalized in relation to foreign direct investment (Rugumanu 2002; Collier and Pattillo 2000). In a comparative perspective, rapid economic growth in successful cases (Asia) has been underpinned by rising rates of savings, investment and exports, linked together in a virtuous circle. Typically, savings and exports both rose faster than income and investment for two to three decades, gradually closing the savings and foreign exchange gaps. Such a process of sustained rapid growth has generally been absent in Africa, with the notable exceptions of Botswana and Mauritius. Hence, besides policy inconsistency, the reversal of the investment boom in Africa appears to have been caused by the failure to establish a virtuous circle of growth involving complementary increases in savings and imports (Akyüz and Gore 2001). Even where adjustment policies have been rigorously implemented, they have failed to establish a sustained process of accumulation linking investment with savings and exports. Consequently, although structural adjustment policies may have contributed to economic recovery in a number of countries, particularly where they were adequately financed, hardly any country has successfully completed its programmes with a return to sustained growth. Growth thus continues to remain at the mercy of the weather, world commodity prices and aid flows (ibid.).

These explanations have been 'spiced up' in recent years with studies emphasizing 'domestic destiny factors' or 'geographical disadvantages' as important causes, while at the same time revising some more orthodox arguments (see above). Instead, poor resource endowments (e.g., poor land quality, human diseases), civil strife and political unrest due to ethnic conflict are stressed as major factors impeding economic growth. Furthermore, many of the countries that have failed to enter global manufacturing markets suffer from the fundamental disadvantages of their land-locked locations. Hence, as Collier and Dollar note (2002:39), these studies show that, even when policies, institutions and infrastructure are 'right', a landlocked and malaria-infested country will not be competitive in manufacturing or in services such as tourism.

For instance, Wood (2002) argues that because Africa is land-abundant, the continent will always have a larger primary sector and a smaller manufacturing sector than the land-scarce (and labour-abundant) regions of Asia and Europe. In addition, as Wood puts it, 'because much of Africa's land is far from the sea, which raises internal transport costs, a prosperous Africa would resemble North America in having a relatively unpopulated interior based on agriculture and mining, with urban industrial concentrations on its coasts' (2002:1). The critical geographical constraints are aggravated by the location of most African countries in the tropics, where agricultural productivity is low due to degrading soil quality, and morbidity is high, as the health of plants, animals and humans is being undermined. Hence, the afflictions of a tropical climate are explanations both for low rates of investment and for low levels of human and agricultural productivity (Wood 2002).[1]

External constraints

A second set of explanations has mainly, but not exclusively, stressed the importance of external market constraints (international trade regulations, non-trade barriers such as food-safety standards, preferential trade agreements, etc.) and the conditions set by the global political economy. We start with the latter.

---

1. However, others have challenged 'the curse of the tropics' argument (Collier and Gunning 1999) by pointing to the agricultural and economic success of some tropical countries in East Asia, where growth was based on the introduction of new technologies in agriculture and the elimination of malaria.

Arrighi (2002) advances a world-historical perspective on the 'African Tragedy' and suggests that the experiences of Africa need to be located within 'the broader bifurcation of Third World destinies that has taken place since 1975' (Arrighi 2002:5). While recognizing that the long-term growth potential of African economies has partly been undermined by the policies of African elites in restraining the growth of agricultural productivity and domestic markets ('perverse growth' in Arrighi's terminology), world capitalism and global circuits of capital have played a key role in constraining and shaping developmental efforts and outcomes at the national level. In comparison with other Third World regions,[1] Africa fared poorly in terms of economic growth rates over the period from 1960 to the late 1990s, but this negative record is almost entirely a post-1975 phenomenon. As Arrighi (2002:16) points out, up to around 1975 the African performance was not significantly worse than the world average and actually better than that of South Asia. However, since 1975, Africa's growth rates have continued to decline relative to the other major Third World regions. Although 'perverse growth' may partially explain the African collapse, it can hardly account for its full extent. The collapse was integral to a broader change in tendencies among First and Third World regions, and the African tragedy must therefore be explained in terms of both the forces that brought about this transformation (and bifurcation between regions) and those that made its impact on Africa particularly severe. Arrighi (2002) provides two main (and interrelated) explanations for the deterioration of economic conditions in Africa from the 1970s onwards:

1. The nature of the crises that overtook world capitalism in the 1970s and the response of the US, the global hegemonic power. The US became the world's main debtor nation and by far the largest recipient of foreign capital in the 1980s (as opposed to earlier decades, when the US had been the major source of world liquidity and of direct investment). This is the single most important determinant of the contemporaneous reversal in the economic fortunes of North America and of the bifurcation in the economic fortunes of Third World regions (Arrighi 2002:18–22).

2. The emergence of the so-called 'Washington consensus', which resulted in a further bifurcation of Third World regions. The Washington consensus succeeded in inducing Third World countries to adapt their economies to the new conditions of accumulation on a world scale that had been created by the redirection of capital flows towards the US.

---

1. Latin America, the Middle East and North Africa, South Asia and East Asia.

Developing countries were forced to open up their national economies to intensified world-market competition and to rival both each other and First World countries in creating the greatest possible freedom of movement and action for capitalist enterprise within their jurisdictions (Arrighi 2002:23).

Within this perspective, recent region-wide initiatives to alter the position of Africa in the global economy are not regarded as significantly changing the situation. According to Taylor and Nel (2002), the 'New African Initiative'[1] might result in a further marginalization of the majority of Africa's peoples, while granting a highly privileged stratum of African elites the potential to benefit from ongoing globalization. The authors argue that the New African Initiative fits the neo-liberal discourse and avoids blaming Africa's marginalization on particular policies or global trade structures (ibid. 164). Instead, African and Northern elites blame the mystical notion that is known as 'globalization'. In addition, leading elements in Africa have gained the North's seal of approval regarding their outward commitment to liberal democracy and market economics. As a result, the message of this group will serve to legitimize existing global power relations rather than restructure them. No analytical attention is paid to other sources and loci of power and privilege in global affairs, such as transnational classes or multinational corporations. Accordingly, Taylor and Nel argue (ibid. 176) that the problem with globalization is not so much that it has restricted state autonomy or eroded sovereignty, but that its logic induces states to opt to be instruments of competition rather than of development.

The impact of global trade dynamics on Africa's marginalization has traditionally been cast as a question of declining export prices and a sharp deterioration in external financial conditions (see, for instance, UNCTAD 1996, 1999, 2003). Conceptualized in the overall perspective of the role of external factors, the marginalization of Africa in world trade is a reflection of the continent's inability to expand its productive capacity, rather than of its resistance to openness. According to UNCTAD (1999), the conventional emphasis on trade, as opposed to investment and accumulation, is thus misplaced. In addition, as noted by UNCTAD (2003), macroeconomic policy reforms in African countries are unlikely to be effective without complementary action being taken at the international level. In particular, this requires a renewed commitment to an international commodity policy

---

1. Launched in July 2001 at a summit of the Organisation of African Unity (subsequently the African Union).

that mitigates the adverse effects of instability and secular decline in commodity prices, as well as providing market access for exports from African countries (UNCTAD 2003:55).

The marginalization issue, however, is increasingly being positioned in the debate over the role of international trade regulations such as the WTO or regional trade organisations (the African Growth and Opportunity Act, the Cotonou Agreement, etc.).[1] As tariffs are falling (including those on agriculture), non-tariff barriers are increasing. Standards such as sanitary and phytosanitary requirements now constitute a potential constraint on the expansion of African agricultural and food exports. The emergence of these standards and technical regulations, including the procedures and technical mechanisms for the assessment of conformity to them, may contribute to the marginalization of ill-equipped countries, especially the least developed countries (UNCTAD 1999, 2001). In relation to international negotiations on standard-setting, the active participation of African countries is not simply a question of attending the meetings of various bodies but, more importantly, the technical capacity to understand and contribute to the process of international standard-setting.[2]

The contents of the book

Somewhat contrary to the writers discussed above, the contributors to this book argue that African countries have been incorporated into present processes of economic globalization in a much more nuanced way. Obviously, structural change and economic growth have not reached the scope seen in other developing country regions, Southeast Asia in particular. But the

---

1. Mattoo et al. (2002) focus on the African Growth and Opportunity Act (AGOA) and argue that, although the AGOA will provide real opportunities for Africa, the medium-term gains could have been much greater if it had not imposed certain conditions and not excluded certain items from its coverage. The most important condition is the stringent rule of origin, i.e., the requirement that exporters source certain inputs from within Africa or the United States. They estimate that the absence of these restrictions would have magnified the impact nearly fivefold, resulting in an overall increase in non-oil exports of US$0.54 billion compared with the US$100–140 million increase that is expected with these restrictions.

2. For instance, within the WTO, sanitary and phytosanitary (SPS) measures are based on 'international standards' that basically reflect developed-country norms and practices. The extent to which these measures may influence the external market access of Africa's agricultural and food products is determined by the compliance ability of African countries to upgrade production and quality-control facilities, as well as laboratories for testing and certification (Otsuki et al. 2001, Oyejide et al. 2000, UNCTAD 2003).

increasing global interaction between functionally integrated foci of production and services also affects Africa in new ways that are substantially changing the material foundations for economic and social life on the continent. These processes are not identical throughout the continent, but affect local, national and regional actors and institutions in many diverse and complex ways. In other words, globalization in Africa is an uneven process, integrating or re-integrating some localities and communities in global flows of goods, finance and information, while marginalizing or excluding others.

The aim of this book is to grasp Africa's diversity of relations in processes of globalization in a systematic manner. The contributors have worked together on the research programme entitled 'Globalization and Economic Restructuring in Africa', in which a common methodology was applied in order to conceptualize and examine the dynamics behind globalization processes. The Global Value Chain (GVC) approach[1] forms the common analytical point of departure for the contributors, who have elaborated on its original form, as developed by the American sociologist Gary Gereffi, by integrating insights from French filière and convention theory as well as from the 'New Institutional Economics' (Raikes et al. 2000). In this volume, commodity chain-specific data in two or more countries are taken as a point of departure for each of the analyses, which examine the variations and similarities in linkages between local, national, regional and global chain segments. The book is based on original quantitative as well as qualitative data collected during fieldwork undertaken by the authors. In addition, official statistics and 'grey' literature have been used: that is to say, reports from government institutions, business associations, private consultancy firms, etc. Furthermore, thanks to the broader context dealt with in the individual chapters, previously published research on specific commodities is also referred to.

In the following chapter (Chapter 2), we outline the key concepts and debates within the GVC approach. We start by introducing the analytical elements that constitute GVC analysis, originally conceptualized as 'dimensions' by Gereffi (1994, 1999). Secondly, we sketch the debate on governance, which is considered to be the most important analytical dimension, as it broadly determines the societal dynamics within the chain, encompassing

---

1. The approach known as 'Global Value Chain' first appeared in the literature under the term 'Global Commodity Chain' (GCC). The 'value chain' concept is thought to be better at capturing a wider variety of products, some of which lack 'commodity' features. However, in this collection of articles, the terms 'value chain' and 'commodity chain' will be used interchangeably.

the social and spatial division of labour among firms and the strategies to maintain or possibly strengthen their relative positions. Thirdly, we consider the role of public regulation in GVC analysis. Fourthly, we provide a brief overview of the different positions and concepts applied in the debate on upgrading, the most salient policy-related issue originating from the academic debate on GVC analysis. Finally, we point out two issues relevant to the delimitation and specification of concrete chains, namely questions about the length and breadth of the GVC.

The chapters in this book deal with these core issues, although their relative importance varies according to the particular objective of the study. In order to illuminate the nature and importance of the key concepts and issues, we use examples from the individual chapters. Hence, Chapter 2 primarily serves to introduce the common analytical framework while at the same time – hopefully – arousing the reader's curiosity about the substantive content of the book.

In Chapter 3, Benoit Daviron provides an account of the historical significance of agricultural policies in shaping competition in international food markets. Drawing on the Food Regime Perspective, Daviron argues that agricultural policies are determined by 'global norms' that define most of the objectives and instruments adopted at national levels in different states under different regimes. Three food regimes are identified, consisting of distinct complexes that have had different significance for the evolution of the participation of developing countries in international trade. The first period, between the mid-nineteenth century and 1914, was characterized by the emergence of world markets for staple food products and led to various territories specializing in the production of staple foodstuffs for export. The second period (1914 to the 1970s) marked the end of the first period of the globalization of foodstuffs markets. In the context of 'nation-centred' growth and the great support given to agricultural protectionism, international trade in agricultural products displayed extremely moderate growth. Developing countries that had previously specialized in food production found themselves being subjected to marginalization in the international food trade by losing their positions as the suppliers of industrialized countries. The third period is characterized by the emergence of the globalization project as an alternative to nation-centred growth, following privatization, deregulation and the opening up of national markets in both OECD countries and developing countries.

Daviron argues that the position of developing regions in international food markets during the last regime has been characterized by a number of different trajectories. Latin America succeeded in preventing its decline in international trade thanks to a double process of diversification: product diversification and geographical diversification. In terms of products, Latin America exports moved from the 'traditional tropical food' complex to the livestock, fresh fruits and vegetables and 'legal drugs' complexes. Asian food exports grew at a rapid pace, pulled by the emergence of the East Asian import food complex (notably meat imports) and the development of export-oriented economic policies. Africa is the only region with a market share that is continuing to decline. However, the composition of its food exports is changing rapidly, with its increasing insertion into the fresh fruits and vegetables and legal drugs complex, for instance, wines from South Africa, tobacco from Malawi and horticultural products from Kenya.

Examining some of these new agricultural export crops in the producing countries, the next two chapters aim to explain the causes of exclusionary effects on producers and regions. In Chapter 4, Charles Mather takes as his starting point a remarkable feature of South Africa's citrus export industry in the previous century, namely the resilience of its single channel system. For almost sixty years, between 1940 and the late 1990s, a single organization coordinated all of the country's citrus exports. Known first as the South African Citrus Exchange and later renamed Outspan International, this organization's control over citrus exports allowed it to establish an impressive infrastructure for citrus production and distribution that included nurseries, research laboratories and cooling and packing facilities, both locally and overseas. By the mid-1990s, Outspan International had also established overseas offices in North America, Europe and Asia. When sanctions against South Africa were lifted in the early 1990s, the single channel exporter responded immediately and soon regained its place as the most important southern hemisphere producer of citrus.

While Outspan International benefited from the lifting of sanctions, its exclusive control over citrus exports came to an end following the broader liberalization of South Africa's economy after apartheid. In 1997, new marketing legislation was introduced and citrus exports were 'deregulated'; for the first time in almost sixty years, independent agents could export South African citrus. The impact of this change on the industry in South Africa, and indeed the entire region, has been far-reaching. In the first year after deregulation, more than 150 new agents, both local and foreign, could be found competing for the produce of some 1,200 citrus growers in South Africa, Zimbabwe, Swaziland and Mozambique. Mather considers three key themes in the re-regulation of citrus markets. First, the issue of 'quality' in the fragmented channel has become a key arena of negotiation and struggle between growers, exporters and importers. Secondly, although the market is in theory more competitive, in the past year export agents and growers have both consolidated their positions, thus leading to the re-regulation of the citrus market. Finally, power relations within the chain have shifted in predictable but also surprising ways, and Mather's chapter considers the impact of deregulation on the power of the various actors in the chain.

Chapter 5 contributes to the general debate on the export potential of smallholder farmers. In it, Michael Friis Jensen focuses on one particular constraint for smallholder participation, namely the use of standards. Specifically, the effect of a number of standards on smallholder participation in the export trade of fresh horticultural products from Kenya is analysed. Standards are defined broadly as any kind of non-price measure, such as buyer requirements for high quality, rules for pesticide residues and demands for so-called ethical production and trading practices. Standards may be either public or private. In the first part of the chapter, the general pros and cons of smallholder participation in the export trade are discussed and an analytical framework using the New Institutional Economics is established. There is a special focus on the role played by measurement costs. In the second part, the historical experience of Kenyan export horticulture is described, especially the role in it played by smallholders. Three stages are identified. During the first, smallholders were frequently involved through open market exchanges; in the second, smallholders became contract farmers; and finally, in the third and current phase, smallholders are being marginalized and replaced by large-scale, vertically integrated, producer-exporter companies.

Jensen concludes that new, stringent buyer requirements – sometimes backed by national legislation – have led to the exclusion of smallholders from the most dynamic and profitable parts of the trade. The main vehicle of change has been the increased incentives for vertical integration provided by demands to make the product traceable back through the commodity chain through all its stages, from final consumer to primary producer. This trend is likely to continue due to increasing standards in selected areas, such as food safety and ethical concerns.

In Chapter 6, Niels Fold and Stefano Ponte also deal with the effects of quality and standards. Although the descriptive and normative parameters of 'quality' have not formally changed with coffee and cocoa market liberalization in Africa, the practice of quality control has. When the opening-up of domestic procurement to the private sector started in the late 1980s and early 1990s, local traders and exporters rushed to secure market shares to avoid being marginalised in the trade. Practices such as offering the same producer price, irrespective of product quality, and buying without proper quality control in order to increase the velocity of capital circulation, have contributed to losses of reputation and of export price premiums. On the other hand, where domestic procurement has not been liberalized, as in Kenya (coffee) and Ghana (cocoa), the quality and reputation of the export commodities have remained fairly constant. On a comparative cross-regional (East vs. West Africa) and cross-commodity (coffee vs. cocoa) basis, Fold and Ponte emphasize the similarities and divergences in different liberalization-cum-quality deterioration processes. Three key sets of questions are considered. First, how was bean quality influenced by the comprehensive liberalization that took place in some national commodity chains and not others? Secondly, what political and regulatory attempts were made by state institutions to maintain specific quality control procedures and incentives? And finally, what is the role of changing corporate strategies on quality and deregulation at the international level?

Shifting the focus to another of Africa's traditional export commodities, in Chapter 7 Marianne Nylandsted Larsen considers contrasting performances and different relations between African cotton-producing countries and the world market. The liberalization of cotton marketing systems and the introduction of private companies have to a large extent enhanced the performance of many cotton systems in sub-Saharan Africa. However, declines in the quality of export crops indicate that liberalization has created serious quality-control problems. Larsen examines different aspects of cotton production and quality in deregulated marketing systems. The first part explores recent changes in the global cotton market, focusing on the structure of world trade, price developments, and the function of international traders as bridges between the spinners and exporters of cotton lint. There is a specific focus on recent developments in lint quality calibration, the changing significance of lint quality in end-markets and the implications of this for international traders' and spinners' sourcing strategies in producing countries.

Against the background of these considerations, the second part explores recent changes in the role of various Anglophone and Francophone cotton-producing countries in the world market. This reflects experiences with different types of cotton market organization and coordination since the implementation of market reforms in the mid-1990s. Larsen argues that the differences between cotton sectors in terms of safeguarding the reputation of the national crop are to a large extent a consequence of the ability of their private players to maintain product quality and, secondly, of whether some form of private coordination has emerged as a 'substitute' for the former state-coordinated quality-control and input-supply systems.

Leaving the 'proper' commodity chains, in Chapter 8 Peter Gibbon examines Africa's changing role within the global value chain for clothing through a discussion of developments in the European and US clothing retail sectors on the one hand, and in the clothing industry of Mauritius on the other. The clothing chain starting in Mauritius is characterized by a high level of end-market segmentation. The great majority of enterprises produce very largely for either the US or EU markets alone. Against this background, Gibbon traces the bifurcation of the export clothing industry of Mauritius with regard to its end market. He argues that differences in end-market orientation correspond systematically to differences concerning ownership, business cultures, overhead structures and labour processes. The US-destined chain was hierarchical and embodied a series of impersonal structures or practices that were lead-agent imposed. The governance structure of the EU-destined chain was more egalitarian and embodied more personally negotiated practices. These differences were associated with the considerably higher bargaining power of suppliers in the EU-destined chain than in the US-destined chain.

Differences in the governance structures of the two sub-chains or filaments of the chain in Mauritius were associated with different kinds of learning opportunities for suppliers. The experience of working in the US-destined chain appeared to give rise to certain narrow but highly structured learning experiences centred on process-related competence. On the other hand, the experience of working in the EU-destined chain allowed for broader but probably also more diffuse learning experiences, centred on competences related to functional versatility. In conclusion, Gibbon critically reviews some of the central elements and unsolved questions of the GVC analysis in the light of recent developments in two Mauritian filaments of the global chain for clothing.

One of the prerequisites of the present phase of globalization has been the reduction of transport costs during the last thirty years, which came about through the so-called logistics revolution, containerization and the rapid restructuring of the transport industry. Together, these led to increased coordination between production and transportation, a focus on multi-modal transportation and an increasing development of hub-and-spoke patterns in transport systems. In Chapter 9, Poul Ove Pedersen shows how slow these processes have been to materialize in Africa. Transport costs are still extremely high compared to most other parts of the world. On the basis of fieldwork in Ghana (cocoa), Zimbabwe (cotton) and Tanzania (coffee), Pedersen examines the changes taking place in three sections of the different transport chains as a result of both national and global structural adjustment, namely the shipping and forwarding industry, inland transport by rail and road and rural transport, mostly head-loading and intermediate means of transport such as bicycles and ox-carts.

Pedersen concludes that the logistical revolution has had only a limited impact on African transport systems, partly because the parastatal organization of the agricultural trade (developed during the import-substitution era) tended to insulate them from its effects. However, structural adjustment policies introduced in both trade and transport organization have led to mutual adaptation and coordination between the commodity and transport chains. Furthermore, with deregulation and privatization, the power to control rural transport and the interest in doing so have both disappeared. As a result, the availability of both motorized and non-motorized intermediate means of transport has increased rapidly in many rural areas.

Finally, in Chapter 10, Tuulikki Pietilä discusses 'World Music' of African origin. She critically reviews some of the findings of previous World Music research and develops a non-traditional approach by adding two different theoretical discussions of globalization: that is, sociological studies of the structures of the global music industry and the political economy discussion of global commodity chains. The point that brings these three otherwise different theoretical traditions together is that power and its distribution constitute central questions in each of the three branches of research.

Existing studies have often concentrated on the system or macro-level of analysis and have seen the World Music industry as either an all-consuming transnational industry, a system that leaves little space for autonomy for minor actors on the one hand, or as a system that leaves the potential for alternative spaces for the minor actors within the system on the other. While acknowledging that existing research gives some idea of the structures and nodes of power in the global music industry and of their changes, Pietiä suggests importing some of the ideas of Global Value Chain analysis, namely its focus on both the structuring and enabling aspects of networks, in order to be able to examine properly questions of power and agency in World Music and to emphasize the role of both African and Western agents in building the institution. The distinction in GVC analysis between power as the ability to control others and power as empowerment avoids the tendency in the

World Music research to take an either–or position in relation to the issues of dominance and agency. The World Music markets are in the West, and the key actors defining what qualifies for release in the World Music market and what that music should sound like are usually people based in or with strong connections to the West. Based on a distinction between what Pietilä calls the celebrity chains (chains that are often initiated by a famous Western musician and take the form of collaboration with a non-Western musician or band) and the regular chains (the less visible but more frequent paths for non-Western music into World Music markets), the chapter considers who the key agents are in the transcultural evaluation of music, what different kinds of agency and control the agents exercise and how these are contested.

References

Akyüz, Y. and C. Gore (2001) 'African Economic Development in a Comparative Perspective', *Cambridge Journal of Economics*, 25:265–88.

Arrighi, G. (2002) 'The African Crisis: World Systemic and Regional Aspects', *New Left Review*, 15:5–36.

Collier, P. and D. Dollar (2002) *Globalization, Growth, and Poverty: Building an Inclusive World Economy.* Washington DC: World Bank and Oxford: Oxford University Press.

Collier, P. and J.W. Gunning (1999) 'Why has Africa Grown Slowly?', *Journal of Economic Perspectives*, 13(3):3–22.

Collier, P. and C. Pattillo (2002) *Investment and Risk in Africa.* Basingstoke and London: Macmillan.

Dorward, A., J. Kydd and C. Poulton (eds) (1998) *Smallholder Cash Crop Production under Market Liberalisation: A New Institutional Economics Perspective.* Oxford and New York: CAB International.

Gereffi, G. (1994) 'The Organization of Buyer-Driven Global Commodity Chains: How US Retailers Shape Overseas Production Networks', in G. Gereffi and M. Korzeniewicz (eds), *Commodity Chains and Global Capitalism.* Westport: Greenwood.

—— (1999) 'International Trade and Industrial Up-Grading in the Apparel Commodity Chain', *Journal of International Economics*, 48(1):37–70.

Mattoo, A., D. Roy and A. Subramania (2002) *The Africa Growth and Opportunity Act and its Rules of Origin: Generosity Undermined?* World Bank Policy Research Working Paper, 2908.

Oyejide, T.A., E.O. Ogunkola and S.A. Bankole (2000) 'Quantifying the Trade Impact of Sanitary and Phytosanitary Standards: What is Known and Issues of Importance for Sub-Saharan Africa'. Paper prepared for the workshop *Quantifying the Trade Effect of Standards and Regulatory Barriers: Is it Possible?* World Bank, Washington DC April 27, 2000.

Otsuki, T. J.S. Wilson and M. Sewadeh (2001) *A Race to the Top? A Case Study of Food Safety Standards and Africa Exports.* World Bank Policy Research Working Paper, 2563.

Raikes, P., M.F. Jensen and S. Ponte (2000) 'Global Commodity Chain Analysis and the French Filiére Approach: Comparison and Critique', *Economy and Society*, Vol. 29(3):390–417.

Rugumanu, S. (2002) 'Globalization and Marginalization in Euro-Africa Relations in the Twenty-First Century', in B.I. Logan (ed.), *Globalization, the Third World State and Poverty-Alleviation in the Twenty-First Century.* Aldershot: Ashgate.

Taylor, I. And P. Nel (2002) '"New Africa', Globalization and the Confines of Elite Reformism: 'Getting the Rhetoric Right, Getting the Strategy Wrong'", *Third World Quarterly*, 33(1):163–80.

UNCTAD (1996) *Globalization and Liberalization: Effects of International Economic Relations on Poverty.* New York and Geneva, UNCTAD.

—— (1999) *African Development in a Comparative Perspective.* UNCTAD, James Currey and Africa World Press.

—— (2000) *Capital Flows and Growth in Africa.* New York and Geneva, United Nations.

—— (2001) *Food Quality Standards: Definitions and Role in International Trade.* New York and Geveva, United Nations.

—— (2003) *Economic Development in Africa: Trade Performance and Commodity Dependence.* New York and Geneva, United Nations.

Wood, A. (2002) *Could Africa Be Like America?* Proceedings of the Annual Bank Conference on Development Economics, April–May 2002, Washington DC: World Bank.

World Bank (1981) *Accelerated Development in Sub-Saharan Africa: An Agenda for Action.* Washington, DC: World Bank.

—— (2000) *Poverty in an Age of Globalization.* www.worldbank.org/research/global.

2. Key Concepts and Core Issues in Global Value Chain Analysis

Niels Fold and Marianne Nylandsted Larsen

Introduction

The contributions to this book aim to provide a detailed examination of globalization dynamics within specific global value chains. Different products are examined and different questions posed in the chapters. The result is a nuanced picture of the complexity, scope and speed of the globalization processes that are incorporating African economies and individual producers.

The book is based on a common analytical framework that focuses on actors, institutions and processes linked to particular material flows, the so-called Global Commodity Chain (GCC) approach, later to be renamed as the Global Value Chain (GVC) approach.[1] With a basis in world systems theory, a global commodity chain was initially conceptualised as 'a network of labour and production processes whose end result is a finished commodity' (Hopkins and Wallerstein 1994). In this version, a commodity chain is constituted of separable processes or 'boxes', each of which encompasses specific production processes with a number of characteristics, such as socially defined and shifting boundaries, different degrees of monopolization, variations in geographical extension, different property arrangements and different modes of labour control. These characteristics may vary over time according to cyclical movements in the world economy, the so-called A and B periods (Hopkins and Wallerstein 1994). The 'boxes' are joined to each other by different linkages reflecting variations in the form and scope of vertical integration between production units in the boxes. These variations tend to be cyclical, as some periods (A) are dominated by vertical integration, while others (B) are marked by concentration and subcontracting, reflecting the trade-off between transaction-cost reductions and labour-cost reductions.

---

1. See footnote 1, p. 17. In this chapter we apply the terminology used by the authors in their original contributions while abstaining from any interpretation of theoretical and methodological significance of the changes in terminology (but see Bair 2005 for an interesting historiography of the analytical approach).

In the more basic and operational form presented by Gereffi (1994a; 1994b), the cyclical nature of the boxes and their linkages is not significant. In this version, a global commodity chain is constituted by three analytical dimensions:

1. An input-output structure that maps out the flow of products and services between value-adding economic activities (cf., the 'boxes' above).

2. A territorial dimension that characterises the spatial concentration and dispersion of production and distribution networks.

3. A governance structure that determines the flows and allocation of resources within the chain. Governance is essential for the coordination and dynamics of global commodity chains.

The input-output structure and the territorial dimension are considered as descriptive categories, whereas Gereffi distinguishes between two different governance structures with theoretical bearings, namely producer-driven and buyer-driven chains. Producer-driven chains are primarily coordinated by transnational companies in industries characterized by high capital intensity in the manufacturing process, as well as by high technological and organisational barriers to entry. Upstream and downstream activities are both organized and controlled by these dominant lead firms, who themselves command substantial productive capacity. Producer-driven chains are typically found in the automobile, aircraft and semiconductor industries. Buyer-driven chains are primarily coordinated by large retailers, brand-name merchandisers or trading companies in industries that are characterized by high labour intensity and high barriers to entry concerning product design, financing and marketing. Whereas downstream activities are controlled through complex, tiered networks of (overseas) contractors, the lead firms do not engage in processing activities. This governance structure is typical of the garment, footwear, toy and consumer electronic industries.

External regulation briefly entered the GCC approach as a fourth dimension, a so-called 'institutional framework that identifies how local, national, and international conditions and policies shape the globalization process at each stage in the chain' (Gereffi 1995:113). In this sense, the analytical framework encompassed public regulation through institutions operating at different geographical levels. However, the institutional framework has never been further elaborated or included as an equally important analytical dimension in subsequent work by Gereffi.

In the remaining parts of this chapter, we outline the debate on the key concepts and core issues within the GVC approach, taking Gereffi's early work as our point of departure. After dealing with governance in the next section, we outline the somewhat strange disappearance of external regulatory issues from the approach, at least as an explicit analytical dimension. Next we examine the different takes on the concept of upgrading, i.e., the process by which firms, regions and/or countries (and even multi-country regions) escalate the value added ladder: this issue is of direct policy relevance and may be considered as the most operational aspect of the analytical approach. Finally, we deal with the methodological and empirical problems involved in delimiting a global value chain. The concepts and issues are illuminated by referring to examples in various chapters in this book where they are implicitly or explicitly addressed.

Governance – and forms of coordination

A sympathetic critique of the conceptual basis of GCCs has come from observers 'outside' the GCC approach (Dicken et al. 2000; Henderson et al. 2002). For this group of authors, the governance structure is overemphasised at the expense of the other two dimensions and – not least – the 'external' institutional regulatory framework (see below). The conceptualization in two ideal forms of governance is far too simplistic, and it is suggested that a major reason for the conceptual fallacy is the heavy bias towards buyer-driven chains in the GCC-inspired empirical studies. In the real world, many GCCs do not resemble the forms or dynamics of ideal forms of governance. Actually, at some point, Gereffi (2001a, 2001b) introduced a third (emerging) governance structure linked to so-called 'internet-oriented chains', while Gibbon (2001) introduced a trader-driven global chain primarily based on the findings of governance structures in the global cotton chain. None of these efforts, however, has been elaborated further in terms of a revised taxonomy.

As for the input-output relationship, the criticism is that it has only been explored superficially because it is treated as a linear and unidirectional flow instead of consisting of flows that are characterized by complexity and multi-directionality. This is far better encapsulated by network approaches in which production and consumption are linked through the examination of more complex social and cultural practices (see also Barrett et al. 2004). Likewise, the territorial dimension is only manifest at very high levels of spatial aggregation (core, periphery and semi-periphery), which is said to reflect world system theory as a seedbed for the GCC approach.[1]

The reaction of Gereffi and his associates to the critique of the simplified types of governance in global value chains is relatively recent. Efforts to develop a theoretically grounded and analytically applicable set of more diversified types of governance (Gereffi et al. 2005) have taken as their point of departure a classification of different buyer-seller relations inspired by transaction-cost theory. Within the spectrum of buyer-seller relationships that stretch from market to hierarchy, different types of network cover the complex inter-firm divisions of labour. Issues like asset specificity, opportunism and coordination costs are handled in different ways by the actors involved through repeat transactions, reputation and social norms. Whereas some networks are constituted by more or less egalitarian relations with mutual dependence between sellers and buyers, others are characterized by pronounced asymmetrical and dependent relations, so-called relational and captive value chains respectively (Humphrey and Schmitz 2002). Besides, research by Sturgeon (2003) has identified buyer-seller relations where transactions bear a strong market resemblance, even though the products exchanged are customized and substantial economies of scale are obtained – the so-called 'modular value chains'.

Theoretically, the different types of buyer-seller relations are justified by a combination of three key factors in GVC governance and a relative measurement of their value, i.e., high or low (Gereffi et al. 2005). The key factors are the complexity of transactions, the codifiability of the information needed for transactions to take place and the capabilities of suppliers. By reflecting on the nature of the possible combinations (eight in total), only five types of buyer–seller relations are considered meaningful and as existing in real life, each of which is claimed to constitute a specific governance structure in particular global value chains. Even though the importance of national regulatory institutions is acknowledged – not only within national territories but also implanted in foreign territory via FDIs – it is the internal variables (cf., the three key factors) that influence the governance of the GVCs, regardless of the institutional context in which they are situated (Gereffi et al. 2005).

---

1. This seems to be an exaggerated and over-simplified interpretation of Gereffi's understandings of the territorial dimension, which is repudiated empirically through the more nuanced use of spatial models in the analysis of the locational pattern of garment exporters to the US market (Gereffi 1999). In a later paper, the critics acknowledge that Gereffi breaks with these static spatial categories (Henderson et al. 2002).

Further, Gereffi et al. (2005) argue that governance patterns are not monolithic, in the sense that they may vary from stage to stage in a particular industry in time and space. Hence, different kinds of buyer-seller relations are considered to be analytically identical to different types of governance structure. But why and how do different combinations of 'bilateral' governance structures between buyers and sellers result in one out of five overarching forms of chain governance? This point is stressed by Gibbon and Ponte (2005), who acknowledge the existence of multiple forms of co-ordination between buyer and seller segments. However, having different forms of coordination within a particular GVC does not rule out a prevalent structure of governance, in particular the tendency towards global value chains being buyer-driven. This is claimed to be a fundamental tendency in present-day global capitalism, caused by salient features of competition, such as the increasing importance of product differentiation and branding, as well as shareholder valorization.

It can be argued, however, that the concept of 'buyer-drivenness' is quite inaccurate when used as a distinct analytical category. In the GVC-related literature, buyers are rarely if ever conceptualized as private consumers. Instead, 'buyers' is traditionally used as a common designation for retailers, marketers and branded manufacturers who are positioned just in front of the consumer market. However, buying operations *per se* are carried out by other actors or companies further up the chain, some of which are involved in production activities. Empirical results reveal that such buyers may assume important and very influential positions in the GVCs in which they are involved. This is particularly the case for so-called contract manufacturers, who supply customized components or intermediate goods to branded manufacturers, for instance, in the food or electronics industries.

As demonstrated in several of the chapters in this volume, different kinds of buyers have significance for how the chains are driven, the nature of the drivenness and thus for the restructuring processes along the chains. In the global cotton chain (Chapter 7), international cotton traders play a key coordinating role by bridging producers (ginning companies) and spinning mills. However, the global cotton chain is far less driven than other agricultural-based chains and there is no clear group of lead firms defining and shaping the division of labour and entry barriers along the chain. As pointed out by Larsen, there has been no marked trend towards global concentration in the trading segment, or immediately downstream in the spinning segment, in the chain. This, in turn, reflects globally dispersed patterns in both supply and demand. Thus, the functions performed by international traders, ginning companies and spinning mills and the functional division of labour in the chain have remained largely unchanged for decades.

This is in contrast to the global coffee chain (Fold and Ponte, Chapter 6), where industrial processors (roasters) have lead-firm status and have expanded their marketing role in recent years. Branded roasters define the key terms of participation in the chain and international coffee traders have either been marginalized by direct purchasing by roasters upstream in the chain or have had to redefine their role significantly. In the global cocoa-chocolate chain, however, lead status has been acquired by companies in two different segment of the chain: the global contract manufacturers (grinders) and the branded chocolate manufacturers. As argued by Fold (2002), the cocoa-chocolate chain can be characterised as a modular value chain (see above), with two groups of firms in different segments of the chain playing the leading role.

The horticultural chain is highly driven by one group of lead firms. The chapters by Mather (Chapter 4) and Jensen (Chapter 5) demonstrate the significant changes in the governance of the global horticultural chain that have occurred in recent years and the role that retailers have assumed in governing the chain. During the last decades, the retailing segment went through enormous concentration. Meanwhile, retailers' sale of fresh fruit and vegetables has displaced wholesale markets, notably in the UK. Due to their size and market power, supermarkets now play the leading role in the horticultural chain and are able define the allocation of activities along the chain. The requirements that supermarkets specify regarding, for instance, product variety, delivery, food safety and quality standards have led to a process of differentiation in producing countries. As Jensen argues, the implementation of food safety requirements by UK retailers has resulted in a (partial) exclusion of smallholders in Kenya previously involved in the production of fresh fruit and vegetables for the export market. In the case of the citrus export chain, Mather shows how different process requirements, food safety and quality standards imposed by buyers in different export markets result in a process of spatial differentiation in South Africa.

Despite the presence of different types of buyers (retailers, branded marketers and industrial processors) in different global value chains, a general trend can be observed in several of the global value chains presented in this volume. Lead firms are increasingly imposing more stringent performance requirements on their suppliers, for instance, in the form of conformity to new quality and process standards.

Institutional framework

In Gereffi's early work, the two types of governance structure are superimposed on a different dichotomy of industrial organization (mass production vs. flexible specialization), although the global perspective in the GCC approach is emphasized. The two types of governance structure are regarded as contrasting but not mutually exclusive poles in a spectrum of industrial organization: that is, as ideal types, rather than representing either a dichotomy or a continuum (Gereffi 1994a, Gereffi 1994b). In addition, the concept of a governance structure is superimposed on two types of industrialization strategy. Industrialization via import substitution (ISI) has been centred on transnational companies (TNCs) and state companies in industries that are typically producer-driven, while export-oriented industrialization (EOI) is channelled through buyer-driven chains in which small to medium-sized local private companies supply the lion's share of manufacturing components and finished goods. Buyer-driven chains and EOI emerged together in the early 1970s, suggesting that the success of the EOI was closely linked to 'the development of new forms of organizational integration in buyer-driven industrial networks' (Gereffi 1994a:100). In a later contribution (Gereffi 1999), the shift from ISI to EOI in developing countries is interpreted as a shift from producer-driven to buyer-driven value chains. Moreover, this shift marks the disconnection of brands from manufacturing companies to retailers and marketers who are able to control and coordinate networks of independent but interconnected companies – that is, brands are increasingly controlled by commercial capital at the expense of productive capital.

Moreover, the important role of the state is stressed in relation to both producer-driven and buyer-driven chains in Gereffi's early work. In the former, state policies are much more interventionist, with regulatory orders in industrial policies and direct involvement in (upstream) manufacturing activities. In the latter, state policies primarily act as facilitating mechanisms for private business accumulation without direct interference in inter-firm relationships or markets. State intervention and policies interfering with markets are also of significance at the end-points of buyer-driven chains, that is, in OECD country markets. Protectionist measures of various sorts, particularly quota systems, heavily influence the global locational pattern of export manufacturing by sub-contracting, as is clearly visible, for instance, in the locational shifts of countries exporting garments to the US (Gereffi 1994a).

The reason we stress this emphasis – albeit in many different forms – on state policies in Gereffi's early work is the somewhat surprising fact that public regulation and the wider institutional framework have actually disappeared as an explicit (fourth) dimension in the succeeding development of the analytical approach (see above). Various multilateral and national regulatory institutions are taken into account in only some of the empirical studies, for instance, in Gereffi's investigations of the apparel chain(s) originating in developing countries that end up in the US market (see Gereffi 1994a, 1999; Bair and Gereffi 2001)

Perhaps the implicit rationale is that it only makes sense to incorporate the institutional framework as a conditioning factor for GVC governance (and upgrading, see below) at the concrete level. Depending on the 'nature' of the product that constitutes the value chain, different sets of regulatory institutions are relevant: it is an empirical question how they interfere with chain dynamics. A GVC originating in agriculture (in the South) and ending on consumers' dinner tables (in the North) is likely to be affected by public and private (i.e., retailer-directed) food safety regulation in addition to ordinary agricultural trade policies implemented at national level (tariffs, domestic subsidies, etc.). In contrast, these types of regulatory mechanisms have far less impact on GVCs in which the end product is a manufactured consumer good. An exceptional but iconic example is the global trade in clothing that until 2005 was constrained by the complex quota system embodied within the Multifibre Agreement. This system determined locational patterns of the global clothing production and inter-country flows of products (including textiles), capital and information. More typical examples of regulatory mechanisms at national level are various product standards that in essence may act as technical barriers to trade: ethical trade codes may unintentionally have the same result.

These latter cases illustrate the opaque distinction between external and internal regulation of GVC dynamics. Technical standards are mostly designed and monitored by public bodies in consultation with trade associations or dominant corporate actors and ethical codes are created by various constituencies of corporations, NGOs, trade unions and/or public bodies. Whether these forms of institutional regulation have to be conceptualized as internalized external regulation or externalized internal regulation is hard to tell. Suffice it to say that external (in whatever sense) regulatory institutions potentially play an important role for GVC dynamics.

This is particularly prevalent in agro-based GVCs. On a global level and in a long term perspective, Daviron (Chapter 3) shows that agricultural policies have been crucial for the form of competition on the international food markets. Despite their apparent complexity and distinctiveness at the national level, these 'rules of the game' (i.e., agricultural policies) are created in particular historical periods on the basis of common global norms for regulatory mechanisms for agricultural production and trade. In relation to African agriculture, exports of food to Europe dramatically increased during two different periods, namely during what is called the imperial autarchy regime (from about 1914 to the late 1950s) and the multilateral regime (somewhat overlapping the former and ending in the 1970s). These periods are characterized by the importance attached to national self-sufficiency in food, and the corresponding (national) agricultural policies therefore structure the role and function of agricultural imports from Africa. In relative terms, Africa is being marginalized in the present period (mainly because of the traditional dependence on the mature market in the EU) while Latin America and the Far East increase their share of the global market for agricultural products.

Looking at particular GVC dynamics, Fold and Ponte (Chapter 6) provide insights into the effects of changing quality control systems caused by fading public regulation in most coffee and cocoa exporting countries in Africa. Parallel to the liberalization of procurement systems, industrial end-users (i.e., coffee roasters and cocoa grinders) increasingly determine and influence quality parameters according to their particular needs. Some of them are even capable of compensating for different crop qualities linked to different origins by homogenizing raw materials via improved process technology, for instance steam-cleaning of coffee beans and advanced roasting-grinding processes. Somewhat contrary to these findings, Larsen (Chapter 7) finds that cotton quality linked to national origins has become increasingly important. Firstly, this is because more advanced spinning technology requires detailed calibration and assessment of fibre properties and, secondly, because the degree of flexibility and inter-substitution in cotton blend formulas is relatively low. Hence, maintenance of traditional and nationally based quality standards is much more important for cotton than for coffee and cocoa. If public regulation of quality is dismantled without replacement by adequate private institutions, there will be a failure to maintain the international reputation of a particular national quality that could result in dramatic loss of premium and/or share on the global market. In general, parastatal marketing boards typically controlled a large part of the transport system, particularly between the rural buying posts and the port, before the implementation of structural adjustment policies in Africa. As pointed out by Pedersen (Chapter 9), the dominant position of parastatals in the marketing of African export crops resulted in a fragmented transport chain with little coordination or integration between rural transport (from field to village/buying posts), and transport from buying posts to the port as well as shipment to Europe or other overseas markets. Following the liberalization of the national marketing systems, international traders (who now function as supply managers for large processors) and contract manufacturers often seek to vertically integrate both domestic and international parts of the marketing and transport chains.

(Agro-)industrial upgrading

As mentioned above, Gereffi discussed modes of industrialization in developing countries (in the traditional terms of ISI and EOI strategies) before, and to some extent overlapping with, the initial development of the conceptual framework of GCCs. The global trend towards a shift from ISI to EOI in developing countries was understood as a parallel shift from producer-driven to buyer-driven GCCs. At this time, upgrading was analyzed at the national level, in the sense that countries traversed different export roles in a particular hierarchical sequencing (Gereffi 1995). Upgrading strategies were basically viewed as different sets of government policies for 'moving up' in the global economy from primary commodity exports to export-processing assembly to component-supply subcontracting, before reaching a position in original equipment manufacturing, and ending as original brand-name manufacturing.

Thus, upgrading was discussed in a manner that was relatively isolated from the analytical framework of GCCs until the late 1990s, when the issue was incorporated into the GCC framework as a process in which companies or economies 'move to more profitable and/or technologically sophisticated capital- and skill-intensive economic niches' (Gereffi 1999:52). Some form of participation in GVCs is considered a *sine qua non* for upgrading in developing countries, as companies and economies are put on dynamic learning curves that benefit them more than various traditional support mechanisms and regulation by national and local institutions.

Analytically Gereffi (1999) distinguished between four different 'levels' of upgrading:

1. within factories (towards more expensive and complex products and larger orders);

2. within inter-firm enterprise networks (from mass production of standard goods towards flexible production of differentiated merchandise);

3. within local or national economies (from simple assembly towards own equipment manufacturer (OEM) and own brand manufacturer (OBM) with greater local and national linkage effects); and

4. within regions (from bilateral, asymmetrical and inter-regional trade flows towards an intra-regional division of labour, including all segments of the particular GCCs).

These categories try to incorporate technological and organizational processes at the company and industry levels, in addition to changes in the geographical and input-output dimensions of the GCC in question. Hence, the result is an extremely broad conceptualization of the upgrading processes, which lacks analytical rigidity. Rather, the categories constitute an empirically grounded generalization of the dominant features in the upgrading process of the garment industry in East Asia (see Gereffi 1996). In this case, some companies developed according to the first and third 'levels' of upgrading and, through subsequent 'triangle manufacturing' transformed the regional dynamics according to the processes sketched in the fourth 'level'.

Humphrey and Schmitz (2002) have outlined another set of more rigid upgrading types. They distinguish between:

1. Process upgrading (inputs are transformed more efficiently by organizational or technical improvements);

2. Product upgrading (production is moved into more sophisticated product lines, measured by, e.g., increased unit values);

3. Functional upgrading (new functions are acquired, leading to the increased skill content of activities); and

4. Inter-sectoral upgrading (new productive activities are entered by clusters of firms).

This typology is more focused on organizational dimensions at the company or industry levels, even though a spatial dimension (cluster) is also included. Distinct types of upgrading process in a particular GVC are claimed to depend on the 'type of value chain', that is, on the nature of the relationships that exist between the actors involved in a transaction: 'Different forms of chain governance have different upgrading implications' (Humphrey and Schmitz 2002:1023).[1]

---

1. For Humphrey and Schmitz (2002), these buyer-seller relationships turn out to be identical to different governance structures (market, network, quasi-hierarchy, hi-

The upgrading issue has been taken into agro-food studies by Gibbon (2001) in his debate with Cramer (1999) over the applicability and suitability of GCC analysis in examining questions of upgrading in developing countries. Gibbon argues that some GCCs based on primary commodities originating in developing countries are driven by another type of lead firm than the retailers and merchandisers, or even branded manufacturers, identified in typical buyer-driven chains. Instead, international trading companies are the main drivers in primary commodity GCCs, as they have historically organized the flow of tropical commodities from numerous small producers in the South to processing companies in the North. Gibbon suggests that different types of lead firm constitute different types of governance structure and argues that different possibilities for upgrading (at the national level) exist in trader-driven GCCs. Moreover, the exclusion of producers from a GCC as a result of initiatives taken by lead firms to reduce coordination costs is incorporated into the analysis. Given the different nature of governance in international trader-driven chains, exclusion dynamics are different and smallholders can be cushioned from the vagaries of lead firms' cost-reduction efforts by combinations of new and old types of public policy instrument (Gibbon 2001).

Besides the sheer volume-based upgrading (i.e., the increase of production by territorially limited producers to a level attractive for international traders in order to reduce system-coordination costs), Gibbon's upgrading typology includes:

1. Increasing the quality, volumes and reliability of supplies and entering into more advanced sale and marketing arrangements. Most of these require some form of public action, the basis for which is unfortunately being undermined by the implementation of SAPs.

2. Producing new forms of existing commodities, for instance, by starting production of GMOs or leapfrogging the world market for standard primary commodities by starting production according to new technical or user-specified commodity forms. The latter are sold directly to trading companies or industrial processors.

3. Localising commodity processing at the intermediate stage as a precondition for entry into the processing of final goods.

---

erarchy). These, in turn, are also designated different forms of chain coordination, leading to considerable conceptual confusion, which comes to the surface again in the discussion of governance structures (see above).

Although there is no exact match between Gibbon's typology and the process, product and functional upgrading defined by Humphrey and Schmitz (2002), the organizational types of upgrading correspond fairly well. The differences may reflect the different nature of the products concerned, that is, agricultural raw materials as opposed to manufacturing goods.

In the absence of a more closely GVC-based theorization of upgrading, Gibbon (2003a) has later suggested that a useful analytical way forward may be to conduct more detailed empirical analyses of the 'reward structures' available to suppliers within global value chains on the one hand, and on the concrete roles releasing these rewards on the other, or, in other words, the 'upgrading preconditions and mechanisms' for arriving at them (Gibbon 2003a:18). As such, this perspective is based on an explicit rejection of the notion that upgrading follows a distinct 'life history' of national economies (e.g., the implicit hierarchies entailed in Gereffi's classification of different levels of upgrading, see above), or that it can take forms that can be defined in the abstract for value chains in general. This critique is reintroduced in Gibbon's contribution to this volume (Chapter 8). In particular, OBM is questioned as the highest stage on the upgrading ladder starting with simple assembly. According to Gibbon, OBM production may embody 'competency traps' where firms are locked-in with highly product-specific competences for design and branding. Instead, a more remunerative strategy for African firms would suggest upgrading by mass-production of a specialised set of products while increasing efficiency in fabric sourcing, work organization and product quality control. This proposition is compatible with the findings from the clothing industry in Mauritius (Chapter 8). Firms participating in the US-destined chain benefited from learning opportunities related to narrow efficiency gains and technical improvements of existing processes, while more diffuse learning opportunities related to functional versatility were obtained by firms participating in the EU-destined chain. Hence, upgrading in the traditional sense should in theory be easier for firms in the EU-destined chain: however, for various reasons the newly acquired competences were inadequate and experiences with OBM positions were costly for locally owned firms.

Instead, Gibbon (2003a) emphasizes that concrete upgrading possibilities for actors below the level of lead firms need to be studied on a case-by-case basis by paying analytical attention to the different concrete roles that seem to offer suppliers higher and more stable returns, as well as the 'routes' for arriving at them (Gibbon 2003a:16; see also Gibbon and Ponte 2005). The reward structures in global value chains refer to the rewards or opportunities available to producers in developing countries and the nature of the roles that trigger special rewards: for example, how premiums and discounts are determined in the international market for a particular crop (e.g., quality grades, securing contracts through forward sales agreements). Upgrading preconditions and mechanisms refer to specific national or local circumstances in which suppliers are able to generate higher and more stable rewards. Gibbon (2003a) provides a first attempt in this direction by linking the discussion of chain-specific reward structures with that of the institutional aspects of the preconditions and mechanisms concerned in producing countries (i.e., the organizational aspects of production and the horizontal coordinating aspects of provision of, for example, public goods).[1]

The issue of upgrading is the subject of ongoing efforts to develop applicable categories with the capacity to assist policy formulation. As indicated, however, there is a risk that the quest for conceptualisation leads to infertile debates for and against idealised classificatory systems. In this respect, Pietilä's contribution (Chapter 10) represents a fresh and inspirational take on the debate, by interpreting increasing fame for African musicians as a form of upgrading. Enhancement in the 'symbolic capital' of fame transforms into increased bargaining power for the musicians, although there may be a trade-off in terms of an artistic integrity: African musicians are expected to reproduce 'the rather stereotypical, essentializing images of Africanness' and to accept 'the symbolic loaded imagery of "otherness"'. On the other hand, product differentiation and branding may be easier and more profitable by exploiting these preferences on the markets in the EU instead of being victimized by the appropriative images.

Chain structure

The delimitation (or shape) of the chain is not unambiguous. This problem is referred to as the question of the 'length' and 'breadth' of the GVC (Gibbon 2003b). The length issue is linked to the analytical range considered in a vertical perspective and deals with the relevant end-points of the chain. Is it, for example, valid to analyse the global garment chain without taking into consideration the dynamics of cotton cultivation, yarn-spinning

---

1. The analysis is based on empirical observations of upgrading opportunities for producers in the global coffee and cotton chains. In addition, Gibbon and Ponte (2005) discuss upgrading possibilities for other global value chains – including cocoa, fresh fruit and vegetables and garments – based on an examination of the reward structures and preconditions and mechanisms for arriving at them in the chains concerned.

and fabric production? How far upstream should one pursue the analysis of the global car industry, with its countless components and intermediate products? Can the governance structure in food industries be grasped if the determinant factors behind shifts in consumer preferences for the specific goods (or cluster of goods) are not incorporated?

In essence, this is a question of how many segments ('boxes' in the original terminology) and matching inter-relations should be incorporated into empirical studies. Sturgeon (2001:3) proposes that value chains be cut out at the intersection of lead firms and suppliers, reflecting the privileged analytical position of lead firms. This section of the chain is then denoted the 'supply chain' in order to specify 'those activities that arise as a response to the impetus of lead firm(s)'. The question of length, however, is mostly 'solved' by practical limitations, being more or less reduced to a simple question of the resources that are available for a particular study. Moreover, some would argue that a basic knowledge of the residual chain is sufficient to consider whether empirical studies are being biased by a focus on a specific 'slice' of the chain.

Whereas a pragmatic solution to the ambiguities concerning the 'length' issue seems acceptable, the 'breadth' issue clearly needs conceptual refinement. Breadth refers to the relevant sections of a particular segment that it is sensible to accommodate in the analysis – the end points viewed from a horizontal perspective, so to speak. The 'mapping issue', linked to the input-output and geographical dimensions, relates to outlining how the GVCs are constituted by different filaments: that is, a sequence of segments in which the filaments coalesce and those in which they ramify. Sturgeon (2001) uses the concept of 'value thread' to describe the homogeneous character of the product in question and to distinguish it from the bundle of goods that may be incorporated in a value chain.[1]

Returning to the set of methodological questions posed above, the relevant question for the garment GVC would be whether the dynamics are similar in the two apparel filaments entering the US market, namely those of fashion and standardized clothing (Gereffi 1994b)? As for the agro-food industry, is it most accurate to consider two GVCs for coffee, one for Robusta and one for Arabica?

There seems to be no particular reason to distinguish between governance structures and lead firms in the two coffee filaments, probably because

---

1. Correspondingly, the concept of a 'supply thread' can be used to specify the activities that result in a particular product, less the activities of the lead firms (see below).

the same international traders and roasters are heavily involved in both. On the contrary, fine and flavoured cocoa constitutes apparently a separate filament due to its intrinsic properties, which make it valued as a luxury product. Fold and Ponte (Chapter 6) focus only on ordinary cocoa beans used for mass-consumed chocolate products and not on cocoa beans with distinctively higher quality. However, as the lead firms in the forastero-based filament are not interested in low volume and geographically dispersed supplies of high quality beans, different governance structures are likely to prevail in the fine and flavoured filament.

In any case, the breadth issue is highly relevant for the relationship between governance structures, upgrading possibilities and end markets. Gibbon (Chapter 8) argues that the clothing chain emanating from Mauritius is segmented into two filaments ('sub-chains') structured according to end-markets, i.e., destined for either the US or the EU. The former filament is hierarchical and embodies a series of impersonal structures imposed by the lead firms. The latter is more egalitarian and embodies more personally negotiated practices. These differences are associated with considerably higher bargaining power by first-tier suppliers within the EU-destined filament. In the same line of thought, Pietilä (Chapter 10) identifies two filaments segmented by end-markets (in the North) for World Music. In the celebrity chain, African musicians are initiated by famous Western musicians and incorporated into mainstream business dominated by global media companies. In the less visible 'alternative' filament (denoted the regular chain), African musicians relate to smaller and nationally based companies. Pietilä argues that the filaments differ significantly with respect to the key actors and mode of functioning, with a resultant substantial impact on the inclusionary and exclusionary dynamics in each filament.

Conclusion

The literature on globalization and economic development in Africa is not overwhelming in scope and most existing studies deal with broader themes, such as the changes in economic regimes caused by the implementation of SAPs, new trends towards regionalization, private sector development, etc. Few books deal with globalization and the specificities of African countries but tend to conceptualise 'globalization' simply as 'international trade' and 'direct foreign investment' (Mshomba 2000).

Rather than concentrating on changes in trade and FDI alone, the contributors to this volume consider additional issues in order to understand the incorporation of African countries into a more broadly conceived globalization process, i.e., changes in corporate strategies, new forms of firm-to-firm relationships, the role of quality standards, etc. The aim of this book is to deal with the consequences of globalization for different groups of actors and provide a background for the formulation and implementation of policies that counteract the exclusionary elements in the present processes.

We maintain that a tangible way to analyze the elusive question of economic globalization in Africa is to adopt a commodity-specific (or product category-specific) approach. The most comprehensive analytical framework is the so-called GVC approach, originally formulated as the GCC approach. This chapter has outlined the important concepts and issues within this analytical tradition and aims to provide a common platform for the individual contributions. None of the authors claims to cover the whole spectrum of intricate flows and relationships that exist within each GVC, nor even within the part of the GVC that is territorially bounded in a given territory, for instance a country in Africa. Instead, each chapter should be perceived as an entry point into the complexity that makes up the present globalization processes in Africa.

References

Bair, J. (2005) 'Global Capitalism and Commodity Chains: Looking Back, Going Forward, *Competition and Change*, 9(2):153–80.

Bair, J. and G. Gereffi, (2001) 'Local Clusters in Global Chains: The Causes and Consequences of Export Dynamism in Torreon's Blue Jeans Industry', *World Development*, 29(11):1885–903.

Barrett, H.R., A.W. Browne and B.W. Ilbery (2004) 'From Farm to Supermarket: The Trade in Fresh Horticultural Produce from sub-Saharan Africa to the United Kingdom', in A. Hughes and S. Reimer (eds), *Geographies of Commodity Chains*. London: Routledge.

Cramer, C. (1999) 'Can Africa Industrialize by Processing Primary Commodities? The Case of Mozambican Cashew Nuts', *World Development*, 27(7):1247–66.

Dicken, P., P. Kelly, K. Olds and H. Wai-Chung Yeung (2001) 'Chains and Networks, Territories and Scales: Towards a Relational Framework for Analysing the Global Economy', *Global Networks*, 1(2):89–112.

Fold, N. (2002) 'Lead Firms and Competition in 'Bi-Polar' Commodity Chains: Grinders and Branders in the Global Cocoa-Chocolate Industry', *Journal of Agrarian Change*, 2(2):228–47.

Gereffi, G. (1994a) 'The Organization of Buyer-Driven Global Commodity Chains: How US Retailers Shape Overseas Production Networks', in G. Gereffi and M. Korzeniewicz (eds), *Commodity Chains and Global Capitalism*. Westport: Greenwood.

—— (1994b) 'The International Economy and Economic Development', in N.J. Smedlser and R. Swedberg (eds), *The Handbook of Economic Sociology*. Princeton, NJ: Princeton University Press.

—— (1995) 'Global Production Systems and Third World Development', in B. Stallings (ed.), *Global Change, Regional Response: The New International Context of Development*. Cambridge: Cambridge University Press.

—— (1996) 'Commodity Chains and Regional Divisions of Labor in East Asia', in E.M. Kim (ed.) *The Four Asian Tigers: Economic Development and the Political Economy*. San Diego, CA: Academic Press.

—— (1999) 'International Trade and Industrial Up-Grading in the Apparel Commodity Chain', *Journal of International Economics*, 48(1):37–70.

—— (2001a) 'Beyond the Producer-Driven/Buyer-Driven Dichotomy: The Evolution of Global Value Chains in the Internet Era', *IDS Bulletin* 32(3):30–40.

—— (2001b) 'Shifting Governance Structures in Global Commodity Chains, with Special Reference to the Internet', *American Behavioral Scientist*, (44)10: 1616–37.

Gereffi, G., J. Humphrey and T. Sturgeon (2005) 'The Governance of Global Value Chains', *Review of International Political Economy*, 12:1, pp. 78–104.

Gibbon, P. (2001) 'Upgrading Primary Production: A Global Commodity Chain Approach', *World Development*, Vol. 29(2):345–63.

—— (2003a) 'Commodities, Donors, Value-Chain Analysis and Upgrading'. Paper prepared for UNCTAD, November 2003.

—— (2003b) 'The African Growth and Opportunity Act and the Global Commodity Chain for Clothing', *World Development*, 31(11):1809–27.

Gibbon, P., and S. Ponte (2005) *Trading Down? Africa, Value Chains and the Global Economy*. Philadelphia: Temple University Press.

Henderson , J., P. Dicken, M. Hess, N. Coe, and H. Wai-Chung Yeung (2002) 'Global Production Networks and the Analysis of Economic Development', *Review of International Political Economy*, 9(3):436–64.

Hopkins, T.K. and I. Wallerstein. (1994) 'Commodity Chains: Construct and Research', in G. Gereffi and M. Korzeniewicz (eds), *Commodity Chains and Global Capitalism*. Westport: Greenwood.

Humphrey, J. and H. Schmitz (2002) 'How Does Insertion in Global Value Chains Affect Upgrading in Industrial Clusters?' *Regional Studies* 36(9):1017–27.

Mshomba, R.E. (2000) *Africa in the Global Economy*. Boulder: Lynne Rienner.

Sturgeon, T.J. (2001) 'How Do We Define Value Chains and Production Networks?' *IDS Bulletin* 32(3):9–18.

—— (2003) 'What Really Goes On in Silicon Valley? Spatial Clustering and Dispersal in Modular Production Networks', *Journal of Economic Geography*, 3:199–225.

Whitley, R. (1996) 'Business Systems and Global Commodity Chains: Competing or Complementary Forms of Economic Organisation?' *Competition & Change*, 1:411–25.

3. The Historical Integration of Africa in the International Food Trade
A Food Regime Perspective

Benoit Daviron

Introduction

This chapter discusses and attempts to explain the evolution of the participation of Africa in the international food trade[1] over a long period. For more than forty years, Africa's share of world food exports has been declining in a quite regular fashion, from 10 per cent of world exports in 1960 to less than 4 per cent in 2001 (see Figure 3.1 below). Since the 1990s, a large number of studies and debates have sought to understand this crisis in the competitiveness of African agriculture, most of which have blamed macroeconomic mismanagement and agricultural policies and, more generally, state involvement in agricultural production and marketing. Consequently, devaluation, reductions in public expenditure, liberalization and privatization have been suggested as the main remedies, and actions have been taken accordingly to try to restore the former competitiveness of African agriculture.

In this chapter, I would like to propose another interpretation of the problem with reference to the long period from the end of the nineteenth century until now. I adopt the perspective of an 'outside world' lecture and place the emphasis on the agricultural policies that have been adopted not only by African countries, but also by the rest of the world. I argue that agricultural policies have played, and still play, a central role in the working and outcomes of international competition in international food markets. Moreover, I argue that agricultural policies are largely determined by global norms that define most of the objectives and instruments used at national levels in different states.

I will also use a food regime approach and adopt a certain number of notions elaborated by Harriet Friedmann and Philip McMichael in a

---

1. This chapter concerns only food products of agricultural origin. Agricultural raw materials (mainly natural fibres and rubber) are therefore excluded, as are products of the sea, although international trade in the latter is flourishing. With regard to data on international trade, the 'food products' category includes SITC items 0, 1, 22 and 4.

series of articles written from the beginning of the 1980s to the present day (Friedmann 1982; Friedmann and McMichael 1989; Friedmann 1991; Friedmann 1994; McMichael 1996a; McMichael 1996b; McMichael 2000b). These authors started with an analysis of the post-Second World War food period, from 1945 to 1975, and have progressively extended their analysis to include both earlier and more recent periods. The first part of the paper discusses this food regime framework and proposes a slightly renewed perspective. The rest of the paper is organized chronologically, as it presents the succession of food regimes and the implications of each food regime for the insertion of developing countries, and Africa in particular, into the international food trade.

Food regimes viewed from an alternative perspective

The concept of a 'food regime' was developed by Friedmann and McMichael (following Hopkins and Puchala 1978a) to describe and interpret the evolution of the international food trade over a long period. The authors identify an initial such food regime as having existed from 1870 to 1914. This regime was characterized by the central role of settler countries in exporting agricultural commodities produced on family farms and supporting the development of the wage relationship in industrialized countries: 'The first food regime was centred on European imports of wheat and meat from the settler states between 1870 and 1914. In return, settler states imported European manufactured goods, labour and capital' (Friedmann and McMichael 1989: 96). At the same time, because of the increasing integration between agriculture and industry in these settler countries, integration exemplified at best by the United States, 'the first food regime was, therefore, a key to the creation of a system of national economies governed by independent states' (Friedmann and McMichael 1989:96).

For the authors, the first regime was also marked by the culmination of the colonial organization of pre-capitalist regions. They note:

> This was the apogee of a centuries-old system of politically-organized colonial empires. As new nations challenged, Britain retreated to empire, moving investment and trade both into tropical colonies, and more significantly into settler states such as Canada and Australia ... Late nineteenth century colonialism expanded the supply of tropical products to metropolitan economies ... In the late nineteenth century colonial administration undertook to organize and extend systematically production for export of sugar, tobacco, coffee, tea and cocoa for expanding European markets. (Friedmann and McMichael 1989:97)

The second food regime, beginning after 1945, is presented as a combination of two opposite movements: on one hand, the extension of the state system previously 'created' by settler states to former colonies, and on the other the 'transnational restructuring of agricultural sectors by agro-food capitals'. In sharp contrast to the first food regime, in this second regime the creation of new states mostly gave rise to new importers of food, imports provided by the concessional sales – food aid – of the United States. Following Hopkins and Puchala (1978a, 1980), Friedmann (1982) sees food aid as having a central role in the post-Second World War food regime, which was based on complementary national policies, that is, on the implicit arrangement between 'American food aid and the cheap food policy of many underdeveloped countries which led them to welcome this aid' (255).

At the same time, national systems of agriculture followed a double process of integration: into the industrial sector, which provides chemical and mechanical inputs and processes agricultural products; and into global value chains. The transnational restructuring of sectors occurred on one hand through the intensification of agricultural specialization and integration across national frontiers in agro-foods chains dominated at both ends by increasingly large industrial capital; and on the other hand through a shift in agricultural products from final use to industrial inputs to manufactured goods. This restructuring was particularly important in two large complexes: the durable food complex (fat and sugar) and the livestock complex. The durable food complex was characterized by 'substitutionism', defined by Goodman et al. (1987:9) as 'a constant drive to diversify possible input sources and achieve greater interchangeability'. Its mode of operation resulted in the import substitution of tropical products. The livestock complex emerged as the result of the development of intensive meat production in Europe and Japan on the basis of soya and corn provided by the United States.

Thus the post-Second World War regime consisted of three distinct complexes (Friedmann 1994): the wheat complex, the durable food complex and the livestock complex. Each of these complexes has had a different significance for the evolution of the participation of developing countries in the international trade. The wheat complex is the source of food dependency. The durable food complex is the source of the declining prices paid for tropical products. Finally, following the food crisis of the 1970s, the livestock complex created new export opportunities with the emergence of the so-called New Agricultural Countries exporting feedstuffs. More recently, McMichael (2000b) and other authors such as Friedland (1994) have described the content of a new food complex, 'the global salad bowl', that is, the international trade in non-traditional fruits and vegetables (other than the traditional citrus fruits and bananas).

My analysis, in being based on a food regime approach, differs from the works presented above in five major respects.

The concept of a food regime

I differ first in my definition of a food regime. Friedmann's and McMichael's definition is actually a very loose and variable one. They define 'food regime' sometimes in a very restrictive sense, as 'a set of rules governing trade among nations' (McMichael 2000a:59), and sometimes in a much broader sense, as linking 'international relations of food production and consumption to forms of accumulation' (Friedmann and McMichael 1989:95) or as 'involving a historically specific set of political relations organizing the global production and circulation of agricultural commodities' (McMichael 2000b: 410). In this chapter, I define an international food regime as a set of agricultural policy objectives and instruments that have been adopted by a large majority of governments in a specific period of history. It takes into account the existence of world norms that define the appropriate agricultural policy that should be adopted. These norms can take the form of formal international institutions defining specific rules, but they can also exist as shared representation of the problems to be addressed by agricultural policies and of the way to address them. This definition, which gives a central role to international norms, clearly distinguishes my approach from that of Friedmann, who considers that 'international stability is not normal, but a fortuitous set of circumstances favouring complementarity among nationally regulated economies' (Friedmann 1991:70). My definition also brings us closer to the approach of the 'international regime' suggested by authors like Ruggie (1998) and Finnemore (1996), who place the emphasis on the role of ideas, not just interests or power, in explaining the behaviour of states.

The forgotten period

In my view, the central component of the post-Second World War food regimes was the objective of national self-sufficiency. Striking a balance between national consumption and national production was and still is an obvious objective of large parts of agricultural policy, one that was also promoted by numerous international organizations such as the FAO or the WFP. The creation of the European Common Agricultural Policy did nothing to contest the principle of self-sufficiency: on the contrary, it was the reproduction at the regional level of the same objectives and the same instruments as those occurring at the national level of different nation states. From this point of view, the EEC and its successor, the EU, differ radically from recent regional agreements such as MERCOSUR or NAFTA.

Actually, the origin of the 'norm' of national self-sufficiency can be found in the First World War and the 'invention' of total war (Shaw 1988). Agricultural policy objectives testify to the strong continuity between the inter-war and post-Second World War periods. But the two world wars and the inter-war period are surprisingly absent from Friedmann's and McMichael's analysis.[1] In my analysis, the wars and the inter-war period do not represent an anomaly or a suspension of the normal course of history, but a crucial era for agricultural policy regarding the legitimacy of objectives, the formation of state bureaucracies and the invention of new institutions and instruments both to manage markets and to govern populations.

The forgotten continent

I fully disagree with the chronology and interpretation of imperial policy adopted by the works discussed above. In their joint paper of 1989, Friedmann and McMichael characterize the first food regime with reference to a rigorous distinction between the tropical products supplied by European colonies and the temperate products (grain, livestock products) supplied by the British dominions and the US (the settler states). The authors note that 'metropoles directly administered (complementary) tropical export agriculture' (1989: 94). This totally ignores the role of Latin American nations in the export of food products. Actually there is no reference at all to Latin America – most of which had been independent since the second decade of the nineteenth century – in the presentation of the first food regime.[2] Yet in 1913, Latin America nations were supplying 21 per cent of world food exports, 94 per cent of the world's coffee exports, 70

---

1. The neglect of war is a classic problem in most social science analysis. On this subject, see Mann (1988).
2. The inclusion of Latin America in the analysis is absolutely necessary to understand the emergence of the 'developing countries' issue in the post-Second World War period. The theoretical framework developed by Latin American intellectuals concerning underdevelopment, centre-periphery relations and so on must be interpreted in close relation with the historical experience of the continent from successful inclusion, during the first period of globalization, to crisis, with the enclosing of the world food market.

per cent of its cocoa (Bairoch and Etemdad 1985), and also 38 per cent of its sugar and 18 per cent of its cereals (Lamartine Yates 1959). During the same year, 1913, Africa supplied no more than 5 per cent of world food exports. In the majority of European colonies, investments (public or private) were very limited before the First World War. According to Kenwood and Lougheed (1992:143), 'Whereas by 1914 almost $11,000m. of British investments were to be found in the United States and the British Dominions, only some $600m. was invested in West Africa, the Straits settlements and the rest of Britain's recent overseas acquisitions'. In 1914, the percentage share of the colonies of French foreign investment was just 5 per cent of the total. Thus, the insertion of Africa, as a part of European empires, occurred after the First World War and, I suggest, must be interpreted as a component, and a transitional one at that, of the national self-sufficiency strategy of European countries.

The concept of the complex

The notion of a 'complex' seems particularly useful in interpreting the existence of international food flows, *in spite of* the worldwide adoption of self-sufficiency policies. In this perspective, a complex must be first defined and described in relation to the specific national agricultural policy instruments and particular international agreements that govern the existence of international trade flows for a commodity or a group of commodities. Thus, by and large I agree with the various complexes that have been proposed to characterize the post-Second World War regime and its recent transformations (the wheat complex, with its predominance of food aid; the durable food complex; the livestock complex; and the more recent fresh fruits and vegetables complex). However, I would like to suggest two modifications:

First, I suggest that the notion of a durable food complex, according to the definition given by Friedmann (1991), is not very useful in identifying a specific component of agricultural policies and/or international trade. The logic of substitutionism is one of national self-sufficiency and is not limited to fat and sugar. Substitutionism is just one component or illustration of the self-sufficiency strategy that was adopted by *all* countries after the Second World War. The search for self-sufficiency implies a search for a substitute for every imported product, and not only for tropical products. Cereals, livestock products and agricultural raw materials have all been the object of substitutionism.

I would also like to introduce two other complexes into the analysis. The first complex includes sugar, the so-called tropical beverages (coffee, cocoa and tea) and the spices. These products have been the core of international food trade for centuries because they were considered 'exotic' and impossible to produce in Europe or North America. I call this complex the 'traditional tropical food complex'. The second complex covers the value chains for alcoholic beverages (mostly beer and wine) and tobacco. During recent years, these products have become increasingly important in international trade. In 2001, their percentage share was 12 per cent of world food exports, as against 7 per cent for tropical beverages (coffee, cocoa and tea). I call this complex the 'legal drugs complex'.

Following McMichael (2000b), for the last period (see Table 3.1) I will use the word 'complex' to identify a specific region, East Asia, not a commodity or a group of commodities. This broadening of the notion of 'complex' may seem confusing and irrelevant. In my view, however, it underlines the shift from a commodity-specific logic to a region-specific logic in the international food trade. This means that, at the present time, agricultural policies are differentiated at the world level not only by commodity but also by region. This also means that at the present time there are no prevailing world norms regarding agricultural policy and that, in relation to the definition proposed previously, there is no active food regime. The level of contestation of the present situation will certainly bring about the emergence of a new food regime in the next few years.

An alternative division of time periods

The present chapter also suggests a reinterpretation of international food trade history and, compared with the work of Friedmann and McMichael, a different division of it into periods, as summarized in Table 3.1.[1]

The first period was from 1870 to 1914 and was characterized by the emergence of world markets for staple food products. This first globalization of markets gave birth to an international division of labour between countries, mostly independent nations, specializing in food production in America, Asia, Oceania and Central and Eastern Europe, and countries specialized in manufacturing production, mostly Western Europe. However, in accordance with Friedmann's and McMichael's (1989) analysis, the United States of America and, more marginally, the British dominions – the so-called 'settler states' – soon evolved towards 'complete' economies characterized by the coexistence and integration of agriculture and industry within the same national economy.

---

1. Obviously, the different periods overlap because it is impossible to identify any single event that one could consider relevant for the whole world.

During and after the First World War, world markets became more and more fragmented into isolated national markets. For the European nations, this war was a decisive experience. From then on, and for more than fifty years, it convinced European countries that the necessities of total war (Shaw 1988) demanded economically self-sufficient nations, in other words the diffusion of the settler state model to Europe and later to all independent countries. Thus, norms relating to the idea of nation-centred economic growth governed international food markets from 1914 to the 1970s.

However, given the insertion of Africa into the international food trade, two sub-periods with particular norms must be distinguished, besides the usual ones connected with the nation-centred growth model. First, just after 1914, the strategy of imperial autarchy emerged as a component of national economic policies. This strategy was dramatically reinforced after the crisis of 1929 and provoked a rapid and dramatic increase in African food exports. Secondly, after Second World War there emerged what I call the 'national self-sufficiency multilateral food regime'. In a world stabilized and ordered by the opposition between the US and the USSR, the dismantling of empires and the independence of colonies stimulated the worldwide diffusion of the nation-centred growth model, while a series of multilateral international organizations promoted the so-called 'development project' (according to the famous expression of McMichael 2000a). In Europe, the Common Market was founded, which followed the imperial autarchy strategy in another form.

Nevertheless the division between the two sub-periods is not actually that clear. The imperial autarchy regime and the multilateral regime interacted and overlapped with each other in several ways:

– In respect of time, it would be misleading to think that the dismantling of imperial markets started right after 1945. At least in France, the chronic balance of payments deficit encouraged governments to maintain, even strengthen, imperial integration wherever possible and to curtail 'foreign' imports whenever they were considered superfluous. Thus, the imperial autarchy project lasted until the signing of the Treaty of Rome in 1957. By that time, and particularly in the Western hemisphere and at the UN level, the development project had already been well and truly 'launched'.

– In respect of institutions managed by independent states, a large number of those concerned with multilateral regimes were set up in the colonial period. This continuity has been more or less pronounced depending on the country and is best exemplified by francophone Africa, with some extreme cases such as Côte d'Ivoire (Losch 1999), rather than by Anglophone Africa. But even there, marketing boards survived independence in most cases.

– In respect of ideology, several aspects are shared by both projects (Arndt 1987; Jackson 1990). Agricultural price stabilization, for example, is a very important common component of both regimes.

After the 1970s, the third period begins with the emergence of the globalization project as an alternative to nation-centred growth. However, the implementation of the globalization project in the agricultural sector occurred in a very incomplete form. Actually, the process of policy reform differs radically according to the level of development in different countries. While in developing countries, the SAP imposed the dismantling of instruments of protection, devices for domestic price stabilization and marketing boards, in developed countries the previous level of agricultural support was maintained. On the one hand, the content of the Uruguay Round Arrangement for Agriculture was limited to defining agricultural policy instruments capable of avoiding trade conflicts between subsidizing nations. On the other hand, market access remained highly restricted. The case of Japan offers a quite different picture. Agricultural support there is very high, perhaps the highest in the world in terms of production value, but the importance of national production in Japanese food consumption is minor and quickly declining. In my view, these contrasted evolutions in agricultural policy are the central characteristic of the last period, one of transition between two regimes, and it explains the diverging trajectories of developing regions in the international food trade.

The (near) absence of Africa in the international food trade: the first globalization period (1870–1914)

The industrial process in England in the nineteenth century was accompanied by a decline of agriculture caused by the opening up of the country to imports of food products. This opening up seemed essential for the prosperity of the industrial sector. Indeed, importing cheap food products on the one hand makes it possible to keep wages low and on the other accelerates the rural exodus and ensures the 'supply' of an increasing amount of labour to the industrial sector. Although the Corn Laws were abolished in 1846, the crisis of English agriculture only really emerged after 1870. However, everything had been settled by 1913. England then depended strongly on

Table 3.1. Summary of the succession of food regimes and Africa's insertion, from the nineteenth century to the present day

	From 1870 to 1929	From 1914 to 1957	From 1950 to the 1970s	From the 1970's to 2003
Objectives of food policies	Access to cheap food (for Western European industrial countries). To produce something to sell in Western European industrial countries (for the other countries).	National self-sufficiency, price stability + imperial autarchy.	National self-sufficiency Price stability Food diplomacy	Double standard in agricultural liberalization implies the coexistence of different objectives: competitiveness for developing countries versus national self-sufficiency and farmers' income stabilization for developed countries.
Instruments of food policies	Free trade, import levies	Control of foreign trade.	Control of foreign trade, Price stabilization policies in domestic and international markets, GATT, International commodity agreement, food aid.	Tariffs, export subsidies, direct financial aid to farmer-norms (technical, sanitary, social...), WTO, regional agreements.
'Motor(s)' of food trade	Production and marketing costs	Imperial protectionism.	Wheat complex, livestock complex, traditional tropical food complex	Livestock complex, fresh fruits and vegetables complex legal drugs complex.
Most dynamic products of food trade	Every product including staple food.	Every product including staple food.	Wheat, feedstuffs, traditional food products (sugar and tropical beverages), citrus and bananas.	Feedstuffs, poultry meat Fresh fruit and vegetables, wine and tobacco.
Most dynamic exporting territories	Independent settler nations/states + continental Europe (e.g., Denmark, Ukraine).	Colonies and subordinated nations/states.	United States.	United States, EU, Far East, MERCOSUR.
Africa's position in food trade	Participation of some colonial islands and coastal regions (mostly vegetable oils and traditional tropical food). Algeria (cereals, wine).	Boom of exports. Every food product. Inclusion of continental Africa.	Marginalization like other developing countries Export specialization in traditional tropical food (sugar and tropical beverages).	Marginalization Participation in the fresh fruit and vegetables and legal drugs complexes.

imports for food, with more than 80 per cent of its wheat and more than 40 per cent of its meat being imported (Perren 1995).

England was not the only country to increase purchases of food from abroad. All the European countries that industrialized adopted the 'English model' to varying degrees during the second half of the nineteenth century. In France, despite its distinctly more protectionist policies, the value of agricultural imports reached 35 per cent of the value of agricultural production just before the First World War (Toutain 1992). The increase in trade was strongest during the third quarter of the nineteenth century. Between 1854 and 1884, wheat sales increased nearly fourfold, those of other grains fivefold, beef sales sixfold and pork sales sevenfold. Growth subsequently slowed somewhat. The volume of food products traded doubled between 1876 and 1890 but increased by only 50 per cent between 1890 and 1913. Until the First World War, Europe (Great Britain and the continent) was without doubt the driving force behind foodstuffs markets. In 1913, it accounted for 72 per cent of world imports of foodstuffs.

Until the mid-nineteenth century, food exports came first from territories that were part of what Curtin (1990) calls the 'plantation complex', whose main features can be summarized by the words spices, large plantation, slavery and colony. Responding to the growth in import demand after 1870, a number of new territories began to specialize in the production of staple foodstuffs for export. Overall, this period of growing trade, which came after the abolition of slavery in the British colonies and Britain's attempts to suppress the slave trade, is characterized by a general movement towards the 'liberation' of agricultural labour. Free workers with the status of full citizens formed the greater part of the labour force in family farming in North America, Oceania and Latin America. A very large part of the labour mobilized in the new exporting territories was European. European labour was found among pioneers in countries receiving mass immigration such as the United States, the British dominions (Canada, Australia and New Zealand), Argentina, Uruguay and southern Brazil (Offer 1989). European labour was also mobilized 'on the spot' by reorienting areas that had long been cultivated but had abandoned mixed cropping plus livestock systems and a weakly merchandised economy in favour of a more or less marked single specialization. This was the case of the Netherlands, Denmark, parts of Russia and the countries along the Danube. The same double process occurred in Asia, with on the one hand migration and pioneering in Burma and Sumatra and on the other hand reorientation of old agricultural regions in, for example, India (Lewis 1970).

Table 3.2. The geographical distribution of world trade in foodstuffs in 1913
(% of the world total)

	Import	Export
United Kingdom and Ireland	25%	4%
Continental Europe	47%	34%
United States and Canada	10%	16%
Oceania	1%	4%
Latin America	6%	21%
Asia	7%	16%
Africa	**4%**	**5%**

Source: Lamartine Yates 1959.

Foodstuff exporters included both completely independent sovereign states (the United States and the Latin American republics), territories that belonged to an empire but enjoyed very great autonomy (the British dominions) and finally colonies in the strict sense (in general, the territories of Africa and Asia). It should nevertheless be stressed that sovereign states were dominant in 1913, at the peak of the trend towards openness. The colonies did not account for more than a quarter of foodstuff exports. In terms of distribution by continent, Latin America alone exported as great a quantity of foodstuffs as Africa and Asia combined. To summarize, the great novelty of the second half of the nineteenth century was the emergence of areas specialized in the exports of staple foodstuffs mobilizing free labour within sovereign, or quasi-sovereign states.

In the 'plantation complex', Africa played a central role as a provider of slave labour but a minor role in the direct supply of food. Mauritius, with its sugar exports, was an exception. Until 1914, the territorial colonization of continental Africa did not result in a large increase in the export of food products. According to Bairoch and Etemdad (1985), Africa exported 9 per cent of Third World food exports in 1860, 11 per cent in 1900 and 10 per cent in 1913. However, at a time of rapid development of world exports, this relatively stable African market share meant an increase in volume. Actually, from 1870 to 1914 Africa's export of food increased by virtue of three separate processes:

– A rebirth of the plantation system, exemplified by the cocoa *roças* of São Tomé. In 1909 São Tomé shared first place among the cocoa-producing territories with Ecuador. In São Tomé, the proximity of Portuguese Africa allowed the planters to use forced labour even after the prohibition of the slave trade and the abolition of slavery in the plantation territories (Tomich 1988). But even there, the organization of a boycott by English and German chocolate manufacturers obliged planters to change the labour mobilization process, thus provoking an irreversible decline in cocoa cultivation after 1910.

– The rapid growth of the 'indigenous' production of agricultural commodities, controlled by African traders as a substitute for the export of slave labour. The dominant place of oilseeds and oil – mostly palm oil and palm kernel from the Niger delta and peanuts from Senegambia – in African exports in 1913 can be interpreted as the expression of this second process (M'Bokolo 1992). The export boom in cloves and copra produced on the East African coast in slave plantations under Zanzibari control is part of the same process of reorientation of the activities of local traders (Cooper 1977).

– The development of European family farms and capitalist estates in North Africa (Algeria, Morocco and Tunisia) producing and exporting wine, fruits and cereals. In 1913, North Africa was exporting almost half of African food exports, and Algeria alone 25 per cent.

Boom and bust in Africa in the international food trade: nation-centred growth (1914 to the 1970s)

The First World War marked the end of this first period of the globalization of foodstuffs markets. The mobilization of the entire economy in the service of the war led to the adoption of agricultural support measures and the application of protective measures on imports. A new stage was reached with the 1929 depression. In addition to increasing customs dues (see Perren 1995 for Britain; Tracy 1989 for Europe; Taylor et al. 1943 and Malenbaum 1953 for the rest of the world), state interventions went from tariff protection to real control of the domestic market and of foreign trade. By favouring self-centred growth, a fair proportion of these national institutions guaranteed the stabilization of domestic prices and producers' incomes.

The imperial autarchy regime and the boom in African exports, 1914–1957

From the First World War to the mid-1950s, the food trade developed increasingly within the framework of the imperial autarchy strategies being followed by the European colonial powers. These strategies were expressed first by infrastructural investment in the colonies and, second, in the introduction of discriminatory mechanisms (taxes, quotas, etc.) against non-empire imports, and incentives (credit, subsidies, higher prices, etc.) to support colonial production. This period of protected relationships between the European countries and their colonies coincided with the boom in African food exports. During that time, Africa's share of world food exports increased continuously from 6 per cent in 1913 to 9 per cent in 1937 and 12 per cent in 1953.

France is an extreme example of the imperial autarchy strategy. The law proposed in 1921 by Albert Sarrault for the 'mise en valeur des colonies' (equivalent in French colonial discourse to the word 'development' in English) is a decisive event in the development of French imperial policy. Sarrault suggested breaking with the financial self-sufficiency of the colonial territories and asked for a massive public investment to build roads, ports and other infrastructure. The shift in commercial policy occurred in 1928. Before and after 1861, even after a new law passed in 1892, the African colonies benefited from very few advantages compared to trade from elsewhere (Poquin 1957). The law of 1928 allowed discriminatory tariffs to be introduced in favour of the colonies. In 1938, the duty on 'foreign' products was as high as 91 per cent for coffee, 110 per cent for cocoa and 34 per cent for palm oil. These different measures were very successful from the point of view of imperial autarchy. From 1913 to 1938, the share of the empire in agricultural imports into metropolitan France increased from 29 per cent to 71 per cent.

Table 3.3. The geographical distribution of world food exports in 1913, 1937 and 1953 (% of the world total)

	1913	1937	1953
United Kingdom and Ireland	4%	5%	4%
Continental Europe	34%	31%	21%
United States and Canada	16%	11%	19%
Latin America	21%	20%	25%
Oceania	4%	7%	7%
Asia	16%	18%	13%
Africa	**6%**	**9%**	**12%**

Source: Lamartine Yates (1959) for 1913 and 1953; League of Nations (1942) for 1937.

Table 3.4. Share of the empire in French imports of agricultural products, 1913–1958 (%)

	1890	1913	1929	1938	1958
Wine	17%	57%	84%	97%	71%
Grains	10%	12%	29%	80%	78%
Table fruits	5%	17%	14%	49%	72%
Coffee	0%	2%	4%	43%	76%
Cocoa	4%	2%	56%	88%	85%
Oilseeds	18%	25%	25%	54%	78%
Sugar	72%	100%	16%	78%	94%
Total agricultural products	19%	29%	38%	71%	71%

Source: Marseille 1984.

In the British Empire, this shift in policy occurred later. In 1932, the Ottawa Conference 'called to discuss the lowering of tariffs within the British Empire on imperial goods produced instead a set of agreements the most important effect of which was to raise British tariffs on non-imperial goods' (Ashworth 1962:244). From 1928 to 1938, the percentage share of Commonwealth imports into the United Kingdom increased from 29 per cent to 40 per cent.

In should be noted that, until their military defeat, Germany and Japan followed similar policies in order to achieve national self-sufficiency. Hirschman (1945) wrote a fascinating account of the role of external trade in the German strategy of influence in Central and Eastern Europe before Second World War. In this way, without direct territorial control, at least until 1938 Germany was able to stabilize and secure part of its supply. The Japanese strategy followed a more traditional path of direct colonization in Korea, Taiwan and later continental China, but it was complemented by the search for regional influence and the building of the so-called 'Co-Prosperity Sphere'.

National self-sufficiency, the multilateral food regime and the 'subordination' of African food exports

After the Second World War, within the framework of 'nation-centred' growth, foreign trade was entirely subordinated to the domestic goals of stability and the full use of resources. In Keynesian policies, exports, like public expenditure, formed part of the re-launching of the economy by increasing the outlets for the nation's companies. From this point of view, as Grjebine (1980) stressed, Keynesian trade policy can be qualified as neo-mercantilist. In the agricultural sector, dumping policies illustrate this neo-mercantilism. In the United States since the 1930s, dumping has been a central tool revindicated and used by the US Department of Agriculture to eliminate surplus production from the domestic market (Wallace 1934).

Ruggie (1982), citing K. Polanyi, suggests that the postwar decades marked by US hegemony can be described as an international order of 'embedded liberalism'. The essence of this international order was that it was multilateral – unlike the economic nationalism of the 1930s – but also that it predicated multilateralism upon domestic interventionism, in contrast with the British gold standard and free trade liberalism. The failure of the negotiations undertaken at the Conference on Trade and Employment and the signing of GATT are clear illustrations of this 'embedded liberalism'. Indeed, GATT first instituted multilateralism (that is to say, non-discrimination), not the abandoning of protectionism. 'Embedded liberalism' acquired a new dimension in agriculture. The initial GATT text permitted very great latitude in the use of non-tariff barriers and export subsidies. The waivers allowed to the United States in 1955 confirmed this exception for agriculture. In fact, until the conclusion of the Uruguay Round, almost all instruments were 'legally' authorized to provide protection for national agricultures (see Hopkins and Puchala 1980 and Cohn 1993).

In this context of 'nation-centred' growth and great tolerance of agricultural protectionism, international trade in agricultural products displayed extremely moderate growth, conspicuously lower than trade in other types of goods and services. The difference in growth rates was a new feature, resulting in a steady downward trend in agriculture's share of trade in goods and services. Before the Second World War and until the 1950s, the proportion of food products in the international trade in goods and services decreased, though only very moderately. For example, it fell from 29 per cent to 26 per cent between 1913 and 1953. This comparative stability of products reflected the international trade logic of the first period of globalization: primary goods were exchanged for manufactured goods. In contrast, the share of food products, and even more of agricultural raw materials, decreased continuously from the end of the Korean War, from 25 per cent in 1953 to 14 per cent in 1972 for food products, and from 14 per cent to 3 per cent for raw materials.

During this period, international markets operated like canal locks between national markets, handling the transfer of products without calling into question the level or stability of prices in the national areas (Johnson 1973). Countries only traded surpluses and shortages on the international market in the quantities required to ensure the equilibrium and hence the stability of the domestic market. Siamwalla and Haykin (1983) described this situation by referring to the rice market as being a 'thin market'. As is well documented in the political economy literature dealing with the food trade, in this context of the national self-sufficiency of agricultural policy two new complexes emerged: the wheat complex and the livestock complex (see Table 3.5). In the wheat complex, trade resulted mainly from the complementarity between US food-aid policy – an institutionalization of the dumping policy – and the search by developing countries for cheap food for their growing urban populations (Hopkins and Puchala 1978b; Hopkins and Puchala 1980; Friedmann 1982). In the livestock complex, a central role was played by corn and wheat on the one hand and soya beans and meals on the other. Mainly exported by the US, these crops provided the basis for the rapidly developing livestock sector in Europe and Japan, exploiting an existing 'protection hole' (Bertrand et al. 1985). On these grain markets, the US secured supply and stabilized international prices by adjusting its stocks and exports according to fluctuations in import demand and in the exports of their competitors (Tubiana 1989).

Although the nationalization of the economy took place first of all in the industrialized countries, the countries that had earlier supplied food products fully adopted the idea of nation-centred development through so-called 'import substitution' policies. These policies were defined as strategies breaking with the 'old international division of labour'. Their aim was to enhance the industrialization of economies that had previously specialized in the production and exports of raw materials. They were called import substitution policies because they were aimed at replacing imports of industrial goods through national production. This is therefore an industrialization strategy focusing on the domestic market[1] in which the state establishes a strict compartmentalization between the national and international markets. Ominami (1986) refers to 'intraverted industrialization' in discussing this development.

Stabilization funds and marketing boards, combined with tariff policies, ensured the strong independence of domestic price movements with regard to international prices on agricultural markets. An important difference, one that does not call into question the autocentric nature of growth, con-

---

1. Import substitution policies are fed by many theoretical and ideological influences, but the work of the secretariat of the United Nations Economic Commission for Latin America (ECLA), headed by Raul Prebisch, doubtless had the most impact (Prebisch, 1949 and 1950).

Table 3.5. Major complexes of the national self-sufficiency multilateral food regime, from 1950 to the 1970s

		Wheat complex	Livestock complex (feed grains, oilseeds and animal feedstuffs)	Traditional tropical food complex	
				Tropical beverages	Sugar
National policies organizing...	Import demand	Marketing board foreign trade monopoly in importing countries	Oilseeds and animal feedstuffs EU protection 'hole' Japanese Agricultural Basic Law (1961)		EU, US and USSR import quotas
	Export supply	US food aid	US international prices stabilization policy for grains (soya, wheat and corn)	Marketing board controlling exports and storage in developing countries	Marketing board controlling exports and storage in producing countries
International rules and agreements		International Wheat Agreement Food Aid Convention World Food Program	FAO sub-committee on surplus disposal Kennedy Round output regarding CAP GATT 'Arrangement concerning certain dairy products' GATT 'Arrangement regarding bovine meat' Lomé Convention (Import quotas for beef)	UNCTAD International coffee agreements International cocoa agreements	International Sugar Convention EU Sugar Protocol

cerns the relationship between agriculture and industry. As the 'Fordism of the poor', import substitution policies were accompanied everywhere by a change in the terms of exchange between agriculture and the rest of the economy that was unfavourable to the former. Explicit or implicit taxation (especially by means of over-valued exchange rates) was the rule in numerous developing countries until the 1970s, and sometimes until the adoption of the SAPs in the 1980s (Bates 1981; World Bank 1986; Krueger 1992).

During the period from the end of the Second World War to the beginning of the 1970s, a large proportion of those countries that had previously specialized in food production found themselves subjected to the trend towards marginalization in the international food trade by losing their positions as suppliers to the industrialized countries (Daviron et al. 1988). The countries suffering this marginalization were developing countries. In otherwords, this trade marginalization forged identity and unity among developing countries.

The marginalization of developing countries in exports of food products can be interpreted as the direct effect of agricultural policies that had been adopted in different parts of the world. Indeed, the so-called 'developed' countries and the so-called 'developing' countries followed opposite agricultural policies. The former closed their food markets and used all means possible to protect their agriculture, including the subsidizing of exports. The latter taxed their agriculture in order to industrialize, increasing taxation when the volume and value of exports tended to peak or even decrease. In a situation of disequilibrium such as this, developing countries could only lose market share to developed countries.

Table 3.6. Share of developing countries in world food exports
(% of the world total, excluding intra-EEC trade)

	1955	1964	1972
Africa	**11%**	**10%**	**7%**
Latin America	22%	17%	16%
Near East	1%	1%	2%
Far East	14%	12%	10%
Total for developing countries	48%	40%	35%

Source: United Nations Conference on Trade and Development 2003.

This contrast in agricultural policies was inherited directly from the first period of globalization. As was argued in the first part of this chapter, the two groups of countries had diametrically opposed positions in the international division of labour. The first exported industrial products and imported food products, while the second produced agricultural products. Turning in on the national area and seeking autocentric growth could only lead the former to protect agriculture and the latter to protect industry.

However, the closing of food markets in the industrialized countries made the industrialization of the former suppliers of food products essential or inevitable, but also made its financing practically impossible.[1] This was the challenge faced by the so-called developing countries. The organization of the first UNCTAD in 1964 can be interpreted as the search for a solution to this problem. The aim of UNCTAD was to define an international framework for solving the trade balance problems of countries undertaking import substitution policies. One of the first demands, which was expressed in the introductory text for the conference written by Prebisch (1964), was for access to the food markets of the industrialized countries. This question was not discussed seriously until the Uruguay Round.

The structure of food exports from Africa and Latin America increased the role of 'exotic' products in parallel with the marginalization in trade. After being expelled from the market for 'temperate' products, these countries found themselves partially limited to 'exotic' products. The tropical beverages group (coffee, cocoa and tea) and sugar regained all the importance that they had enjoyed during the period of the plantation complex. This was particularly marked in Africa. The percentage of exotic products (tropical beverages and sugar), which had accounted for 10 per cent of food exports in 1913 (Lamartine Yates 1959), increased to 26 per cent in 1937/38 (Bairoch and Etemdad 1985), 40 per cent in 1962 and 52 per cent in 1972 (FAO 2003).

The search for international agreements on commodities responded partly to this evolution. With the priority being placed on tropical beverages, the agreements were intended to maximize export income from these products, the aim still being to reduce trade imbalances. From this point of view, the approach put forward within the framework of UNCTAD was substantially different from that which had prevailed immediately after the

1. This is doubtless what underlies the distinction between the former British dominions and developing countries. Although the former were foodstuff suppliers, they established tariff policies aimed to protect the development of industry at a very early date, that is to say, when the food markets of the industrialized countries were still open (see Knowles 1924).

war. The Havana Charter saw the agreements as exceptional temporary measures for the management of unbalanced situations to enable an adaptation to depressed sectors. The objective was henceforth one of setting up permanent price support mechanisms (Prebisch 1964). Thanks to UNCTAD, developing countries explicitly received the right, or at least international legitimacy, to organize cartels of tropical commodity exporting nations. The International Coffee Agreement (ICA) is one of the best concretizations of this right, with a very large participation by producing *and* consuming countries, including the US (see Table 3.5).

The marginalization of Africa in the international food trade: from the 1970s to the present day

For the last thirty years, a series of 'shocks' – oil price and dollar fluctuations, debt and financial crisis, the rise of NICs – has shaken the nation-centred growth model. Since the mid-1970s, the OECD countries have begun to reform their economies in response to these shocks. Privatization, deregulation and the opening of national markets have been the basic ingredients in the liberal regime that has been adopted by these countries. However, until now OECD agricultural policies have escaped most of these reforms. In spite of the inclusion of agriculture on the agenda for trade negotiations during the GATT Uruguay Round, a large majority of OECD countries still protect their domestic food markets and support their own domestic agricultural production.

According to recent OECD secretariat estimates, 'in 2002, the level of support provided to farmers (the Producer Support Estimate) was USD 235 billions, which represented 31% of total farm receipts in the OECD area, compared with an average of 38% between 1986 and 1988. Output-based support and input subsidies accounted for 76% of support to farmers in 2002, compared to 90% in 1986–88' (OECD 2003:30). Indeed, implicitly, the objective of national food self-sufficiency has survived the dismantling of the nation-centred growth model in OECD countries.

This general realization hides considerable disparity between countries. OXFAM (2002:99) has produced a 'Double Standard Index' to compare 'the level of protectionist trade policies employed by the richest and more powerful trading nations against exports from developing countries'. According to this index, the EU comes first in the level of protection that is opposed to the exports of developing countries, being followed by the US and then Japan. The European CAP is being reformed at an extremely slow pace. The objective of promoting a multifunctional agriculture, in being linked to commodity production support, looks more like a new way of justifying protectionism than a really new project. For its part, in 2002 the US adopted a new farm bill, the Farm Security and Rural Investment Bill, which was more oriented towards producer and export subsidies than the act it replaced.

In contrast to the EU and the US, Japan seems to be moving towards a more open trade policy for agricultural products. A new fundamental law on agriculture has been drafted to replace a framework of regulations that has remained practically unchanged for thirty-five years. Its main provisions imply replacing controlled prices by measures aimed at stabilizing the agricultural economy (in other words, direct aid), the introduction of agro-environmental measures and finally the promotion of multifunctional agriculture. The food security concern is still very present in the ongoing discussions. However, as has already been shown by Japan's positions during the Uruguay Round, the food security aim is certainly based on support for national production, though also, and to an even greater extent, on the promotion of an international framework guaranteeing the stability of imports (Rapkin and George 1993). Even the rice policy– a highly sensitive topic for the conference – underwent its first reform in 1997, with import quota restrictions being replaced by customs dues.

The very laborious revision of the agricultural policies of developed countries, harshly negotiated in a multilateral framework, took place at the same time as the more rapid and sudden withdrawal of the state in those developing countries that had 'adopted' structural adjustment policies. The reduction of import barriers and the closing of state marketing boards proceeded much more quickly and more drastically within this framework. It would be tedious to draw up here an inventory of the liberalized sectors in the developing countries. As an illustration, state withdrawal from coffee production, for which marketing boards had existed in *all* the producer countries until the end of the 1980s, is now practically complete. Only Colombia still has a public body, Fedecafè.

This worldwide reform process, which is being followed in very different ways according to the country concerned and its level of wealth, has generated very different trajectories for the insertion of developing regions into the international food trade: the stabilization of market share in Latin America, rapid growth in the Far East and continuous decline in Africa. The rest of this chapter provides a brief summary and interpretation of these trajectories.

Figure 3.1. Share of developing regions in world food exports, 1955–2000
(% of the world total, excluding intra-EU trade)

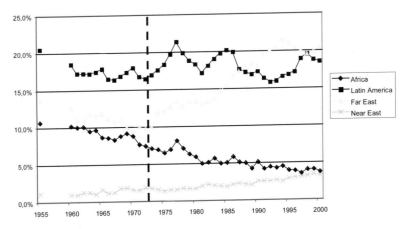

Source: UNCTAD (2003).

Figure 3.2. Share of developing countries in world food imports, 1955–2000
(% of the world total, excluding intra-EU trade)

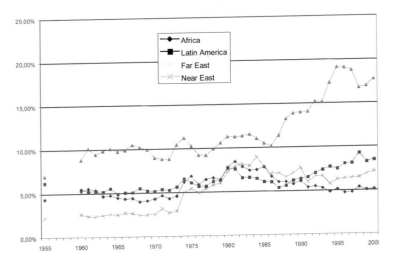

Source: UNCTAD (2003).

The successful diversification of Latin American food exports

Latin America succeeded in preventing its decline in the international food trade thanks to a double process of diversification: product diversification and geographical diversification. In terms of products, Latin America exports moved from the 'traditional tropical food complex' to the livestock, fresh fruits and vegetables and 'legal drugs' complexes (see Table 3.7). During the last fifteen years, tropical beverages and sugar have lost most of their importance, from 50 per cent at the end of the 1980s to less than 20 per cent in 2001. During that last year, oilseeds and derived products accounted for 25 per cent of food exports, fruits and vegetables for 23 per cent and wine and tobacco for 10 per cent.

The insertion of Latin America into the livestock complex started at the beginning of the 1970s, with the export of soya to Europe by Brazil and then by Argentina. Both countries replaced the US as a supplier of feedstuffs for European livestock (Bertrand et al. 1985; Bertrand and Hillcoat 1996). The development of competition with US soya producers was due to copying the North American model of agricultural modernization: the same kind of large family farm, and the same level of access to technology (seeds, equipments), credit and relatively stable markets (Leclercq 1988). Brazil also 'invaded' the other side of the livestock complex, as the country has been exporting poultry meat for twenty years and more recently, increasing incredibly rapidly, pork.

Secondly, from the very beginning of the 1980s, new fresh fruits and vegetables appeared in the inventory of exports. Latin America benefited from a relatively lower level of protection for fresh fruits and vegetables in OECD countries. According to Llambi (1994:196): 'Most fruits and vegetables, particularly when they are not processed, encounter less restrictive tariff barriers in the major industrial countries than do the mass-consumed durable food commodities ... In the United States, most fresh fruit and vegetable products enjoy duty-free treatment under the Generalized System of Preference. Lastly, at the end of the 1980s, the export of 'legal drugs' increased dramatically, following a path very similar to that taken by fresh fruits and vegetables.

Geographically speaking, Latin American exports shifted from the US to Western Europe and the Near East in the 1970s, then to regional trade after 1989 and more recently to Asia. Today Latin America's share of EU imports is equal to its share of US imports, the EU accounting for 29 per cent of Latin American exports as against 26 per cent to the US.

Table 3.7. Major complexes from the 1970s to 2003

		Wheat complex	Livestock complex	Traditional tropical food complex		Fresh Fruit and Vegetables + Legal drugs complexes	East Asian Import Complex
				Tropical beverages	Sugar		
National policies organizing…	Import demand	Unprotected food markets in developing countries	Norms Oilseeds and animal feedstuffs EU protection 'hole' Unprotected food markets in developing countries	Norms	EU and US quotas Unprotected food markets in developing countries	Seasonal import quotas in OECD Low tariff protection in OECD	Japan and Korean opening policy Unprotected food markets in developing countries
	Export supply	Food aid EU export subsidies US Export Enhancement Program US export credit policy	EU export subsidies US Export Enhancement Program for grains US Dairy Export Incentive Program US export credit policy		EU export subsidies		US export credit policy
International rules and agreements		Food Aid Convention Uruguay Round Agreement on Agriculture (URAA) MERCOSUR	MERCOSUR URAA SPS	SPS agreement	EU sugar protocole URAA	SPS agreement	Uruguay Round Agreement on Agriculture (URAA) ASEAN

*The rapid growth of Far Eastern exports and the emergence of an
East Asian import complex*

From the beginning of the 1970s to the financial crisis of 1997, the percentage share of the Far East in world food exports increased steadily from 10 per cent to 20 per cent. This remarkable performance was closely linked to the emergence of what McMichael (2000b) called the East Asian import complex (see Table 3.7). Indeed, 60 per cent of Far East food exports are sent to Asia.

In the food sector, since the 1960s Japan has depended to a very considerable extent (80–100 per cent) on other countries for its supplies of wheat, secondary grains and oil seeds. This strong food dependence has recently been intensified by the extremely rapid growth of meat imports. The proportion of imports for consumption has increased sharply since 1985, from 30 per cent to 60 per cent for beef and veal, 15 per cent to 40 per cent for pork and finally 10 per cent to 30 per cent for poultry. This growth began with the Uruguay Round negotiations. It is partly a response to pressure from the United States, but also from a number of domestic groups. It also forms part of the questioning of modern agriculture, whose environmental externalities are absorbed with difficulty in the crowded national territory of Japan. Meat imports are a direct substitute for the grain imports intended as feedstuffs for livestock. The evolution of the value of food imports in Japan clearly summarizes these continuing changes, tripling from 1986 to 1996 and increasing from 18 to 54 billion dollars.

This dynamism in food imports is found throughout so-called 'developing' Asia, where the value increased from 16 to 57 billion dollars between 1986 and 1996. Asian import demand from both developed and developing countries has grown as a proportion of the international trade in food products since 1985. Western Europe had 'always' been at the heart of the international food trade, but it lost its central position and role as a main outlet over a ten-year period. In 2000, the share of Asian imports in the international trade in food products totalled 31 per cent, against 19 per cent for Western Europe.

Japanese firms organize links to East Asian importing countries and Far East exporting countries. According to McDonald (2000:487), 'since 1986, many firms have leapt offshore to organize fresh, frozen and processed foods for the Japanese market, and to manufacture abroad for markets abroad'.

Table 3.8. Share of world food imports for the Far East, Japan and Western Europe
(% of the world total, excluding intra-EU trade)

	1972	1980	1990	2000
Japan	6%	7%	14%	13%
Far East	9%	11%	14%	18%
Total Asia	15%	17%	28%	31%
Western Europe (Intra-EU excluded)	42%	28%	25%	19%

Source: United Nations Conference on Trade and Development 2003.

The marginalization of Africa

Africa alone remained on the path shared by the developing countries in the three decades following the Second World War. After 1972, Latin American countries and, to an even greater extent, Asian countries regained the market shares they had lost during previous years. By contrast, at the beginning of the twenty-first century the market share of Africa is less than 4 per cent, well below its market share in 1913.

First, the decreasing part played by Africa can be explained with reference to the closeness of its relationship with the EU. Fifty per cent of African food exports go to the EU, the only region where Africa has an important market share, namely 11 per cent of EU food imports. However, EU imports are increasing very slowly, more slowly than imports to Japan or Far Eastern countries before the 1997 crisis. Even the US, despite its protectionist agricultural policy, is increasing its food imports at a higher rate.

In spite of the various reforms implemented over the past twenty years, the CAP retains its objective of self-sufficiency. Some countries can still use the 'flaws' in protection[?], like Latin America in the feedstuffs market. Some products which have enjoyed more recent increases in consumption are also less protected, like fruits and vegetables. But fundamentally, the EU still aims at food self-sufficiency. Compared to how the Far East has benefited from Japan's import strategy, Africa is clearly being penalized by the policy of her 'centre'.

Secondly, Africa has lost almost all its markets outside the EU. The case of the United States, where the percentage share of food imports from Japanese firms organize links to East Asian importing countries and Far East exporting countries. According to McDonald (2000:487), 'since 1986, many firms have leapt offshore to organize fresh, frozen and processed foods for the Japanese market, and to manufacture abroad for markets abroad'.

Table 3.9. Origin of food imports of the main importing countries and regions, 1990–2000

	World (intra-EU trade excluded)	Japan	Far East	US	EU (intra trade excluded)
Far East	19.9%	34.7%	45.2%	13.4%	13.9%
Australia/NZ	5.8%	7.8%	8.2%	4.4%	4.1%
US	17.3%	30.9%	17.0%	–	13.6%
Latin America	18.9%	6.9%	8.3%	33.4%	30.9%
EU (intra-trade excluded)	16.6%	10.0%	10.1%	19.0%	–
Near East	3.2%	0.2%	1.8%	0.7%	4.0%
Africa	3.9%	2.0%	1.4%	1.3%	11.4%
World	100 %	100%	100%	100%	100%

Source: United Nations Conference on Trade and Development 2003.

Table 3.10. Destination of food exports of developing regions, 1998–2000

	World	Japan	US	EU	Far East	Latin America	Africa
Far East	100%	21.8%	10.1%	12.1%	38.9%	–	–
Latin America	100%	4.6%	25.6%	29.2%	7.5%	18.5%	–
Africa	100%	6.4%	4.9%	52.3%	–	–	12.1%
World	100%	12.5%	14.5%	17.9%	17.1%	8.6%	5.2%

Source: United Nations Conference on Trade and Development 2003.

However, an analysis of the composition of African exports presents us with a slightly different view of the situation. African food exports are concentrated in three complexes: traditional tropical foods, legal drugs and fresh fruits and vegetables (see Table 3.7). In 2001, these products together accounted for seventy-eight per cent of African food exports. Participation in the traditional tropical food complex is a product of the past: more specifically, it is a legacy of the specialization allowed by the national self-sufficiency multilateral food regime. African exports were protected from competition in relation to these products, thanks to the existence of international agreements for coffee and cocoa and the sugar protocol. The percentage share of these two groups in the international food trade has decreased dramatically during the last fifteen years (see Table 3.9). It also decreased as a proportion of African exports, but it remains very important compared to the situation in Latin America or Asia.

The two other complexes – legal drugs and fresh fruits and vegetables – include products with a much higher growth rate in the international food trade. Their share of African exports is increasing at a rapid pace, for instance wines from South Africa, tobacco from Malawi and horticultural products from Kenya.

Table 3.11. Composition of international food trade and of African food exports, 1986–89 and 1999–2001 (intra-EU trade excluded)

	% of world trade (intra-EU excluded)		% of African exports	
	1986/1989	1999/2001	1986/1989	1999/2001
Meat and meat preparations	8%	9%	2%	2%
Dairy products and eggs	4%	4%	0%	1%
Cereals	15%	15%	4%	4%
Oilseeds	5%	5%	1%	2%
Animal and vegetable oils	5%	6%	3%	1%
Feedstuffs	5%	5%	1%	1%
Tropical beverages and spices	12%	7%	53%	33%
Sugar and honey	7%	4%	9%	9%
Beverages and Tobacco	9%	12%	6%	14%
Fruit and vegetables	16%	18%	15%	22%

Source: FAO 2003.

Conclusion

The opening up of European countries to food imports in response to the growth requirements of the industrial sector led to various territories specializing in the production of staple foodstuffs for export between the mid-nineteenth century and 1914. The development of exports of foodstuffs was undoubtedly synonymous with wealth for sovereign states such as the American republics and quasi-sovereign states like the British dominions. Although history then condemned this 'outward' growth model, it was an effective solution in seeking 'wealth and modernity' until 1914.

Africa played a minor role in this first food regime. It was only after the First World War, and more especially after the 1929 crisis, that the governments of European countries really began to find and organize sources of supply in their African colonies as a component of their policies of self-sufficiency in food products. The export sectors in these colonies developed in a context that had already been affected strongly by market fragmentation, protectionism and state intervention. To some extent, the increase in African exports after 1914 can be interpreted as a particular manifestation of the substitutionism underlined by Friedmann (1991; 1994).

The division of labour on a world scale, through which a number of territories (with very varied history, political, economic and social situations) specialized in the production of foodstuffs and others in industrial products, was seriously called into question by the gradual nationalization of agricultural markets after the First World War and decolonization after the Second World War. The industrialization policies involving the substitution of imports, adopted first by Latin American countries and then by the newly independent nations of Asia and Africa, can be seen as a response to the closing of food markets in the industrialized countries. This status of being a former exporter of food products faced with a loss of outlets, combined with the difficulty of domestic industrialization, created the developing country status, at least as instituted by UNCTAD. All these countries were then subjected to a process of marginalization with regard to their integration into the trade in foodstuffs. The decline of Africa in the international food trade began a little later, after independence and the development of the CAP, but it soon followed the same path as Latin America and Asia.

In retrospect, the 1970s and the first half of the 1980s look like the golden age of the internationalization – in the literal sense of the word – of agricultural markets. Although there was clearly an increase in the interdependence of national markets, they remained isolated from one another. In other words, the development of trade was not accompanied by any market unification at the world level. On the contrary, this period was characterized by an increasing differentiation of trading conditions, with price differentiation according to destination, specific credit conditions, the development of barter operations, etc.

The liberalization introduced after the oil price hike and the debt crisis, as well as the conclusion of the Uruguay Round, was supposed to change this situation radically and bring about the unification of the world market for agricultural goods. However, the liberalization of agriculture is being realized at very different paces in the developed and developing countries. In the latter, SAPs have dramatically reduced state intervention and largely opened the domestic market to foreign competition. The developed countries, conversely, with the notable exception of Japan, have retained their national self-sufficiency policies.

In this context, the position of developing regions in the international food markets during the last thirty years has been characterized by a number of different trajectories. Latin America, or at least some of it, has been able to participate in the livestock complex by supplying animal feedstuffs first to Europe and then to East Asia, as well as, more recently, poultry meat to the latter. The growth of Latin American exports has also been supported by the development of new food complexes for fresh fruits and vegetables and legal drugs. Asian food exports grew at a rapid pace, pulled by the emergence of the East Asian import food complex (McMichael 2000b) and the development of export-oriented economic policies.

Africa is the only region with a market share that is continuing to decline. By some criteria, Africa seems to be 'jammed' in the 1960s, even after fifteen years of reform of economic policy. However, the composition of its food exports is changing rapidly, with its increasing insertion into the fresh fruits and vegetables complex and the legal drugs complex. Thus, the continued decline in Africa's position in world food markets can be broken down into three components:

—   First, the close relationship with Europe, a 'centre' with a particularly low pace of food import growth.

—   Second, its inability to participate in the livestock complex by exporting feedstuffs like Brazil and Argentina, or exporting poultry meat, again like Brazil or, more recently, China.

—   Third, its delayed involvement, compared to other developing regions, in the fresh fruits and vegetables complex and the legal drugs complex.

Ironically, Africa is increasingly exporting another 'commodity' not mentioned in this chapter – labour. In several countries, migrants' remittances are playing a central role in supporting the balance of payments and now account for a larger share of external income than the traditional food products. Thus, having almost arrived at the end of a cycle of agricultural boom and bust lasting for more than a century, Africa seems to be returning to a very old and in many ways unpleasant type of specialization, namely the export of human labour.

References

Arndt, H.W. (1987) *Economic Development: The History of an Idea*. Chicago: University of Chicago Press.

Ashworth, W. (1962) *A Short History of the International Economy since 1850*. London: Longman.

Bairoch, P. and B. Etemdad, (1985) *Structure par produits des exportations du Tiers-Monde, 1830–1937*, Genève: Droz.

Bates, R.H. (1981) *Markets and States in Tropical Africa: The Political Basis of Agricultural Policies*. Berkeley: University of California Press.

Bertrand, J.P. and G. Hillcoat (1996) *Brésil et Argentine: La compétitivité agricole et agro-alimentaire en question*. Paris: L'Harmattan.

Bertrand, J.P., C. Laurent et al. (1985) *Le monde du soja*. Paris: La Découverte.

Cohn, T.H. (1993) 'The Changing Role of the United States in the Global Agricultural Trade Regime', in W.P. Avery (ed.) *World Agriculture and the GATT*. London: Lynne Rienner.

Cooper, F. (1977) *Plantation Slavery on the East Coast of Africa*. New Haven: Yale University Press.

Curtin, P.D. (1990) *The Rise and Fall of the Plantation Complex: Essays in Atlantic history*. Cambridge & New York: Cambridge University Press.

Daviron, B., M. Petit, et al. (1988) 'Sécurité alimentaire et commerce alimentaire dans les pays en développement', Rapport d'étude pour la CNUCED, Montpellier.

FAO (2003) *FAOSTAT: Agricultural and Food Trade Data 2003*.

Finnemore, M. (1996) *National Interests in International Society*. Ithaca: Cornell University Press.

Friedland, W.H. (1994) 'The Global Fresh Fruit and Vegetable System: An Industrial Organization Analysis', in P. McMichael (ed.) *The Global Restructuring of Agro-food Systems*. Ithaca: Cornell University Press.

Friedmann, H. (1982) 'The Political Economy of Food: The Rise and Fall of the Postwar International Food Order', *American Journal of Sociology*, 88(Supplement): 248–86.

—— (1991) 'Changes in the International Division of Labour: Agri-food Complexes and Export Agriculture', in W.H. Fridland, L. Busch, F.H. Buttel and A.P. Rudy (eds) *Towards a New Political Economy of Agriculture*. Boulder: Westview.

—— (1994) 'Distance and Durability: Shaky Foundations of the World Food Economy', in P. McMichael (ed.) *The Global Restructuring of Agro-food Systems*. Ithaca: Cornell University Press.

Friedmann, H. and P. McMichael, (1989) 'Agriculture and the State System. The Rise and Decline of National Agricultures, 1870 to the Present', *Sociologia Ruralis*, 39(2):93–117.

Goodman, D., B. Sorj, et al. (1987) *From Farming to Biotechnology*. Oxford: Blackwell.

Grjebine, A. (1980) *La nouvelle économie internationale*. Paris: PUF.

Hirschman, A.O. (1945) *National Power and the Structure of Foreign Trade*. Berkeley: University of California Press.

Hopkins, R. and D. Puchala, (1978a) 'Perspectives on the International Relations of Foods', *International Organization*, 32(3):581–616.

—— (1978b) 'Toward Innovation in the Global Food Regime', *International Organisation*, 32(3):855–68.

—— (1980) *Global Food Interdependence: Challenge to American Foreign Policy*. New York: Columbia University Press.

Jackson, R.H. (1990) *Quasi-states: Sovereignty, International Relations, and the Third World*. Cambridge: Cambridge University Press.

Johnson, D.G. (1973) *World Agriculture in Disarray*. London: Macmillan.

Kenwood, A.G. and A.L. Lougheed (1992) *The Growth of the International Economy 1820–1990: An Introductory Text*. London: Routledge.

Knowles, L.C.A. (1924) *The Economic Development of the British Overseas Empire*. London: Routledge.

Krueger, A.O. (1992) *The Political Economy of Agricultural Pricing Policy: A Synthesis of the Political Economy in Developing Countries*. Baltimore: Johns Hopkins University Press.

Lamartine Yates, P. (1959) *Forty Years of Foreign Trade: A Statistical Handbook with Special Reference to Primary Products and Under-developed Countries*. London: Allen & Unwin.

League of Nations (1942) *The Network of International Trade*. Genève: League of Nations: 172.

Leclercq, V. (1988) *Conditions et limites de l'insertion du Brésil dans les échanges mondiaux du soja*. Montpellier: INRA/ESR.

Lewis, W.A. (1970) *Tropical Development, 1880–1913: Studies in Economic Progress*. London: Allen & Unwin.

Llambi, L. (1994) 'Comparative Advantages and Disadvantages in Latin American Nontraditional Fruit and Vegetables Exports', in P. McMichael (ed.) *The Global Restructuring of Agro-food Systems*. Ithaca: Cornell University Press.

Losch, B. (1999) *Le complexe café-cacao de la Côte d'Ivoire*. Montpellier: Faculté de Sciences Economiques Montpellier.

McDonald, M.G. (2000) 'Food Firms and Food Flows in Japan 1945–98', *World Development,* 28(3):487–512.

McMichael, P. (1996a) *Development and Social Change: A Global Perspective.* Thousand Oaks, CA: Pine Forge Press.

—— (1996b) 'Global Restructuring and Agri-food Systems', Communication at conference *Restructuration of Perennial Crops,* Manizales, Colombia.

—— (2000a) *Development and Social Change: A Global Perspective.* Thousand Oaks, CA: Pine Forge Press.

—— (2000b) 'A Global Interpretation of the Rise of the East Asian Food Import Complex', *World Development,* 28(3):409–24.

Malenbaum, W. (1953) *The World Wheat Wconomy, 1885–1939.* Cambridge: Harvard University Press.

Mann, M. (1988) *States, War, and Capitalism: Studies in Political Sociology.* Oxford: Blackwell.

Marseille, J. (1984) *Empire colonial et capitalisme français: histoire d'un divorce.* Paris: Albin Michel.

M'Bokolo, E. (1992) *Afrique noire: histoire et civilisations, XIXe–XXe siècles.* Paris: Hatier-AUPELF.

OECD (2003) *Agricultural Policies in OECD Countries: Monitoring and Evaluation 2003.* Paris: OECD: 260.

Offer, A. (1989) *The First World War: An Agrarian Interpretation.* Oxford: Clarendon Press.

Ominami, C. (1986) *Le tiers-monde dans la crise.* Paris: La Découverte.

OXFAM (2002): 'Rigged Rules and Double Standards: Trade, Globalization, and the Fight against Poverty', in *Make Trade Fair.* London: OXFAM.

Perren, R. (1995) *Agriculture in Depresion.* Cambridge: Cambridge University Press.

Poquin, J.-J. (1957) *Les relations économiques extérieures des pays d'Afrique Noire de L'Union Française.* Paris: Librairie Armand Colin.

Prebisch, R. (1949) 'El desarrollo economico de la American Latina y algunos de sus principales problemas', *Estudio Economico de la America Latina 1948.* Santiago: CEPALp.

—— (1950) 'Crecimiento, desequilibrio y disparidades: interpretacion del proceso de desarrollo economico', *Estudio economico de la America Latina 1949.* Santiago: CEPALp.

—— (1964) *Nueva política comercial para el desarrollo.* México: Fondo de Cultura Económica.

Rapkin, D. and A. George (1993) 'Rice: Liberalization and Japan's Role in the Uruguay Round: A Two-level Game Approach', in W.P. Avery (ed.) *World Agriculture and the GATT.* Boulder: Lynne Rienner.

Ruggie, J.G. (1982) 'International Trade, Transactions, and Change: Embedded Liberalism in the Postwar Economic Order', *International Organization,* 36(2):379–415.

—— (1998) *Constructing the World Polity: Essays on International Institutionalization.* London: Routledge.

Shaw, M. (1988) *Dialectics of War: An Essay in the Social Theory of Total War and Peace.* London: Pluto.

Siamwalla, A. and S. Haykin, (1983) *The World Rice Market: Structure, Conduct and Performance.* Washington: IFPRI.

Taylor, H.C., A.D. Taylor et al. (1943) *World Trade in Agricultural Products.* New York: Macmillan.

Tomich, D. (1988) 'The 'Second-Slavery': Bonded Labour and the Transformation of the Nineteenth-century World Economy', in F.O. Ramirez (ed.) *Rethinking the Nineteenth Century.* New York: Greenwood.

Toutain, J.C. (1992) 'La production agricole de la France de 1810 à 1990: départements et régions', *Economies et Sociétés,* 11–12:1–142.

Tracy, M. (1989) *Government and Agriculture in Western Europe 1880–1988.* New York: New York University Press.

Tubiana, L. (1989) 'World Trade in Agriculture Products: From Global Regulation to Market Fragmentation', in D. Goodman and M. Redclift (eds) *The International Farm Crisis.* New York: St Martin's Press.

UNCTAD (2003) Handbook of Statistics 2003. United Nations Conference on Trade and Development. Online. Available at HTTP: <http://www.unctad.org/Templates/Page.asp?intItemID=1890>

United Nations Conference on Trade and Development (2003) *Handbook of Statistics 2003.*

Wallace, H.A. (1934) *New Frontiers.* New York: Reynal & Hitchcock.

World Bank (1986) *World Development Report 1986.* New York: Oxford University Press.

4. The Structural and Spatial Implications of Changes in the Regulation of South Africa's Citrus Export Chain

Charles Mather[1]

Introduction

In 2000, the South African citrus export industry declared itself in crisis. Export earnings plummeted by 600 million rand to a level that had not been seen in almost a decade. There were several *proximate* causes of the crisis facing domestic producers and exporters of fresh citrus. When South Africa's early maturing varieties of citrus arrived in Europe, exporters faced fierce competition from large volumes of unsold northern hemisphere-produced citrus. While the ensuing competition affected all citrus exporters and producers, the South African industry felt the brunt of oversupply: unseasonal weather in the early part of the growing season resulted in a much higher than normal percentage of smaller sized fruit, which in Europe fetches much lower prices. An additional contributing factor, according to industry analysts, was the large number of new exporters that had emerged in the wake of liberalization in 1997: these new agents lacked the experience of dealing with difficult market conditions. Industry stalwarts suggested that if the citrus sector had still been regulated through a single desk, the very experienced single channel agent would have managed the crisis far more effectively. In late 2000, the industry responded by establishing a Citrus Southern Africa, a producer's organization aimed at regulating the activities of private exporters.

These proximate causes veil a range of *structural* problems facing primary producers and exporters of South African citrus. In the last two decades, the consumption of fresh citrus has either stagnated or declined in the most important European, North American and Asian markets (FAO 1998). At the same time, production has increased rapidly through intensification in

---

1. Thanks to the editors for their critical comments on an earlier draft of this chapter. Funding for the research in South Africa and the UK was provided by the Centre for Development Research, Copenhagen (now Danish Institute for International Studies). Thanks also to Wendy Job, Cartography Unit, Wits University for preparing the diagrams.

traditional citrus exporting countries and through the spread of citrus farming to new sites in both the northern and southern hemispheres. Increases in the global supply of fresh citrus have been exacerbated by improved storage techniques and longer growing seasons in both hemispheres, which have eroded the counter-seasonal advantage that southern hemisphere exporters had enjoyed since the 1970s (USDA 2004). The situation of oversupply and frequent overlaps of production has led to intense competition between producing countries, a situation appropriately described by McKenna and Murray (2002) as the 'jungle law of the orchard'. Gaining a competitive edge is based on improving the quality and variety of fruit and decreasing costs through 'chain efficiency' and 'chain shortening'.

Retailers in Europe and North America have played a central role in driving producers and exporters to produce higher quality and new varieties of fruit (Le Heron and Roche 1995; Barrett et al. 1999; Dolan and Humphrey 2000). In the last decade, retailer fruit sales have displaced wholesale markets and small corner stores, especially in the UK and also in several other European countries (Rabobank 1997b). Fresh fruit is very important to large multiple retailers, as margins are relatively higher in this category than they are for other commodities sold on supermarket shelves. Retailers also position themselves in relation to their competitors on the quality and variety of their fresh fruit. These increasingly powerful agents within the food system have benefited from a situation of oversupply by demanding much higher quality, greater variety and cheaper prices for fruit. The liberalization of agricultural markets in the early 1990s in some fruit-producing countries has allowed retailers to further press home their advantage in the fresh fruit trade (cf., van der Laan et al. 1999). Liberalization has removed whatever power producers might have had in the past against retailers and international buyers.

The changes described for the citrus export chain associated with market liberalization in the producing country and the growing power of agents downstream of the farm – notably processors and retailers – have been an important area of research in recent studies of African agro-export commodity chains (e.g., Larsen 2002; Ponte 2002a, 2002b; Mather and Greenberg 2003; Raikes and Gibbon 2000; Gibbon 2003; Fold 2002). Much of this research is based on analyses of various fresh or processed products, and employs the global value chain (GVC) concept of 'governance' to explore changes in the regulation of these export chains. In many export chains, governance has shifted from producers to buyers, with important implications for producers, exporters and farm workers in African countries.

This chapter builds on this research by exploring changes in the governance of South Africa's citrus export industry. The first part of the chapter suggests that in the period prior to the liberalization of citrus exports, the chain was producer driven in the sense that the single channel exporter was able to exercise considerable power over agents both upstream and downstream of itself. Yet the governance of this chain is unlike the archetypal producer-driven chains associated with automobile and aircraft manufactures. In his analysis of tropical agro-commodity chains, Gibbon notes that these were 'not driven by manufacturing TNCs and did not involve "dedicated" supply relations of any kind ... But producers participated actively in setting the rules of the game, both in price terms and in terms of arbitrating quality and the relation of quality to price' (Gibbon 2001:61). This section of the chapter suggests that the citrus chain was governed in a similar fashion to traditional African agro-exports. For several decades in the period after the 1960s, South Africa's single channel exporter was also able to set the 'rules of the game' for fresh citrus in destination markets. The chapter also shows, however, that its ability to govern the chain was fragile and increasingly vulnerable to competition from other exporting countries and the growing demands of powerful retailers.

The next three sections of the chapter explore the impact of market liberalization on the South African citrus industry after 1997. The first of these sections examines changing quality criteria for citrus in the country's most important export markets. This section suggests that although South Africa's single channel agent for citrus was able to manage quality problems during the regulated era, these systems broke down after 1997 with a more fragmented supply system. Importers and buyers in Europe were able to exploit the quality problems that emerged after 1997 by discounting all South African citrus. The third section of the paper explores the structural impact of new market demands in a post-liberalization era. Here, the chapter suggests that liberalization has led to a process of differentiation that has affected both growers and packers. The process of differentiation is shaped by the new quality and process requirements now demanded by both private and public agencies in destination markets. In the last section of the chapter, the theme of differentiation is explored in spatial terms. Several citrus-growing regions are now linked to specific high-value citrus chains, and production systems in these regions are being reshaped in line with the specific quality and process requirements of these markets. This process of 'inclusion' is matched by a process of exclusion: citrus-growing regions unable to meet the process or quality requirements are being marginalized and are now

Figure 4.1. Southern hemisphere fresh citrus exports

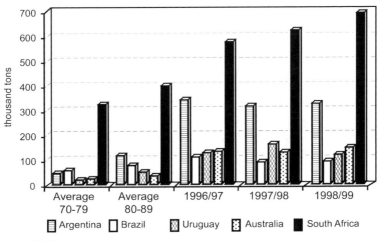

Source: FAO, 2000.

forced to supply local or regional markets where the returns are far lower. The conclusion of the chapter reflects critically on this process of structural and spatial differentiation.

A producer-driven citrus chain

Between the 1940s and the late 1980s, the South African citrus export sector was in a position to set the 'rules of the game' through a statutory single-channel marketing scheme and by virtue of its dominant position as a counter-seasonal exporter of fresh citrus. The single channel system for citrus, set in place through the Marketing Act (1937), meant that citrus producers were not permitted to export their fruit outside the infrastructure established by the South African Cooperative Citrus Exchange (SACCE). The position of the Citrus Exchange was strengthened through the postwar period as South Africa entrenched itself as the most important southern hemisphere exporter of fresh citrus. Indeed, for most of this period South Africa exported more fresh citrus than the combined crop of all other exporters south of the equator (Figure 4.1).

The Citrus Exchange played a key role in increasing the volume of citrus exported. Payments to growers were based on a pooling system, which rewarded larger volumes of fruit, albeit at the expense of quality. In addition, the Exchange established an impressive extension and laboratory infrastructure to advise farmers on cultivar selection and farming methods and techniques. From the late 1980s, the Citrus Exchange was also assisting and sourcing fruit from black farmers on agricultural projects in the former homelands. These projects had been set up in the 1980s – along the lines of World Bank farmer settlement schemes – and several of the projects produced fruit of high quality, although with strong support from consultants, the Citrus Exchange and officials of the former homeland departments of agriculture.

With enormous volumes of fresh citrus, sourced first from the warmer northern parts of South Africa, Zimbabwe, Mozambique and Swaziland and later from the cooler Cape regions (Figure 4.2), the Citrus Exchange established itself as a reliable supplier to European importers, fresh fruit markets and retailers. From the 1960s, the Citrus Exchange used its command of large volumes of citrus to exercise greater control over markets in Europe. In a strikingly 'commodity chain'-like statement, in 1960 the chairman of the Citrus Exchange called for greater control over distribution: 'It was always our policy to control the distribution of fruit down to the first point of sale ... we are now adopting a policy which is designed to enable us to control the flow of our fruit right down to the ultimate consumer' (cited in Cartwright 1977:84). To this end, the Exchange established a panel of 'master agents' throughout Europe who were responsible for specific country or regional markets. Using the master agents, and by controlling huge volumes of citrus that could be stored for limited periods of time, the Exchange was able to influence prices, even when the crop itself was of poor quality.[1] The Exchange was also heavily involved in promoting its Outspan brand, which it did vigorously until these activities were disrupted by anti-apartheid protestors in the UK and elsewhere in Europe (Mather and Rowcroft 2004).

While the Citrus Exchange was able to influence agents downstream of production, its reliance on *volumes* alone as its leverage exposed it to competition from both northern and southern hemisphere producers. Overlaps between citrus produced in the northern and southern hemisphere are more common now, but they were a problem for South African exporters as early as the late 1970s. The Citrus Board's 1984 report noted that market

---

1. A long time employee of the Exchange based in the UK described this process as follows: "When the knew what the crops was we decided that we would keep count 56s tight (large sized fruit). We used promotional efforts for the 88s and 105s (less popular small fruit) to get rid of them. We used campaigns like 'the small ones are more juicy'".

Figure 4.2. Citrus production in South Africa

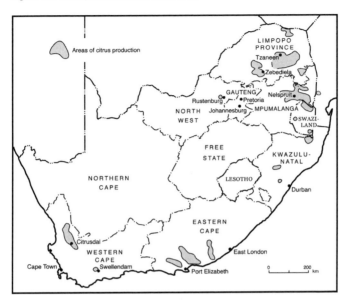

Source: Cartography Unit, University of the Witwatersrand.

conditions had been difficult due to 'a record European overlap of unsold Mediterranean citrus' and by the 'all time record US Valencia crop' (Citrus Board 1983/4). Larger volumes of citrus from new southern hemisphere producers and larger volumes of unsold citrus produced in Spain and Italy compromised the Exchange's ability to manage the chain.

A more serious problem facing the Citrus Exchange was the uneven quality of South African citrus exports. The goal of increasing volumes of fresh citrus exports had come at a considerable cost, which was not easily remedied. Grapefruit provides a vivid illustration of the problem: citrus producers were encouraged to establish grapefruit trees on rough lemon rootstocks, which deliver large volumes of low quality fruit. As one former high-ranking Citrus Exchange employee noted: 'Farmers kept on planting grapefruit on rootstocks that gave high yields but low quality. The Japanese want high internal quality, and that is the only way to sustain that market, but the farmers planted on rough lemon rootstock. It gives good yields, but the quality of the fruit is mediocre' (senior manager of the South African Cooperative Citrus Exchange, June 2001, Pretoria).

Improving the quality of grapefruit required significant capital investment, which explains why the Exchange's own overseas office was often unable to meet the demands being made on it by retailers:

> At the UK office we were really a branch of the head office based in South Africa. By implication we were grower driven. But we couldn't get growers to do what we wanted them to do. There were huge pow-wows over quality standards. We tried to set a common standard for the sugar acid ratio of grapefruit – this was one of Tesco's demands. But the growers couldn't agree so in the end we had to say to Tesco 'Do you want the fruit or don't you?'(senior manager, Capespan, October 2001, Southampton).

Fruit buyers for the main UK multiple retailers also complained that the Citrus Exchange was unresponsive to requests for new varieties. A retail buyer based in the UK argued:

> Whilst there was generally speaking a controlled marketing of fruit in a disciplined and fairly sophisticated way, when retailers wanted specific requirements of size, varieties, and different standards it used to be extremely frustrating. We always found it frustrating because we couldn't necessarily get what we wanted. And that would be from a size point of view, an eating quality point of view, and from a varietal point of view (fruit buyer for UK supermarket, October 2001, London).

By the late 1980s, the Citrus Exchange was aware of the problems it faced in adapting to the new competitive environment in the fruit trade. From this period, it commissioned several external and internally produced reports, all of which conveyed the same message: while the Exchange had developed an impressive infrastructure for the production of large volumes of citrus, its marketing efforts were outdated and out of touch with the realities of the international trading environment. Moreover, the organization had failed to meet new market demands for a commodity that was increasingly oversupplied and under pressure from retailers pressing for better quality and more variety. The consultants recommended that the organization restructure with a focus on becoming more 'market driven' through a review of its overseas marketing methods and strategies and by introducing 'performance-linked' incentives to growers (Citrus Board 1990). The Exchange's own 'in-house' investigation completed two years later confirmed the earlier consultant's report: the Citrus Exchange had failed to adapt to a radically different global trading environment for citrus. In outlining a new strategy, the Exchange stressed the need for flexibility in products, in fruit delivery and in pricing. It also confirmed the need for incentives to improve the quality of citrus produced by South African growers.

In response to the assessments of its competitive position, the Citrus Exchange embarked on two strategies. First, it attempted to encourage better quality products from its growers through restructuring the pooling system. Previously, growers had been paid by cultivar pool, and the returns over the season or for a large part of the season were averaged for growers. The Exchange changed the system so that returns were averaged over a shorter period of time, to reward producers more directly for better quality citrus or early and late season varieties. The organization also began to brand extra-special quality fruit for retailers in the UK. Citrus producers with a reputation for producing good quality fruit were singled out for these brands or for the programmes for Tesco, Marks & Spencer and Sainsbury's. To meet the growing demands for new varieties of citrus, the Exchange intensified its efforts in developing new and preferred citrus categories.

Although the Exchange was able to begin to meet the demand of overseas importers and retailers, there was a great deal of inertia in the system. For some farmers, responding to the new demands required a complete overhaul of their farming operations, something that they were unwilling to do before it was absolutely necessary. There was also inertia in the cooperatives that supplied the Citrus Exchange fruit, especially the larger ones located in the Western and Eastern Cape. The infrastructure that had been designed to pack millions of cartons of standard citrus was not flexible enough to meet the new demands for quality and variety (Mather and Greenberg 2003). As one UK-based importer argued, the Citrus Exchange's efforts to 'incentivize' for quality was 'blunted' by the big cooperative packers, who did not want to incur penalties for fruit that had problems (Manager, Fruit import company, October 2001, Southampton).

The Citrus Exchange's second strategy was to establish itself as an international fruit trader in the mould of Dole and Del Monte. The cooperative started this process at home by transforming itself into a private company called Outspan, and then later Capespan through a merger with the single channel exporter responsible for deciduous fruit. Shares in the new company were disbursed to individual growers or cooperatives based on the volumes supplied in the three previous citrus seasons. The new company also shifted from its previous focus on 'production' to 'marketing'. This shift involved downsizing and later privatizing the extension and research infrastructure and increasing its capacity in marketing. In citrus-growing regions, the result was that extension officers with a great deal of expertise in citrus propagation were now involved in setting up business plans for their grower members.

From the late 1980s, Capespan also embarked on an aggressive asset acquisition campaign, mainly in the form of cooling and port facilities. It restructured its marketing structure overseas by discontinuing its relationship with its dedicated 'master buyers' and presented itself to retailers and importers as a preferred supplier of fresh citrus and later deciduous fruit, tropical fruit and even wine. Controversially, Capespan also acquired the intellectual property rights for various citrus cultivars and distributed these to a limited number of growers in return for exclusive supply rights. Capespan's strategy through the 1990s had much in common with the strategies of other large fruit traders who were under intense competitive pressure due to the oversupply of fruit and the growing influence of retailers in global fruit chains (Rabobank 1997a). In response, traders have attempted to cut costs, innovate in terms of product and presentation and improve the efficiency of the distribution network.

This section of the chapter has suggested that the Citrus Exchange was in a position to set the 'rules of the game' for producers and agents downstream of production. Its leverage was based on its position as the largest producer of southern hemisphere citrus. Through the 1980s, however, the Citrus Exchange found it increasingly difficult to use volume alone to leverage UK retailers and other large buyers in Europe. Unlike classic producer-driven chains – where barriers to entry are high due to the capital- and technology-intensive nature of production – the barriers to entry in citrus production are much lower. As a consequence, the basis of its ability to 'drive' the chain was always under threat. From the late 1980s, it faced the additional challenge of a retail sector that was demanding higher quality and more variety from its fruit suppliers.

Quality and South African citrus after liberalization

One of the consequences of market liberalization in African agriculture has been deterioration in the quality of the continent's agro-exports. For African exports crops as a whole, Raikes and Gibbon (2000) argue that lower quality partly explains the decline in the continent's unit values for a range of export crops. Several writers have linked problems with quality to the dismantling of quality controls – usually performed by parastatal marketing boards – in the post-liberalization period (Shepherd and Farolfi 1999; van der Laan et al. 1999; Friis-Hansen 2000). Although parastatals were often regarded as inefficient, the role they played in quality controls is now being reassessed, especially given that the private sector has not taken over the quality monitoring functions of the parastatals (Shepherd and Farolfi 1999; although see Larsen 2002).

In the period after the liberalization of the South African citrus export chain, quality problems were also reported by importers, especially in the UK and continental Europe. Interviews with importers and retailers in the UK suggest that the reliable supply of reasonably good quality citrus was severely disrupted after 1997. Quality problems were related in part to the challenges faced by the country's export quality control agency, the Perishable Products Export Control Board (PPECB). The PPECB faced considerable difficulties inspecting fruit packed in both packhouses and at the ports in the period after the citrus chain was liberalized. During the single channel era, most fruit was packed in a limited number of large co-operative packhouses or several very large privately owned packing facilities. In the period after liberalization, the number of smaller packing facilities and independent exporters increased dramatically: in the case of exporters from one to more than two hundred. This new complexity to the citrus export chain placed huge pressure on the organization's limited infrastructure and inspection staff, and compromised the PPECB's ability to effectively monitor the quality of citrus exports in the immediate post-liberalization period.

Yet the problems of quality in South African citrus after liberalization were more complex and not restricted to the limited capacity of the PPECB. As noted earlier, when citrus exports were controlled through a single channel, the single desk exporter played an important role in managing quality problems when the fruit was loaded on to ships in South Africa and also when the fruit was offloaded at ports like Southampton, Bremen and Antwerp. Managing the quality of citrus involved diverting 'distressed fruit' to less discerning markets – usually to Eastern Europe and Russia – or destroying the fruit when it could not be sold. With many new agents handling South African citrus, this system of quality control broke down. Smaller agents lacked the infrastructure or the networks to divert fruit in the destination markets, and they also preferred to sell the fruit at any price rather than have it destroyed. Importers in Europe were able to take advantage of the fragmented supply by discounting the value of all South African citrus, a situation that has contributed to lower unit prices for fresh citrus in both the UK and continental Europe (Figures 4.3 and 4.4).

Figure 4.3. Citrus exports to the United Kingdom from South Africa

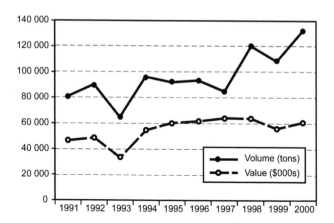

Figure 4.4. Citrus exports to continental Europe from South Africa

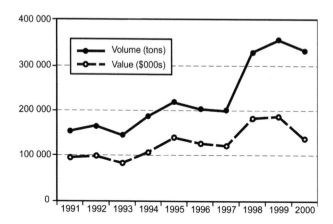

Sources: OECD International Trade by Commodity (2002), SITC rev. 3.

Figure 4.5. Global supply patterns of citrus

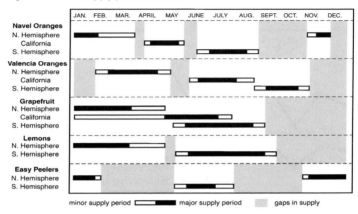

Source: Adapted from Dixie, 1995.

The problems South African producers and exporters faced in managing quality in the post-liberalization period must also be seen in terms of the stricter quality criteria for fresh citrus. From the late 1980s, citrus producers all over the world were facing two sets of pressures around quality. In traditional varieties of citrus, for which there is a situation of oversupply, the pressure on producers is on colour, size, acceptable sugar-acid ratios and ensuring that the fruit has few or no seeds. In new and preferred varieties of citrus – notably navel oranges and easy peelers – the pressure on producers is to fill windows in the season where the global supply is limited or absent. For easy peelers there are significant gaps in seasonal supply (Figure 4.5): the pressure on suppliers to meet retailers' demands for year-around supply of all varieties especially in this category is considerable.

Quality in fresh fruit is also now defined according to a set of increasingly rigorous process requirements. As early as 1990, the UK's Food Safety Act required retailers to exercise 'due diligence' in their sourcing practices. Since 1990, the range of process requirements has become more numerous and more complex. There are private process standards – the best known of which is EurepGap – which set down production criteria for traceability, food safety and environmental responsibility. Without EurepGap accreditation, producers cannot supply the members of this private consortium of European retailers. Public standards for individual countries or regional trading blocs have also become stricter through the 1990s, with much higher minimum residue levels for pesticides and other chemicals, and a longer list of banned chemicals.

Although the imposition of quality and process standards is becoming more widespread, there are markets where quality and process standards are much less important. Eastern Europe, Russia and the Middle East (mainly Saudi Arabia) are generally regarded as markets where quality and process criteria are either weak or absent. In non-citrus producing countries of the Middle East, it is also possible to export fruit that may have been exposed to citrus diseases that are not harmful to humans but are restricted in Europe. African countries north of South Africa and Indian Ocean islands are also considered to be 'second tier' markets where quality and traceability requirements are not important. Finally, the local domestic market is another outlet for fruit that does not meet export criteria, although it tends to be heavily over-supplied and returns are very poor.

South African producers and exporters in the post-liberalization period face rising quality standards and process criteria in what are considered to be the industry's traditional markets of the UK and Europe. Process standards that were previously restricted to the UK – for instance traceability – are now being extended throughout Europe. At the same time, there are other markets where quality standards and process requirements are weakly enforced or non-existent. Unfortunately for producers, prices for citrus in these markets are significantly lower. The next section of the chapter considers the changing landscape of quality and process requirements for South African producers and packers of fresh citrus.

Structural differentiation

The response by the South African citrus industry to these quality and process demands has been very uneven. For almost six decades, the industry encouraged producers to increase volumes and it has been difficult for exporters to convince producers and cooperative packers of the need to improve the quality and variety of their fresh citrus. Indeed, many producers remain unconvinced that their farming enterprises can be economically sustainable based on smaller volumes of higher quality fruit. Producer culture is not, however, the only problem facing citrus exporters. The local industry has found it difficult to meet the demand for new varieties that are more difficult to handle, like easy peelers, with an infrastructure that was geared to producing large volumes of hardier oranges and grapefruit. This problem is especially evident within cooperative packhouses where the legacy of the single channel has been fixed into the design structure of the huge assembly lines geared to packing two or three million boxes of citrus a season (Mather and Greenberg 2003).

Growers

The new demands for quality, variety and the higher phytosanitary standards for both traditional and new 'protocol' markets have led to sharp differentiation between citrus producers in South Africa. Many citrus growers have been excluded from export chains due to their inability, or reluctance, to meet the quality standards now being demanded by retailers and importers. Those farmers who have not gone bankrupt are shifting their emphasis to tourism opportunities or to less risky agricultural crops (Mather and Greenberg 2003). Black citrus farmers on agricultural projects in the former homelands have found it especially difficult to meet the new standards in citrus export markets. The assistance they had from the single channel exporter has been withdrawn, as has the financial and other support provided by former homeland governments. Citrus farming in these regions has all but collapsed since liberalization (Greenberg 2002; Mann 2001).

While a category of grower is being excluded from the global citrus chain, the ostensible winners in this process are those farming operations that are more attractive to overseas buyers. These farms normally have larger volumes of fruit, they often have attractive varieties including easy peelers, navels and other seedless citrus cultivars, and they usually have their own packing infrastructure. Several of these growers have moved up the chain by establishing their own marketing companies, with varying degrees of success. Indeed, most of these growers talk of the need to get 'closer to the customer' and express the desire to 'shorten the chain' to cut costs, much in the same way that retailers talk about establishing closer ties to producers. Although farmers in this category appear to have succeeded in the post-liberalization era, they operate in what remains a buyer-driven chain. Improving the quality and variety of the fruit produced is not so much a way of 'upgrading' or moving up the value chain: upgrading is imperative for remaining in global chains. Even the most highly sought-after growers, who are known by name to UK retailers, complain of buying practices and prices they say make it difficult for them to farm sustainably.

Packers

Cooperative packhouses have also faced very difficult circumstances in the period since liberalization. Those that exist outside the Western and Eastern

Cape citrus-growing regions have tended to be small, with a limited membership of growers and relatively small volumes of fruit. After the end of the single channel in 1998, many of these cooperatives have been dissolved and the packing facility, usually outdated and requiring significant investment to meet internationally recognised process standards such as Hazard Analysis and Critical Control Point (HACCP), has been sold or simply abandoned. The situation in the Western and Eastern Cape is considerably more complex. The cooperatives in these two regions are large, with memberships of between one hundred and three hundred growers. During the single channel, these cooperatives established a large packhouse infrastructure geared to sorting and packing millions of cartons of fruit during the four or five months of the citrus harvest season. Many cooperatives in these two regions also invested in retail stores, packing factories and other facilities that allowed them to decrease input costs for their grower members. By the mid-1990s, most had a complex asset base that went far beyond the packhouse.

These large cooperatives have faced enormous challenges adapting to liberalization of the citrus export chain after 1997. Before and after 1997, a considerable number of growers with a reputation for good quality citrus – and often larger volumes of fruit – broke away from the cooperatives and established private packing facilities. The loss of volume has severely compromised their profitability, which was based on using economies of scale to pack as cheaply as possible. Losing volume is not the only challenge facing packhouses: cooperative packhouses with a large membership of producers are finding it difficult to meet new process requirements. As noted earlier, traceability has been a requirement in the UK since the 1990 Food Safety Act, which has required retailers to apply 'due diligence' in their sourcing practices (Marsden et al. 2001). In 'protocol markets', including the US, Japan, Korea and Taiwan, traceability is a basic requirement for exporters. Indeed, in Taiwan traceability is required to the orchard and not only to the farm. Although the ability to trace an orange back to the farm has not been a demand for exports to continental Europe, it is a key requirement for EurepGap accreditation, which came into force at the end of 2003. Without EurepGap certification, producers and packers face the prospect of being excluded from selling to EurepGap members and will be forced to sell their fruit in less lucrative markets, or on wholesale markets where they are more vulnerable to discounting. Achieving traceability in a packhouse designed to pack millions of cartons of fruit for two hundred or more growers has proved to be a significant challenge for cooperative packhouses.

The inflexibility of packhouses and the difficulties they face in achieving traceability has excluded them, at least until they can guarantee traceability, from some UK retailer programmes. Several retail buyers in the UK interviewed in 2001 expressed their reluctance to source from former cooperatives, preferring instead to establish relationships with grower packers with large volumes of fruit:

> In terms of cooperatives, our technologist and myself aren't that keen on cooperatives. It is almost impossible to guarantee traceability; our preference is to work with larger players that can offer traceability; they have due diligence; all the things you would expect. In fact I haven't visited a citrus grower in South Africa who doesn't have his own packhouse (fruit buyer for UK supermarket, October 2001, London).

Large cooperatives have responded differently to the challenges they face in a fragmented and increasingly demanding citrus export chain. In Citrusdal, the Goodehoop cooperative decided to meet the new market demands 'head on' by selling its various assets and focusing on its 'core business' of fruit packing. In order to meet the demands for traceability, it was forced to restructure its packing operations. It has also successfully achieved HACCP accreditation in one packhouse and is in the process of meeting this standard for the other two packhouses it owns. Not surprisingly, the HACCP accredited packhouse is the newest of the three: achieving accreditation with the other two is a major obstacle for the company. The restructuring process has been difficult, with significant job losses, the impact of which is evident in the small town of Citrusdal , where unemployment levels have increased dramatically. In the Eastern Cape, Patensie Citrus decided on a more conservative route: in order to shore up losses in volume to other privately owned facilities it has enforced a 'pack-right' clause on its members. This regulation forces growers to deliver fruit to the company's packhouses or face huge charges for their contribution to previous capital investments. This strategy has failed in that growers have taken Patensie's claim to the competition commission for arbitration. After long deliberation, the commission found in favour of growers and rejected pack-right as 'non-competitive behaviour'. The different responses of these two cooperatives appear to have been a consequence of management culture, but also perhaps differences in the financial situation of the two cooperatives. Due to various large investments in the late 1980s and early 1990s, Patensie's debt situation was considerably worse than Goodehoop's. Despite their different responses, both face considerable difficulties in meeting the new quality and process requirements of a liberalized market environment.

Spatial differentiation

During the single channel era, citrus exports were presented to overseas markets as a South African product branded under the 'Outspan' label. In the period since liberalization, this 'national product' has fragmented with many new brand names for South African citrus. Citrus-growing regions within the country have also become more prominent than they were before: several regions are now better known for higher quality or specific varieties of citrus. One of the outcomes of spatial differentiation is that regions – and producers within regions – are establishing close links to specific overseas markets where the returns for high quality citrus are usually very good. Stricter quality criteria and new process demands are playing an important role in shaping this simultaneous process of spatial differentiation and the establishment of links to specific citrus-producing regions. The remainder of this section considers two regions that have established links to specific export markets based on process requirements and quality demands.

Western Cape and the United States

From the early 1990s, South African citrus producers began supplying several countries described locally as 'protocol markets'. Japan, South Korea and Taiwan have sanitary and phytosanitary protocols that are far stricter and more rigorous than those imposed by private or public agencies in other parts of the world. Meeting these phytosanitary protocols involves considerable effort, cost and risk, although if the fruit passes inspection the rewards are high. Producers must be registered and audited prior to supplying protocol markets. Once approved, producers must meet an additional set of logistical demands. Fruit destined for Japan, for instance, must be 'cold sterilized', which means the fruit must be maintained at a temperature of -0.6°C for at least 12 days. The fruit is inspected at South African ports by Japanese plant quarantine authorities and on arrival in Japan. Fruit that fails to meet the protocol after arrival in Japan must be incinerated at the expense of the exporter.

Until recently, supplying a protocol market has been an option for all citrus producers in South Africa. When the citrus industry gained access to the US market in the late 1990s, however, the process criteria excluded all producers outside the Western Cape, a region of the country that has a Mediterranean climate with winter rainfall (see Figure 4.2). The basis of this partial and geographically specific market access was a phytosanitary disease called citrus black spot (CBS). This phytosanitary problem is both controversial and difficult to control: it affects the fruit but, unlike many other citrus pathogens, not the tree itself. The disease is present in all summer rainfall regions in both the northern and southern hemispheres. In winter rainfall regions, notably the Mediterranean, California and the Western Cape province of South Africa, CBS is absent (FAO 2003). Even though there has been no recorded case of CBS-infected fruit affecting orchards in winter rainfall regions, the US Department of Agriculture (USDA) was only prepared to grant Western Cape producers access to US markets.

Since gaining access to the US, Western Cape producers have focused much of their effort on improving the volume and quality of citrus exported to this lucrative market. Exports to the US from the Western Cape have, as a result, risen from thirty thousand cartons in 1997 to over one and a half million in 2002. Although this volume is only three per cent of total exports from South Africa, it represents seventeen per cent of total export earnings. There have been very active local efforts to reduce the amount of fruit that does not pass USDA inspections at packhouses and at the port. Rejections were high in the first years of citrus exports, primarily due to a pest called mealybug. Efforts by industry representatives have since led to dramatic improvements in the amount of fruit approved by the USDA inspectors (Citrus Southern Africa 2002). Western Cape citrus growers have also been active in improving the quality of fruit, especially the colour of navel oranges and the quality of easy peelers, which initially resulted in a poor reputation of South African citrus in the US. Not surprisingly, there are several other regions of South Africa now claiming to be 'black-spot free'.

The extent to which Western Cape citrus producers now see their future tied to the US market was underlined with George Bush's visit to South Africa in 2003. While his visit was marked by various protests against the US-led invasion of Iraq in cities like Pretoria, Johannesburg and Cape Town, farmers and farm workers in Citrusdal, the heart of the Western Cape's citrus industry, 'paraded in decorated tractors and trucks' to celebrate his visit and their access to this lucrative market (*Business Report*, 10 July 2003).

While Western Cape citrus producers have benefited from US regulations on citrus black spot, other parts of the country are facing significant challenges associated with the disease. Before 1993, the EU did not consider CBS as a risk to its citrus producers. After all, South Africa had been ex-

6. Are (Market) Stimulants Injurious to Quality?
Liberalization, Quality Changes and the Reputation of African Coffee and Cocoa Exports

Niels Fold and Stefano Ponte

Introduction

This chapter examines the relationship between changing forms of regulation, quality control procedures and performance and the organization of value chains for two 'traditional' African export crops, coffee and cocoa. It focuses on operations that take place within the boundaries of producing countries in the context of a larger discussion of the overall governance of these Global Value Chains (GVCs) that has been carried out elsewhere (Daviron and Ponte 2005; Ponte 2002; Giovannucci and Ponte 2005; Fold 2005; Fold 2002). In particular, this chapter analyzes how domestic market reforms have impacted on the incentive system for small-scale producers to deliver 'high-quality' products in different regulatory environments, and what this entails in specific value chains with varying degrees of quality and/or volume demands.

Experiences of commodity market reform and outcomes in terms of supply response have varied enormously in Africa, depending on the specific commodity in question, the country concerned and conditions in domestic markets before the implementation of reforms. Yet certain common traits have emerged. Market reforms have in many instances led to prompt cash payments and a higher proportion of the export price being paid to farmers, although domestic price volatility increased with the end of price stabilization mechanisms (Akiyama et al. 2001). Peripheral farmers are particularly affected by the elimination of pan-territorial pricing and market failures in input distribution. Access to credit for local traders and farmers becomes more difficult (Ponte 2002b; Poulton et al. 2004; Shepherd and Farolfi 1999). The private sector becomes substantially involved in producer-country processing. Finally, cooperatives and former parastatals lose substantial proportions of their market share to private traders, especially those owned or financed by multinational corporations (MNCs) (Ponte 2002a).

While these are important traits of commodity market reform, another area of inquiry has been relatively neglected in the literature on liberalization until recently, namely changes in the assessment, monitoring and evaluation of the quality parameters of the traded commodity. This has led to a series of new contributions focusing on: (1) how 'drivenness' is exercised along GVCs through the negotiation of quality (Daviron and Ponte 2005; Larsen 2003; Ponte 2002a; Ponte and Gibbon 2005); (2) how policies and institutions affect market performance, including aspects related to quality (Aksoy and Beghin 2005; Baffes 2004; 2005; 2006); and (3) how private coordination can complement and/or substitute regulation in providing quality-related incentives in liberalized agricultural markets (Dorward et al. 2005; Kydd and Dorward 2004; Poulton et al. 2004).

Analyzing the quality aspects of commodities is germane to understanding the dynamics of liberalized markets, because reforms affect the form, timing and price formation of commodity trade, thus impacting on farmers' welfare through possible changes in reputation and price premiums. Changes in quality also affect the role of a national or sub-national crop in a GVC and the organization of marketing operations.

One of the results of market liberalization that is eagerly underlined by the promoters of reforms is increased buyer competition. Yet, when this results in early buying rather than in price competition or the search for higher quality crops, buyer competition may lead to the purchasing of a crop that is not ready to be marketed, for example, unripe cotton or wet cocoa and coffee beans. Also, where the private sector has not set up a system of buying in grades, there is no direct incentive for producers to improve crop quality. Quality control functions in the single-channel marketing system take place at both the cooperative level and the marketing board level for export. In the post-liberalization regime, the first level of quality control has often been lost, the second being retained by the public sector in some cases (coffee in Tanzania and Uganda), or contracted to the private sector in others (coffee and cocoa in Côte d'Ivoire). The loss of primary-level quality control since the liberalization of the domestic commodity trade and processing has led to deteriorating export crop quality in several countries, and in some cases to a fall in or erosion of price premiums within groups of African agricultural commodities and a loss of reputation for some 'national' crops (Ponte 2002a; Fold 2001).

Changes in the specific quality parameters and organizational practices (cultivation, harvesting, primary processing, storing, etc.) of a commodity result in variations in its use value. These use values are transformed operationally into standards that are determined in complex negotiating processes between global buyers and suppliers of the commodity in question. Different use values are reflected in various price premiums compared to a broadly accepted 'standard' commodity. These premiums are often linked to the country where the commodity originates (the 'origin'). Hence, changes in premiums to a large degree reflect a change in the exporter's organizational practices – the way 'things are being done' in the exporting country. This raises the question of the relationship between specific elements in market liberalization processes and changes in organizational practices that simultaneously lead to (short-term) domestic price increases and (long-term) quality deterioration with a loss of price premium (or a growing discount). Moreover, some countries have managed to preserve price premiums on certain commodities, even though they have implemented other reforms at the general macroeconomic level.

In order to examine these issues, this chapter deals with coffee and cocoa, both of which are 'traditional' African export crops. We discuss the two commodities in different regional settings: coffee exports from East Africa (Kenya, Tanzania and Uganda) and cocoa exports from West Africa (Cameroon, Côte d'Ivoire, Ghana and Nigeria). We suggest that drawing on cross-commodity and cross-regional material enables us to make a comparative analysis of changing regulatory instruments and institutional settings and their impact on quality and premiums. We analyze cases where liberalization has led to a deterioration in quality (Nigeria, Cameroon and Côte d'Ivoire for cocoa, Tanzania for coffee), where deterioration has been followed by partial recovery (Uganda for coffee) and where limited liberalization has led to the preservation of quality (Ghana for cocoa and Kenya for coffee). Because of space limitations, we provide only a general picture in this chapter. Further details and primary data can be found elsewhere (Ponte 2001; 2002a; Fold 2001; 2002). Also, we focus on 'material' quality attributes, which are the key dimension of quality negotiation in producing countries. For a discussion of 'symbolic' and 'in-person service' quality attributes in commodity trade, see Daviron and Ponte (2005).

The chapter is structured as follows. First, we map out the 'inherent' parameters that shape the material quality of coffee and cocoa and the influence on quality exerted by external factors (e.g., farming practices, primary processing, handling and storage) and regional grading practices. Second, we briefly outline the various ways in which domestic value chain segments have been affected by liberalization processes in countries where the average quality of coffee and cocoa exports declined badly, with or without a later recovery. Third, we examine two countries that had not implemented comprehensive liberalization of the coffee and cocoa value chains at the time of fieldwork (early 2000s), namely Kenya and Ghana. In these countries, existing quality-control procedures and incentives had been more or less maintained and quality levels and a 'good' reputation kept intact. The analysis of commonalities and divergences between the cocoa and coffee value chains and among different regulatory environments inform our concluding discussion.

Quality parameters and grading practices

Coffee

Quality standards and quality control procedures are key aspects of the domestic coffee trade in producing countries. At this level, quality is mainly assessed for its 'material' attributes, including sometimes aroma and taste. Except for Ethiopia, African producer countries do not have substantial populations of coffee consumers. Thus, symbolic attributes generated through branding, packaging, retailing and consumption do not play an important role (on sustainability and origin as symbolic attributes, see Daviron and Ponte 2005).

Mainstream coffees are normally evaluated in producing countries on the basis of material quality through what the industry calls 'objective' physical parameters (colour, size, defects, etc.). These are measurable by means of sensory inspection and more or less sophisticated mechanical and optical processes of separation and sorting. Some types of coffee (especially higher quality Mild Arabicas) are also assessed for aroma and taste before export. This is a much more subjective evaluation, although it is shrouded in a 'scientific' aura. Professional tasters (also called liquorers or cuppers) in white laboratory gowns slurp and spit from long lines of white coffee cups, writing down their scores on pre-printed evaluation forms. In reality, the taster performs art, craft and science at the same time.

Cup testing in the country of origin is not sufficient for the complete disclosure of quality that is sometimes demanded by importers and roasters. As a result, especially for higher-end coffees, cuppers based in the consuming country may carry out their own evaluation on pre-purchase samples. In the past, aroma and taste were based on rough description. Sensory analysis, however, is now becoming more of a science, having been born in the wine industry, though it is now spreading to other products. One of the problems in the coffee industry is that cuppers operating in one producer country have only limited comparative knowledge of what other origins taste like.

The material quality of coffee is generated by inherent and external factors. So-called 'inherent' factors include: (1) the genetic type of coffee tree (Arabica, Robusta); (2) the cultivar (Bourbon, Blue Mountain, Kent, etc.); and (3) agro-climatic conditions (soil type, rainfall, altitude). So-called 'external' factors include: (1) farm practices (input application, pruning, weeding, mulching, irrigation when available, sun- or shade-growing); (2) harvesting procedures (picking only ripe cherries); (3) primary processing (wet or dry methods); (4) export preparation; and (5) handling and storage during passage from one stage to the next in the value chain (Brown 1991).

Primary processing of coffee does not 'improve' material quality: its aim is to maintain the original quality of the bean, which is only possible when the bean is dry. Therefore, quality control at every stage of processing and trading is critical to the final quality. Poor handling, pulping, fermentation, drying, storage or shipping result in deteriorations in the appearance of the bean and the flavour of the liquor extracted from it. Inadequate sorting, grading or cleaning increase the proportion of defects in the sample and reduce the price and acceptability of a coffee consignment for export (Brown 1991).

Smallholder coffee-producers relate to quality mostly through farm practices rather than their own consumption experiences. Therefore, quality is seen as the outcome of what they do on the farm. The main indicator of quality is what the coffee beans look like in the first 'change of hands' between the farmer and the primary-level trader or processor. At this point, both actors have only limited information on the material properties of coffee quality. If dry cherry is sold (Hard Arabica, Robusta), quality is assessed by making sure that the coffee is properly dried and that there is no foreign matter mixed in with it. If the consignment is larger, the buyer may hull a small sample to assess the quality of the bean inside. If fresh cherry is sold (Mild Arabica processed at centralized pulperies), quality checks are also limited to discarding unripe cherries (of green colour) and foreign matter. Sometimes, a rough grading procedure can be carried out by floating a consignment in a water tank (lighter cherries will float). If parchment coffee is sold (Mild Arabica processed by individual farmers with small pulpers), more attributes can be evaluated in addition to moisture and absence of foreign matter, such as the size of coffee beans, their colour and their smell.

In no case, however, can taste characteristics be assessed. The primary buyer relies on the reputation of the seller or the area in which the coffee is bought to minimize the 'quality risk'. The higher the quality risk, the higher the price discount that will be applied to all coffee bought from a specific farmer or area. The amount of quality information accessible to the primary buyer usually depends on the degree of vertical integration in the value chain: the more fragmented the chain, the more difficult the flow of quality information. However, there are exceptions to this rule (see below), as quality management depends heavily on the regulatory framework of the coffee trade in producing countries.

In most coffee-producing countries, the analytical valuation of coffee at the export point is achieved through official grade standards (see Daviron and Ponte 2005). These standards vary from country to country, but generally describe the size of the bean, its density, colour, shape, moisture content and the number of defects in a standard weight sample. In the Robusta and Hard Arabica trade, this information, sometimes together with a report of 'clean cup' (absence of spoiled or foreign flavours assessed through cup testing), is generally sufficient for export. The coffee is then sold 'on description' using the vocabulary defined in a specific national grade.

In the Mild Arabica trade, and especially where quality variation within an origin is high (as in East Africa), additional information is needed. After grading, coffee is evaluated on the basis of a points system that combines scores for the raw appearance of the beans, its roast qualities and its liquor. By looking at a roasted coffee sample, a seller or buyer can check the evenness of the roast and assess whether the coffee has been over-dried (in which case the beans will break). By looking at the colour of the roast, sellers and buyers can detect whether the coffee has been over-fermented or poorly washed. Cup testing consists of brewing a sample of coffee and evaluating its body, acidity, aroma and the presence of foreign flavours in descriptive terms (similar to wine tasting). These qualifications are then combined in a matrix that takes into consideration the grade of the coffee as well. The final result is the coffee 'class', the overall indicator of coffee quality in Mild Arabica (at least in East Africa). These classes achieve a fairly complete analytical valuation from the point of view of the exporter. To what extent they are sufficient for the importer will depend on the kind of coffee, the relationship between exporter and importer and the possibility for the importer to assess pre-shipment samples. Prices in the physical trade of Arabica coffees of various origins are set as differentials in relation to the futures price of Colombian Milds ('C' contract) quoted on the New York Coffee, Sugar and Cocoa Exchange (CSCE). The reference price for Robusta is set at the London International Financial Futures and Options

Exchange (LIFFE). Price differentials for a particular coffee are the indicators of its commercial valuation and are set in relation to market demand, analytical quality and reputation.

Cocoa

The basic quality requirements in the cocoa trade are determined by the chocolate manufacturers, by far the most important group among the industrial end-users of the crop. For technical and economic reasons, the flavour and content of edible material in the individual cocoa bean are of great significance for chocolate manufacturers. Flavour is made up of several descriptors, but taste and odour are of major importance. Since the flavour of the beans cannot be measured objectively, professional taste panels are normally used to determine the quality of a particular consignment or origin of beans. The panels assess flavour on the basis of either cocoa liquor (the result of roasting and grinding the beans) or chocolate samples (cocoa liquor with additional cocoa butter; cocoa butter and cocoa cake are the residues left over from pressing cocoa liquor).

A suitable flavour depends on the proper fermentation and drying processes of the cocoa beans on the farm or plantation. However, it is the industrial roasting process that is particularly important for flavour development (see Becket 1999). Roasting also reduces the moisture content and loosens the shell, making it easier to remove by winnowing the beans before grinding them into cocoa liquor. Several factors influence the flavour and proportion of edible material of cocoa beans and therefore also affect the assessment of the price of a particular parcel. Until recently, the determinants of flavour were rather opaque, but now certain practices at the field and factory stages are recognized as influencing quality, which is also affected by any additional flavour notes and the presence of flavour defects.

The 'inherent' potential flavour is determined by the three main cocoa varieties, namely Criollo, Trinitario and Forastero (Ahmoa 1998). Whereas Criollo and Trinitario are usually referred to as 'fine and flavoured' cocoa, Forastero is known as 'bulk' cocoa. In the context of quality, these terms refer to the type of cocoa, not the flavour or other aspects of quality. Forastero beans constitute about 95% of the world market in volume terms and are dominant in the major producing areas, despite the much higher unit price for fine and flavoured cocoa, which is cultivated in the Caribbean and certain parts of South America. Also influencing bean quality are climatic conditions such as rainfall and temperature, the latter being particularly important in the determination of the hardness of the cocoa butter.

Criollo is a milder variety of cocoa bean yielding a nutty type of chocolate described as weak and delicate. These trees require particular soils and climatic conditions and lack vigour compared to the much more robust Forastero tree. Forastero beans produce a hard, relatively bitter, strong and pure chocolate flavour that is preferred by most chocolate manufacturers. Trinitario is a mixed variety of Criollo and Forastero types: the beans produce a mild flavour and are mostly used for blending with Forastero beans to obtain a distinctive flavour in specific finished products.

Significant differences exist between Forastero beans from different countries, largely because of variations in farming and handling practices, as well as national quality-control procedures. Therefore, manufacturers take country of origin into account in determining what flavour to expect from specific consignments. New methods of the 'flat' storage of cocoa beans transported by bulk carriers from exporting countries to logistics centres in the North reflect these concerns by separating stored beans according to origin countries but not other criteria (e.g., size, purity, etc.). Considerable variations in flavour may be caused by inconsistent practices, resulting in demanding and costly compensatory readjustments of processing equipment. Hence, consistency in itself is a quality parameter, which to some extent compensates for a less desired flavour.

Sloppy or incorrect farming practices may produce off-flavours (mouldy or smoky), excess acidity or bitterness, which cannot be removed in the industrial processing of the beans. Off-flavours and other flavour defects are produced especially during the fermentation and drying phase at the farm level by wrong timing, inadequate physical facilities or contamination by foreign matter (smoke, mineral fuel, etc.). Another factor influencing the quality of cocoa beans is the extent of any impurities that might affect the finished goods, such as pesticide residues, bacteria or infestation.

Last but not least, the potential yield of the beans affects their value to manufacturers and is reflected in price differentials. Unlike flavour, this aspect can be objectively measured through various criteria. Bean size and uniformity of parcels are important parameters, as smaller beans have a higher shell content and therefore a lower fat content. Uniformity is necessary to avoid having to adjust factory equipment for cleaning and roasting. An adequate moisture content that is not too high (leading to a risk of mould and bacterial growth) or too low (leading to a high level of broken beans, which are removed during cleaning) is also important. In general, factors causing a loss of edible material also reduce bean quality.

In the past, most exporting countries operated their own system of internal quality control and standards in order to assess and secure the reputation of their exports as an origin. However, cocoa on the world market is traded according to standard contracts drafted by the most important national cocoa associations, which are those in the UK, France and the US. These contracts are based on objective measures in which flavour quality is indicated by the so-called 'cut test'. This is a sample consisting of 300 mixed beans – irrespective of size, shape and condition – each cut lengthwise through the middle and examined. The test can detect flavour defects indicated by a high proportion of slaty beans (causing bitterness) or mouldy or infested beans (causing musty notes). Bean size is not included in any of the contracts, but the increasing cultivation of hybrids producing beans with relatively large size variations has been used recently as an argument by some chocolate producers to include size criteria in contracts.

The standards in the contract do not reflect acceptability by chocolate manufacturers but serve as reference levels for possible arbitration procedures which are provided by all three cocoa associations. The UK and French contracts operate with two grades, namely good fermented and fair fermented, measured by a maximum level of 5% and 10% respectively of slaty beans and 'other defects', that is, beans that are internally mouldy, infested or damaged. Standards in the US contract are more similar to the FAO standard and stipulate a maximum of 4% mouldy or infested beans or a maximum of 6% for the two combined. Standards for the futures markets in London and New York lay down rules for deciding whether a particular parcel is suitable for tendering at the contract price, or with a premium or discount.

Summing up, quality conceptions linked to world market prices for both coffee and cocoa beans are set by the industrial end-users, that is, the roasters and grinders respectively. Flavour, a non-measurable parameter, is of crucial importance for the finished products of both crops. Tests by experienced teams of tasters are used as major determinants of quality. Inherent parameters such as genetic type and cultivar to some extent dichotomize the demand for each crop (e.g., Arabica and Robusta; Fine & Flavoured and Forastero), although blends are used in some finished products (this is the norm in the case of coffee). In addition, differences related to origin fragment the market, as some beans are in higher demand than others, despite the fact that compositions of mixed beans of different origins may have a particular use value for some industrial end-users.

Proper practices within and between the different stages in the value chain reduce the proportion of spoiled crops, but fermentation, drying and primary processing seem to be of particular importance in developing flavour. Grading systems used for the international trade, on the other hand, are fairly simple in comparison to the complex flavour patterns. Consistency is also an important quality criterion because the industrial end-user must identify a certain mix of raw materials that suits specific finished goods. Hence, unpredictable variations in quality seem to be even more harmful to an origin's reputation than beans of more or less consistently low quality.

Liberalization and quality changes in African coffee and cocoa exports

Coffee in East Africa

Payment systems and quality control prior to liberalization

Prior to market liberalization, in Kenya, Tanzania and Uganda the domestic coffee trade was under the control of cooperative societies or unions and marketing boards. Formally, coffee did not change hands until it was sold at auction (Kenya, Tanzania) or to importers (Uganda). Therefore, through the cooperatives farmers owned the coffee up to the point of export and bore the risk of price fluctuations. However, the payment systems allowed price variations to be smoothed out within the marketing year. Farmers were paid the same price, irrespective of when they delivered the coffee to the cooperative or when that particular consignment of coffee was sold. Furthermore, in both countries, farmers received payments in relation to the quality of the Mild Arabica coffee they delivered. The handling and payment systems were fairly labour- and resource-intensive and slowed down the flow of coffee from the farmer to the importer. Overhead costs associated with these procedures were high, meaning that farmers received a lower proportion of the export price than they would have done in a more efficient system (quality considerations being equal). Payments to farmers were often late and resources were siphoned off from the system at various levels. However, price stabilization was ensured within one season. Most importantly, the system provided quality incentives to cooperative societies and, less directly, to farmers.

Quality considerations are generally more important for Mild Arabica than for Robusta and Hard Arabica. For Robusta and Hard Arabica, it is virtually impossible to determine the quality of the bean inside the dry cherry when it is delivered. Quality control at the primary level is then limited to removing foreign matter and under-dried cherries. For large consignments, a hulling operator can take a sample of dry cherry, hull it and assess out-turn, humidity level, defect count and smell. This is not feasible when collecting relatively small amounts from smallholders. Therefore in the Robusta sector, there is necessarily a less direct link between quality and price at the farmer level. However, at least in Tanzania, prior to liberalization there was a quality incentive for the output delivered by cooperative societies. Societies that delivered bigger beans with a lower defect count were paid more, as were their farmers.

The impact of liberalization on quality in Tanzania and Uganda

Tanzania produces Mild Arabica, Hard Arabica and Robusta coffees, although it is best known for its Mild Arabicas. The process of reforming coffee marketing started in 1994–95 and has resulted in the complete liberalization of the domestic trade up to auction. The auction system has been maintained and private curing plants have been allowed to operate. Domestic traders can buy parchment or dry cherry coffee only at authorised buying posts. High barriers to entry (due to licensing requirements) have facilitated consolidation. Some exporters (subsidiaries of major international trading and/or roasting companies) have vertically integrated themselves into curing and domestic procurement, and in some cases even into estate production and primary processing (Ponte 2002a).

In Tanzania, at least on paper, quality control procedures at the primary buying level have not changed with liberalization. In reality, one price is paid for any kind of parchment/dry cherry bought at the primary level. Buying of wet coffee to 'beat' the competition has also been a major problem. The one-price-for-all buying practice means that there is no direct incentive for farmers to deliver better quality coffee. Cooperatives, which in the past offered differentiated prices in relation to quality, have had to adapt to the new market situation and now operate in a very similar way to private traders in terms of pricing. They have also discontinued the provision of inputs on credit to their farmers. However, the quality-control procedures of cooperative societies are still stricter than at private buying posts.

Contrary to what happens in the domestic trade, quality-control procedures at the auction and export levels have been maintained. Also, liberalization of the curing sector has increased the speed of coffee turnaround. The new plants also have superior technology, which allows for better grading and fewer losses. More efficient marketing and curing operations have led to lower overheads and a higher proportion of the export price being paid to farmers. Maintaining the auction provides transparency to the market, but due to the vertical integration of exporters into domestic buying, most of the coffee sold at auction does not actually change hands but is simply repurchased by the same company (Baffes 2005; Ponte 2004; Temu 2001; Winter-Nelson and Temu 2002). Lower international prices and a lack of price competition in the domestic trade have led to lower farm-gate prices. There has also been a serious quality decline in green coffee, reflected in the decreasing proportion of top-quality coffees sold at auction since liberalization (see Ponte 2001). This has further affected the reputation and the premium paid for Tanzanian coffee in the international market.

Uganda started to liberalize its coffee sector in 1990–91. The process was carried out quickly and efficiently. Licensing requirements for private-sector actors are minimal, and coffee can be bought anywhere, in any form and be sold anywhere else in the country. Regulatory powers were transferred to the newly-created Uganda Coffee Development Authority (UCDA), which is in charge of testing export consignments for minimum quality standards and releasing export certificates. The Coffee Marketing Board (CMB) was closed down and the cooperative sector has almost disappeared.

Uganda is a major world producer of Robusta coffee. As mentioned above, quality considerations for Robusta coffee are much less stringent than for Arabica. Proper differentiation of the product at the primary buying stage is not simple unless large deliveries of dry cherry are made. The most pressing factors at this level are the separation of extraneous matter and the moisture content of the hulled coffee. The maximum level of moisture in hulled coffee suitable for trade is set by UCDA but rarely enforced.

Prior to liberalization, the coffee board was the only exporter. After liberalization, all the major international trading companies established procurement and export operations in the country or pre-financed local exporters. In the first few years, there was massive competition among buyers to establish market share. Large export companies vertically integrated themselves into the field as much as they could, even to the point of buying dry cherry instead of hulled coffee. As in the case of Tanzania, this created incentives to 'buy fast' without proper quality monitoring. According to industry actors, this led to a massive decrease in quality because of the increased trade in and hulling of cherry coffee that was not dry enough.

Large profits were made in the coffee trade after liberalization, especially in the 1994–96 period. Since 1996–97, however, exporters have been buying at a loss. Because Ugandan Robusta plays a key role in major blends, international traders need to be present in Uganda even if they do not make profits, just to keep their major clients happy. This has led to the consolidation of the industry. In 1994–95, there were 117 registered exporters, in 2001–02 only 29. Exporters have restructured their operations dramatically since 1997. They have withdrawn from buying in the field and now buy only hulled coffee, mostly in Kampala and a few other major towns. Restructuring has also led to greater care being taken over quality controls. Local trade and hulling are now almost completely in the hands of independent local operators. Some of the major exporters have started to apply quality-related pricing conventions in their buying posts. Because buying is now more centralized, quality control is easier to carry out and its incentive effects more likely to reach actors upstream (see Ponte 2001).

The liberalization of domestic marketing in Uganda led to a period of quality deterioration followed by a recovery. This did not lead to a loss of reputation for Ugandan Robusta because export quality was maintained through UCDA monitoring. If coffee does not reach 'clean cup' quality or does not pass screen, humidity and defect count tests, it cannot be exported and needs to be re-sorted. The special characteristics of Ugandan Robusta lie in the fact that it is grown at higher altitudes than most other Robustas. Therefore, the most important quality trait is embedded in the product and it is consequently less easy to spoil than the Mild Arabicas. From this point of view liberalization has not affected the reputation of Ugandan Robusta, but it has benefited farmers, who are paid a higher share of the export price than in the pre-liberalization period (see also Baffes 2006).

Cocoa in West Africa

Payment systems and quality control prior to liberalization

Before the implementation of SAPs in West Africa, domestic cocoa purchases, trading and exports were regulated by marketing boards or, in the former French colonies, *caisses de stabilisation*. The regulative power of these institutions varied from country to country, depending on temporary variations in state policies and former colonial practices. However, irrespective of whether commercial activities were carried out by state-owned or private licensed companies, farmers handed over control of the cocoa after selling it in villages at a fixed price. Even though various grading practices existed, purchases were mostly made on an accept-or-reject basis, leaving no incentive to farmers to do anything beyond having their beans accepted. In essence, the fixed pan-seasonal and pan-territorial producer price system acted as the basis for a system built upon pre-determined margins for each participant, ending with state-controlled export companies reaping the potential windfall profits – or dramatic losses – due to fluctuations in world market prices.

The impact of liberalization on cocoa quality in Nigeria, Cameroon and Côte d'Ivoire

In Nigeria, the marketing board was dismantled in 1986 in an effort to cut the costs of state institutions and eradicate entrenched sources of corruption. The dismantling took place virtually overnight, with no alternative institutions ready to take over regulation. Due to the monopsony of the Nigerian Cocoa Board (NCB), no experienced private companies were active in the industry, and therefore the scene was left open for new entrants, who found it profitable to take over purchasing and exporting activities. Some of the experienced personnel in the NCB tried to form new companies, building on traditional practices and the quality-control system that was already in place. However, these companies were not able to compete with a group of new traders with easy access to credit. For these individuals and companies, cocoa only became interesting as a means of obtaining foreign exchange. As the foreign exchange market was not liberalized, revenues from cocoa exports were kept in overseas banks (capital flight) or used to pay for the importation of consumer goods to be sold on the lucrative domestic market. Hence, quality control was of minor importance, as traders rushed to the farmers to get hold of as much cocoa as possible, thus driving producer prices up to a level that 'real' cocoa companies could not match (Gilbert 1997; Walker 2000).

As a result of the decline in quality and poorer contract reliability, the premium on Nigerian cocoa has now been transformed into a small but stable discount compared to Côte d'Ivoire prices. This has not changed, even though the industry was consolidated during the latter part of the 1990s, primarily due to the presence of European trading houses and processors. These companies buy a large share of total production and have established buying operations in Lagos in order to ensure the reliability of supplies and quality (Simmons 1999). There are no signs, however, that the general level of quality of Nigerian beans has improved along with the increase in production in recent years. Rather, production seems to fluctuate closely with the world market price, indicating the sector's heavy reliance on old, decaying trees that are only harvested if prices are considered sufficiently high.

In Cameroon, the liberalization of exports started in the early 1990s, but the *caisse* system was not dismantled until 1994–95, when it went bankrupt. The state was not able and donors were unwilling to bail it out. Hence, the existing domestic trading companies could not rely on this usual source of finance and in addition many incurred losses as a result of the bankruptcy. Instead, they had to turn to the national banking sector for credits, bear the high interest rates and compete with new entrants with access to credit but without experience in the cocoa trade. The result was a perceptible decline in quality, as farmers were able to sell beans that had not been properly dried and fermented. This trend was strongly reinforced by the geographical shift in cocoa production towards the more humid southwest of Cameroon, where the necessarily artificial drying often imparts a smoky flavour to the beans.

A decade later, the industry has consolidated, as the vast bulk of the harvest is purchased by the agents of three European companies, one of which also operates a processing plant in the country. These companies specialise in producing cocoa powder and have particular interests in securing adequate supplies of Cameroon cocoa beans that, after processing, yield a highly desired red powder. The market power of the three foreign giants has squeezed domestic prices and transformed local trading and exporting companies into purchasing agents. No premium is paid on purchases made at the port, and most exports now take the form of in-house transactions, thereby avoiding European trading operations. Demand for Cameroon cocoa over and above that by the specialised companies is limited, and the beans are sold at a discount on the open market. The decline in the premium is therefore not only caused by declining quality as such, but is also a product of the new industrial structure that emerged after liberalization (Gilbert 1997; Simmons 1999). Furthermore, recent press reports report a further decline in quality due to the practice of mixing acceptable beans with beans that should have been rejected due to inferior fermentation and drying.

Before liberalization, Côte d'Ivoire had a reputation as a cocoa producer of large volumes of average, undifferentiated and stable quality beans (Losch 2002). The quality was close to that of beans from Ghana due to the similarities in agro-climatic and technical conditions, although large-scale mechanised drying – considered to produce a quality inferior to sun-drying – was widespread in ports and other reception areas.

Liberalization of the marketing system started in the early 1990s but was reversed a couple of times during the mid-1990s. In the late 1990s, the process was revived, and full liberalization of the export trade was introduced in the 1999–2000 season. However, the export sector had already been concentrated into a small number of international companies: at the turn of the century the three major global cocoa processors controlled about 50 per cent of the country's annual harvest, with another 30 per cent of the harvest being handled by five foreign trading companies that had taken over local exporters.

Quality has deteriorated at the same time as exporters have taken over full responsibility for quality control. Traders continue to pay the same price for all beans, regardless of quality, and beans are no longer graded at village level (Atse 1999). Low quality is caused primarily by high bean humidity at the arrival points in the port of shipment and the resulting mould that easily develops. High humidity content is a consequence of inappropriate and reduced drying times at village level, which in turn is caused by 'the logic of the farm-gate buyer' who aims to buy as much as possible on each visit to the village in order to keep costs down and reduce circulation time (Losch 2002). During the 2000–01 season, average quality sunk to such a low level that a considerable part of the beans were rendered unacceptable to Northern exporters and grinders (*Marchés Tropicaux* 2000: 2566).

The recent years of military unrest provoked by increased tensions over access to land and labour between indigenous groups and migrant farmers from the Sahel countries (see Wood 2004) have done nothing to restore quality levels. Harassment of migrant farmers has resulted in a mass exodus of farmer families and labour from cocoa-producing areas in the government-controlled south of the country and disrupted the proper maintenance and harvesting of cocoa trees. Due to the sheer size of cocoa exports from Côte d'Ivoire on the global market, world market prices increased markedly at the end of 2001, when the violence erupted and reached its maximum in the main season of 2002–03. Since mid-2003 the market has calmed down and prices have stayed relatively constant but low, as bumper crops occurred in West Africa in 2003–04 and cocoa flows in Côte d'Ivoire resumed, despite rebel 'cocoa transport taxes' and substantial volumes of cocoa being smuggled into neighbouring Ghana. However, neither the increase nor the decrease in the world market price served to change the price discount – estimated at US$ 130 per ton in 2004 – on Côte d'Ivoire beans compared to cocoa from Ghana (see www.otal.com/commodities/cocoa).

In conclusion, certain differences existed between the general payment systems applied to the two crops in the pre-liberalization phase, that is, up to the early and mid-1990s. In East Africa, coffee farmers were paid in several tranches, only the first of which was fixed. Therefore, through the cooperatives they carried some of the risk of international price movements. Cocoa in West Africa was traded at pre-seasonal fixed purchasing prices with one single payment. Within a single season, this system provided complete cover for farmers against the vagaries of world market prices. Systems operating on producer price differentials according to quality existed for Mild Arabica coffee in East Africa, although a simple system based on bean size also operated in the Robusta trade in Tanzania. Cocoa, on the other hand, was traded in all the West African countries examined above on an accept-or-reject basis at the village level. Hence, there were no systems in operation in the cocoa trade that stimulated different degrees of quality concerns at the farm level beyond requirements related primarily to foreign matter and moisture content.

In both the coffee and cocoa markets, present post-liberalization systems seem to have developed into rather uniform structures. After liberalization, an initial rush for market share by both experienced and new domestic traders resulted in higher producer prices and less buyer concern for traditional quality requirements. Insufficient and costly capital compelled domestic traders to reduce the time between borrowing and repayment and to increase the velocity of capital turnaround in order to maximise profits. As a result, farmers were pushed into selling their crops before they had been properly processed. Insufficient time for the drying process was a common and serious problem, resulting in the erosion of the general quality level, loss of previous consistency and reduction of price premiums. This situation has remained substantially the same ever since the first 'post-liberalization rush' for both crops. However, in the case of Ugandan coffee, things may have started to turn around. The most important quality trait in Ugandan Robusta (cultivation at a relatively high altitude) is embedded in the product and is less easy to spoil than in the case of Mild Arabica coffee. Therefore, quality deterioration at the domestic trade level did not necessarily lead to a proportional loss of reputation at the export level. Also, the recent re-introduction of basic quality-price mechanisms by exporters buying in bulk seems to have improved the quality profile of the Ugandan crop.

Gradually, consolidation has taken place in all the producer countries analyzed above, primarily through the adoption of purchasing and exporting activities by the dominant transnational industrial end-users and trading companies. Increasing proportions of the domestic trade now take the form of intra-company flows of commodities. Vertical integration upstream from export to processing, local trade and (in some estates) farm-level production have taken place in the coffee trade in Tanzania (but this may be changing due to new regulations; see Ponte 2004). In Uganda, the process of vertical integration into the local trade has recently receded, and major export companies buy coffee from intermediaries in a few towns, or in Kampala itself. One of the consequences of the entry of Northern companies into the domestic trade is the introduction of standards in accordance with intra-company quality requirements and company-specific systems of price differentials in purchasing activities.

Gradual and partial liberalization and premium preservation

Kenya

In the 1990s, East African exports represented on average 35 per cent of total African exports of green coffee and 6 per cent of total world exports (FAO data). Kenya, even with a low proportion of global coffee exports, plays an important role in the category of Colombian Milds (a sub-sector of Mild Arabicas). In the 1990s, coffee exports from Kenya remained in the range of 1.4 to 1.6 million bags a year, with the exception of lower production in 1991–92 and 1992–93, and a peak of almost 1.9 million bags in 1994–95.

Kenya is world famous for its fine quality coffees. Small amounts of top Kenyan coffee find their way into most coffee blends, giving them a specific flavour. Good Kenyan coffee is also sought by the speciality coffee industry. Generally, though, the quality of Kenyan coffee is very uneven. According to exporters based in Nairobi, although there are very fine coffees in the country, there is also 'a lot of very poor coffee', which is usually over-fermented. However, they argue that what makes Kenya so special is its top-end coffees. As long as these are available, they push up the price of all the other types of coffee as well.

The liberalization of coffee marketing in Kenya started in the early 1990s, but it has progressed only very slowly since then. The basic structure of the domestic value chain has remained almost the same, even after the passing of a new Coffee Act in 2001. The basic quality control and payment procedures have been maintained. As a result of the maintenance of the old quality-control system – and unlike other countries, where the process of liberalization has been more far-reaching – the overall class performance of Kenyan coffee actually improved in the second half of the 1990s (for details, see Ponte 2001). This happened even though the coffee marketing system in the country was marred by financial mismanagement and production volumes were decreasing. In particular, performance improved substantially in the top coffee classes[repetition], although the proportion of *mbuni* (non-washed coffee of the lowest quality) also increased. It is also clear that small-holders achieved a higher proportion of top-end coffees than estates.

The full liberalization of domestic marketing was the next step in the (donor-pushed) government agenda in the early 2000s. The revision of the Coffee Act was a hot issue and figured frequently in the local press. In 2000, the Coffee Board of Kenya (CBK) carried out consultations with 'key stake-holders' on this topic. These meetings were very tense and have occasionally resulted in riots. One of the surprising aspects of this process is that many exporters did not express any support for liberalization in interviews with one of the authors, even though they were one of the driving forces behind coffee market liberalization in Tanzania and Uganda. These exporters argued that liberalization would not do any good for the quality of Kenyan coffee. They thought that it would lead to more homogenous mixtures, with the result that, while the average quality of bad coffees would improve, the quality of the top coffees would deteriorate. [repetition]The top export companies also feared that with liberalization a lot of business-minded people with limited coffee-buying experience would jump into the trade, leading to lower quality control and undifferentiated trade.

Despite these reservations even within the industry, in late 2001 the new Coffee Act was passed, which provided for a more extensive liberalization of the industry, including the end of CBK's monopoly of marketing. Yet the pace of implementation has been very slow. A few companies (including a large parastatal mill) have been allowed to market coffee for farmers and cooperatives at auction on an agency basis. These agents are not allowed to buy coffee outright at the farm gate or ex-cooperative, nor are they allowed to export outside the auction. In essence, competition at the farm gate is limited and prices are set at auction, not in private negotiations between buyers and sellers (at least in theory). In early 2005, the government started to consider amendments to the 2001 Coffee Act that would allow out-of-auction exports for the first time in the country's history. To begin with, it seemed that direct sales at the farm gate would still be outlawed (*The Nation*, 1 February 2005). Later on, the possibility of allowing direct sales acquired new political weight and legitimacy, partially through the publication of a World Bank-commissioned report recommending exactly that (GDS 2004). In August 2005, parliament passed two amendments to the 2001 Coffee Act making direct sales possible, but (again) real implementation has been delayed (*The Nation*, 24 January 2006).

If full liberalization takes place at the farm-gate and export levels, Kenyan coffee quality is likely to plummet. As in Tanzania, full liberalization is likely to lead to more homogenous mixtures, with the result that the average quality of bad coffees will improve, but also that the quality of top coffees will deteriorate. This is likely to lead to lower differentials for Kenyan coffees in general, without guaranteeing a supply response. At the same time, the proportion of the export price paid to producers is likely to increase. The overall price impact at the farm level will depend on the ratio between the gain in the price transmission ratio from export point to farm and the loss in quality premium.

Ghana

Production in and exports from Ghana have recovered tremendously since a historical low point in the early 1980s. Ghana is now one of world's largest and most important producers and exporters of cocoa. During the late 1990s, the country's annual production of about 400,000 tonnes was second only to Côte d'Ivoire's (1,100,000 tonnes), and about the same level as Indonesia's (350,000 tonnes). Ghana's production is now far larger than the next tiers of major producing countries, namely Cameroon, Nigeria and Brazil (all about 130,000–180,000 tonnes), and Ecuador and Malaysia (70,000–100,000 tonnes). The present export volume has increased to about 600,000 tonnes, primarily due to state-financed spraying campaigns, improved smallholder access to fertilizers and favourable world market prices. A large but unknown quantity of exports consists of cocoa beans smuggled in from Cote d'Ivoire, as middlemen took advantage of the higher government-fixed farm gate price and easy access from rebel-controlled areas.

In 1992, a programme of liberalization and privatization was implemented for the cocoa chain in Ghana as part of a series of SAPs. Prior to that, extension services to farmers and the purchase, handling, transportation, grading, processing, marketing and shipping of cocoa beans were carried out by various subsidiaries of a state-controlled marketing board (Cocobod). In the restructuring process presently going on, each of these subsidiaries is either going to be incorporated into another state regulatory body (e.g., extension services in the ministry of agriculture) or privatized after the removal of its monopolistic or monopsonistic position in the chain.

Most importantly, the monopsony of the purchasing arm of the marketing board has been removed and a score of private companies, so-called licensed buyer companies (LBCs), have obtained a licence to buy beans from farmers. About half of these are to varying degrees actively buying beans, while the rest are dormant due to a lack of financial and/or management capacity. Exports are still fully controlled by CMC (the marketing company of Cocobod), although LBCs have formally been allowed to export a minor share of their purchases since October 2000 (Fold 2004). In practice, however, all the LBCs have handed over their cocoa beans to CMC, as no export licences had been issued up to the 2005–06 season.

Under the existing price system, most LBCs try to control and externalize the purchase operations of individual agents, who are contractually linked to the company but not employed by it. The LBCs have internalized transport operations, and it is expected that some LBCs will move into some kind of contractual relationship with overseas customers in order to obtain pre-finance and gradually build up experience in exports and marketing. On a global scale, international processors seem to be able to squeeze commodity traders out of business by entering into direct purchase agreements with LBCs. This is now a general trend in the region, although not so pronounced in Ghana – yet.

Despite the initiatives taken towards liberalization, a pan-seasonal and pan-territorial producer price is still determined by the state in advance of the harvest season for the main crop (November–February), and recently prices were also adjusted before the mid-crop (May–July). The producer price can be settled because Ghana beans earn a premium on the world market (about £60 per tonne compared to beans from Côte d'Ivoire) due to their high fat content and rich flavour. International customers are willing to buy the beans eight to fourteen months in advance of harvest, and the marketing board sells a large part of the expected harvest at known prices. This revenue, combined with price forecasts, constitutes the basis for the domestic producer price.

The premium is generated through careful fermentation and drying carried out by farmers and a well-established quality control and standardization system throughout the chain. Control starts at buying posts, where trained clerks (or agents) accept beans from farmers on the basis of inspection for dryness, smell, colour, infestation and size homogeneity. After weighing and re-bagging into ordinary sacks, Cocobod's quality-control division is invited to take samples from piles of thirty bags. Beans are checked for moisture content, size homogeneity and defects using the cut test. Depending on the extent of mould, slaty beans and other defects, beans are graded into grades 1 and 2, and the sacks are sealed so that time, location and grader can be determined at a later stage. Beans of substandard quality are rejected. The beans are then transported to regional depots, from where they are taken to the ports at a later stage. Quality control is also implemented upon arrival at the port and again before overseas shipment.

Even though all the key actors in principle support the maintenance of the quality-control system, a move towards a more flexible and less rigid system seems inevitable. This is mainly due to pressure from the LBCs, who wish to speed up circulation time by reducing the number of quality checks along the chain and to increase the number of licensed quality-control companies – which presently amounts to one, namely a subsidiary of Cocobod.

It seems reasonable to argue that only the Northern chocolate industry segment that depends heavily on the specific quality parameters for Ghanaian beans is in a position to maintain the present chain structure and dynamics in the country. Being willing to pay a premium, it may stimulate the LBCs to maintain a somewhat changed but still coherent and efficient quality-control system. Keeping up industrial standards is, in turn, the basis for the present pricing system, although this must also be modified in order to accommodate changes in the composition of harvested beans due to the recent planting of hybrids (which have no clear seasonality regarding the size of beans).

Challenges to the present value chain organisation come from two sides. First, the World Bank is still putting pressure on the government for a full penetration of world market prices throughout the chain. Secondly, the market is dominated by a few transnational grinding companies, whose operations are based on non-flavour-specific parameters of quality. The demand of these companies may gradually lead to the dismantling of the quality-control system by stimulating the LBCs to emphasize circulation time and volume in preference to industrial standards. The transnational grinders, on the other hand, are the most likely participants in a future upgrading of the value chain in Ghana, although some chocolate producers may find it worthwhile to invest in grinding facilities capable of supplying the chocolate factories of the parent company with tailor-made cocoa mass and cocoa butter.

Conclusion

Coffee beans from Kenya and cocoa beans from Ghana have a worldwide reputation for high-quality flavour. They are often indispensable in blends with other coffee or cocoa beans used for relatively expensive finished products with distinctive profiles. Even though quality varies within each of the origins, the top-quality sectors serve to push average bean prices upwards. In these two countries, basic pre-liberalization structures and institutions have been preserved in state-regulated marketing systems (until very recently in the case of Kenya), and quality-control systems have changed only partially. The price premiums that these countries attract in international markets have been maintained.

Interestingly, some of the major buyers (i.e., industrial end-users and international traders) of Kenyan coffee and Ghanaian cocoa support the preservation of the still existing non-liberalized aspects of these marketing systems. In particular, they are concerned about the risk of losing the ability to source above-average quality beans from the two origins. This concern is partly due to their own (or their customers') traditional preferences for a particular quality related to a particular origin.

At the same time, some industrial users are homogenizing different crop qualities linked to origin by improving processing technology – for example, steam-cleaning of Robusta, and new roasting and grinding procedures for Forastero beans. These new technologies are based on the premise that: (1) only experts are able to tell the difference between the 'industrial' products and origin-based products or blends; and (2) due to the non-measurability of flavour, certain origin qualities are only qualities for manufacturers with specific and traditional preferences because of their technological capacity or reputation linked to brand names (e.g., 'made from the finest Ghana beans' or 'pure Kenyan coffee').

Quality preservation may not be an important feature for origins where volume rather than quality represents the historical 'insertion point' in a GVC, or where quality deterioration is less vulnerable to changes in marketing systems. Uganda, for example, has often been used as the 'textbook' success story of commodity market liberalization, having witnessed improved market efficiency, increased price competition and higher producer/world price ratios. However, increasing substitutability between beans of different origins leads to growing competition among producers and a further erosion of their bargaining power. In this context, dismantling national quality-control systems is particularly detrimental in origins where quality reputation is important (Cameroonian and Ghanaian cocoa, Kenyan coffee, Kilimanjaro coffee from Tanzania). Viewed from this perspective, the question is whether quality premiums are high enough to justify producer countries' efforts to preserve and improve the quality and reputation of their crops. The fragmentation of consumption in the North has resulted in widening price ranges for finished goods, but this fragmentation has not been (though it should be) reflected in the price differentials paid to producers of quality crops (see Fitter and Kaplinsky 2001). Moreover, consumer prices do not reflect the downward movements in world market prices paid to producers. Hence, in the phase of dwindling coffee and cocoa prices of the early 2000s, massive transfers of resources have taken place to international traders and roasters as well as grinders and chocolate manufacturers in consuming countries.

The case studies discussed in this chapter suggest that market liberalization may be the best option for some countries and sectors, while highly regulated markets may be the best for others. However, at the more global level and in the long term, a focus on quantity rather than quality is counter-productive for developing countries as a whole in view of the ever-worsening terms of trade for 'traditional' commodity exports. New openings provided by increased product differentiation and the emergence of 'niche' markets can be exploited through product differentiation and the improvement of 'material' quality standards and reputation in producer countries. However, this is not sufficient. With increased product differentiation, consumers pay proportionally less for the 'material' attributes of coffee quality, and more for their 'symbolic' and 'in-person service' attributes – including branding, packaging, consumption ambience and 'sustainability' content. But many developing countries are largely stuck in producing and exporting goods that are valued for their material quality attributes. Symbolic and in-person service quality attributes are generated and controlled elsewhere (Daviron and Ponte 2005).

In the last twenty years, several 'solutions' have been proposed with a view to the 'decommoditizing' of agricultural products, mostly based on the idea of supplying different product forms. Creating new material attributes is one of these solutions, as we have argued above. But the agro-food processors and retailers that buy these agricultural products do not necessarily demand differentiated material offerings. Their own differentiation strategy is based on the ability to create differences from the same raw material and above all to add symbolic quality attributes to the products they sell.

Adding 'new' symbolic attributes is another solution, one that is at the core of specialty markets and various 'sustainability' initiatives. However, agro-food processors and retailers have also entered the fray of 'new' symbolic offerings and are proposing their own concepts of 'specialty' and 'sustainable' products. In this process of mainstreaming, producers have been cut off from many standard-setting processes, nor do they seem to gain much from some of the initiatives that have been marketed as being for their own benefit (Giovannucci and Ponte 2005). As the standards that producers have to match proliferate and become more complex and stringent, doubts have also emerged concerning the long-term feasibility of small-scale production in Africa more generally. Given that many agro-food commodities are produced overwhelmingly by smallholders on the continent, the potential impact of such an evolution should not be taken lightly.

References

Akiyama, T., J. Baffes, D.F. Larson and P. Varangis (eds) (2001) *Commodity Market Reforms: Lessons of Two Decades.* Washington DC: World Bank.

Aksoy, A. and J.C. Beghin (eds) (2005) *Global Agricultural Trade and Developing Countries.* Washington, DC: World Bank.

Amoah, J.E.K. (1995) *Development of Consumption, Commercial Production and Marketing.* Cocoa Outline Series 1. Accra: Jemre Enterprise.

Atse, D. (1999) *Reforming the Cocoa Sector in Cote d'Ivoire: The Case of the Electronic Trading* System. International Development Department Paper 34, School of Public Policy, University of Birmingham.

Baffes, J. (2005) 'Tanzania's coffee sector: constraints and challenges', *Journal of International Development,* 17(1):21–43.

_____ (2006) 'Restructuring Uganda's coffee industry: why the basics matter', mimeo. Washington DC: World Bank.

Beckett, S.T. (ed) (1999) *Industrial Chocolate: Manufacture and Use.* Oxford: Blackwell.

Brown, J.G. (1991) 'Agro-Industry Profiles: Coffee'. *EDI Working Papers.* Washington DC: World Bank.

Daviron, B. and S. Ponte (2005) *The Coffee Paradox: Global Markets, Commodity Trade and the Elusive Promise of Development.* London and New York: Zed.

Dorward, A.R., J.G. Kydd, J.A. Morrison and C. Poulton (2005) 'Institutions, Markets and Economic Coordination: Linking Development Policy to Theory and Praxis', *Development and Change,* 36(1):1–25.

Fitter, R. and R. Kaplinsky (2001) 'Can an Agricultural "Commodity" be Decommodified, and If So, Who is To Gain?' *IDS Working Paper* 37. Brighton: Institute for Development Studies.

Fold, N. (2001) 'Restructuring of the European Chocolate Industry and its Impact on Cocoa Production in West Africa', *Journal of Economic Geography,* 1(3): 405–420.

—— (2002) 'Lead Firms and Competition in 'Bi-polar' Commodity Chains: Grinders and Branders in the Global Cocoa-Chocolate Industry', *Journal of Agrarian Change,* 2(2):228–47.

—— (2004) 'Spilling the Beans on a Tough Nut: Liberalization and Local Supply System Changes in Ghana's Cocoa and Shea Chains', in Hughes, A. and S. Reimer (eds) *Geographies of Commodity Chains.* London: Routledge (pp. 63–80).

—— (2005) 'Global Cocoa Sourcing Patterns', in Fold, N. and B. Pritchard (eds) *Cross-Continental Food Chains*. London: Routledge (pp. 223–38).

Gibbon, P. and S. Ponte (2005) *Trading Down: Africa, Value Chains and the Global Economy*. Philadelphia: Temple University Press.

Gilbert, C.L. (1997) *Cocoa Market Liberalization: Its Effects on Quality, Futures Trading and Prices*. London: Cocoa Association of London.

Giovannucci, D. and S. Ponte (2005) 'Standards as a New Form of Social Contract? Sustainability Initiatives in the Coffee Industry', *Food Policy*, 30(3):284–301.

Kydd, J.G. and A.R. Dorward (2004) 'Implications of Market and Coordination Failures for Rural Development in Least Developed Countries', *Journal of International Development*, 16:951–70.

Larsen, M.N. (2003) 'Quality Standard-setting in the Global Cotton Chain and Cotton Sector Reforms in Sub-Saharan Africa', *DIIS Working Paper* 03.7. Copenhagen: Danish Institute for International Studies.

Losch, B. (2002) 'Global Restructuring and Liberalization: Côte d'Ivoire and the End of the International Cocoa Market?' *Journal of Agrarian Change*, 2(2):206–27.

Ponte, S. (2001) 'Coffee Markets in East Africa: Local Responses to Global Challenges or Global Responses to Local Challenges?' *CDR Working Paper* No. 01.5. Copenhagen: Centre for Development Research.

—— (2002a) 'Brewing a Bitter Cup? Deregulation, Quality and the Re-organization of the Coffee Marketing Chain in East Africa', *Journal of Agrarian Change*, 2(2):248–72.

—— (2002b) *Farmers and Markets in Tanzania: How Policy Reforms Affect Rural Livelihoods in Africa*. London, Portsmouth, NH and Dar es Salaam: James Currey, Heinemann and Mkuki na Nyota.

—— (2002c) 'The "Latte Revolution"? Regulation, Markets and Consumption in the Global Coffee Chain', *World Development*, 30(7):1099–122.

—— (2004) 'The Politics of Ownership: Tanzanian Coffee Policy in the Age of Liberal Reformism', *African Affairs*, 103/413:615–33.

Ponte, S. and P. Gibbon (2005) 'Quality Standards, Conventions and the Governance of Global Value Chains', *Economy and Society*, 34(1):1–31.

Poulton, C., P. Gibbon, B. Hanyani-Mlambo, J.G. Kydd, M.N. Larsen, W. Maro, A. Osario, D. Tshirley and B. Zulu (2004), 'Competition and Coordination in Liberalized African Cotton Market Systems', *World Development*, 32(3): 519–36.

Shepherd, A.W. and S. Farolfi (1999) 'Export Crop Liberalization in Africa: A Review', *FAO Agricultural Services Bulletin* 135. Rome: FAO.

Simmons, R. (1999) 'Cocoa Market Liberalization', *The Manufacturing Confectioner*, December: 74–5

Temu, A. (2001) 'Market Liberalisation, Vertical Integration and Price Behaviour in Tanzania's Coffee Auction', *Development Policy Review*, 19(2):207–24.

Walker, E.A. (2000) '"Happy days are here again": Cocoa Farmers, Middlemen Traders and the Structural Adjustment Program in Southwestern Nigeria, 1986–1990s", *Africa Today*, 47:151–69.

Winter-Nelson, A. and A. Temu (2002) 'Institutional Adjustment and Transaction Costs: Product and Inputs Markets in the Tanzanian Coffee System', *World Development,* 30(4):561–74.

Wood, D. (2004) 'Predatory Elites, Rents and Cocoa: A Comparative Analysis of Ghana and Ivory Coast', *Commonwealth & Comparative Politics,* 42(2):224–41.

7. The Global Cotton Market and Cotton Sector Reforms in Sub-Saharan Africa

Marianne Nylandsted Larsen[1]

Introduction

Cotton is one of the rare recent agricultural success stories in sub-Saharan Africa. Production has increased twice as fast as in the rest of the world over the past two decades, and the continent has become the world's leading tropical region for cotton exports. At the same time, most public monopolies have been progressively abolished through privatization and liberalization, although in varying degree. In eastern and southern Anglophone Africa, parastatal cotton-marketing boards have been dismantled and private companies now dominate input supply, ginning (a simple mechanical process in which lint is separated from seed) and marketing activities. The Francophone countries are still highly regulated, although here private companies have also entered the ginning and marketing levels and all countries are under increasing pressure to liberalize. Meanwhile, an animated debate has emerged over the nature of the changes brought about by market liberalization. In general, it is accepted that policy changes have led to more efficient flows in the marketing channel and that farmers have benefited from prompter payments and now receive a higher share of the export price than they did before liberalization, trends noted in different countries and for different export crops. On the other hand, one of the key issues in the current debate is whether crop quality and, correspondingly, relative unit prices have deteriorated as a result of the dismantling of the single-channel marketing systems.

An argument frequently advanced in the more pro-liberalization literature is that 'producers, exporters and importers alike have adequate incentives to maintain minimum quality standards' (Gilbert and Tollens 2002: 4). It is further suggested that if export quality (and hence price premiums) does fall following market liberalization, this would indicate that in the pre-liberalization marketing system parastatals were demanding quality standards in excess of what the market was willing to pay. In other words,

---

1. I am indebted to Peter Gibbon, Niels Fold and Colin Poulton for their valuable comments on earlier drafts of this paper. The usual caveats apply.

any recent changes in quality are a result of what industrial end-users are willing to pay for the product: that is, they are market-driven (Gilbert and Tollens 2002).

In this chapter, I argue that while this line of thought may have some merit in relation to other agricultural export crops where there has been a worldwide erosion of quality premiums (e.g., in the cocoa-chocolate chain[1]), recent changes in lint quality emanating from Africa are not so much the result of end-market 'demand' as of a failure to transfer quality control and input supply from public institutions to the private sector in most post-liberalized markets. The management of lint quality has actually become more important in the spinning market due to technological developments and increased competition, and spinners have imposed new demands for quality as well as for greater accuracy in assessing fibre properties upstream in the chain. At the same time, not only do premiums and discounts attached to internationally traded lint persist, but they derive (partly) from reputation linked to *national* origins: once the reputation of a national crop has suffered, it becomes difficult for it to re-enter or regain a specific market segment. Thus, in order to safeguard the reputation of the national crop, some kind of collective action – private and/or public coordination – is required in order to prevent the liquidation of public goods (i.e., quality reputation) and to ensure that short-term interests do not undermine the long-term profitability of the sector.

The chapter starts with an outline of the global cotton market, focusing on the structure of world trade, price developments and the function of international traders as bridges between spinners and ginners/exporters. It then discusses recent developments in lint quality calibration, the (changing) significance of lint quality in end markets and the implications of this for international traders' and spinners' sourcing strategies in producing countries. Against the background of these considerations, the chapter explores recent changes in the role of various Anglophone and Francophone cotton-producing countries[2] on the world market. This reflects experiences with different types of cotton market organization and coordination since

---

1. As Fold notes (2002), as a result of new processing techniques used by industrial consumers (grinders and chocolate manufactures) it is now technically possible to compensate for variations in cocoa bean quality, although within certain limits. Thus intrinsic quality (and national origin) has become less important in the cocoa-chocolate chain (see Fold ibid. for a detailed discussion).
2. The largest producers and exporters in the Anglophone region are Zimbabwe, Zambia, Tanzania and Uganda, and in the Francophone region Mali, Côte d'Ivoire, Benin and Burkina Faso.

the implementation of market reforms in the mid-1990s. This leads to some general reflections on the importance of quality attributes, the role of quality considerations in countries' respective positions in the world market and their role in the longer-term development of cotton sectors.[1]

The global cotton market

Cotton is one of the rare agricultural products for which both production and consumption is more or less global in extent. There are more than seventy cotton-producing and -exporting countries, while many developed and developing countries depend on imports of lint for their spinning and textile industries. Worldwide cotton production and consumption has increased significantly during the last four decades, from 9.8 million tons in 1960–61 to 18.5 million in 1998–99, reaching 21.1 million tons in 2001–02[2] (Badiane et al. 2002). Most world cotton production is located in the developed world, the US being by far the largest producer. Over the last two decades, however, cotton production has increased twice as fast in sub-Saharan Africa as in the rest of the world, especially in Francophone Africa, where production has increased fourfold, making the region as a whole the third (occasionally the second) largest current exporter of lint. Other major national producers are China, India, Pakistan and Uzbekistan. Around 30 per cent of world production is exported internationally every year, and four dominant exporters – the US, Francophone Africa, Uzbekistan and Australia – account for more than two-thirds of all exports. In addition to the increasing production worldwide, the past decades have been characterized by major shifts in trade flows as a result of a geographical shift in international cotton yarn and fabric production. The main cotton trade flows are now from the four main exporting countries and regions to countries in Asia. The latter region has become the leading importer of cotton in line with its expansion in spinning and textiles. This is especially true of Thailand and Indonesia. Asia's import share has expanded steadily, from 35 per cent at the beginning of the 1980s to 46 per cent in 1995. In general, the structure of lint imports is less concentrated than exports. Eight countries –

---

1. Part of the paper is based on interviews conducted with Liverpool-based international trading companies engaged in cotton purchasing in Francophone and Anglophone countries, as well as the Liverpool Cotton Association and Cotton Outlook. The latter company is the founder of the Cotlook A Index, the principal measure of international cotton prices.
2. The international market season begins on 1 August and ends on 31 July the following year.

Indonesia, India, Mexico, Thailand, Turkey, Russia, Italy and the Republic of Korea – accounted for half of world imports in 2000-01 (Heijbroek and Husken 1996; ICAC 2001).

Although cotton remains the world's most important fibre in textile production, with a share of about 40 per cent in recent years (Badiane et al. 2002), world cotton prices have been under intense pressure, with a downward turn since the mid-1990s: in 2000-01 the A Index[1] dropped to its lowest level since 1972 (Goreux 2003). The significant downward trend in prices is due to a number of factors. First, while world consumption has remained virtually unchanged for cotton, synthetic fibres have increased their share of the textile fibre market from 48 per cent in 1995 to 59 per cent in 2000. Second, as a result of the recent slow down in economic activity, world cotton demand has remained virtually unchanged (approximately 20 million tons), while world production rose by 12 per cent between 1999 and 2002 (Badiane et al. 2002; Goreux and Macrae 2003). As a result, stocks increased to their highest level in fifteen years at the end of 2002, thus preventing much recovery in prices for the next couple of seasons. Third, cotton prices have been pushed down by increased government support to cotton exporters, notably in the US.[2] This has led to increasing production in and export from the US, from levels that were already historically high (see Goreux 2003; Minot and Daniels 2002 for a discussion of the impact of producer-country subsidies on world cotton prices).

International trading companies play a key role as bridges between producers (ginning companies) and spinning mills, although it is also common for spinners to source directly from ginning companies in exporting countries. Nevertheless, the majority of internationally traded lint is handled by trading companies and the functions they perform have remained largely unchanged for several decades. These functions are to act as intermediaries between producers/ginning companies and the immediate downstream consumer (spinners). Traders provide purchasing services when producers/ginning companies want to sell, bulk cotton supplies (volume and national

---

1. The A index price is an average of the cheapest five quotations from a selection of sixteen upland cottons traded internationally. In addition to the A Index, there are quotations for coarser quality cotton (the B Index), which is the average of the three least expensive of eight styles.
2. Several other major producing countries – for instance China – subsidize cotton production. However, cotton subsidies in China are likely to decline as a result of ongoing reforms to meet the requirements for WTO entry. Recently, Brazil has complained about US cotton subsidies to the WTO and requested a panel to be established in the dispute settlement body of the WTO. Benin has taken third party status.

Figure 7.1. Index prices, 1980–2002 (US$ per pound)

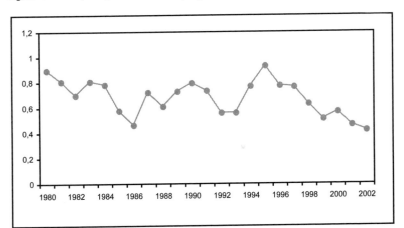

Source: Cotton Outlook, various years; Baffes 2002.

origins) to provide lots demanded by spinning mills, hedge price risk and arrange transport to destination (Heijbroek and Husken 1996).

The cotton trade is far less concentrated than is the case for the international trade in other agricultural commodities (e.g., the global cocoa-chocolate and coffee chains),[1] but some consolidation has occurred in this trading sector during the last decade. The nineteen largest international trading companies (handling more than 200,000 tons per year) increased their share of world production from 35 per cent in 1995 to 39 per cent in 2000 (Larsen 2003b; ICAC 2002). In addition, many international trading companies expanded their operations significantly in terms of increases in the number of supplying countries they purchase from and also upstream in terms of investments in ginneries and involvement in local purchasing activities, as well as the provision of inputs to smallholders. This has happened in a context where many cotton-producing countries in the southern hemisphere have liberalized their markets, and it partly reflects a reaction to deregulation in those countries. Since the liberalization of national cotton sectors, international traders have found themselves dependent on multiple, often small- to medium-sized local private companies (as opposed to a few parastatals and/or cooperatives prior to liberalization). This has prompted international traders to become more involved in producing countries in

---

1. See, for instance, Fold (2002) and Ponte (2002) respectively, on the structures of the international cocoa and coffee trades.

order to ensure a constant supply of a variety of origins and sufficient volumes to spinners.

Although spinners increasingly impose new demands for the detailed assessment of lint fibre properties upstream in the chain, many international trading companies have apparently been reluctant to perform any kind of pre-sale quality management for spinners. The next section discusses developments in the arbitration of lint quality and the changing role of quality management in the global cotton chain, as well as its implications for international traders' sourcing strategies in producing countries.

Lint quality and fibre calibration

Until about the 1980s, lint properties were commercially assessed in a manner that had remained largely unchanged since the beginning of the century. An international cotton classification system was initially developed and promoted by the US Department of Agriculture in the 1920s and accepted as the basis of an international grading system. This 'universal' classification system was used as a reference for drafting national standards and grading systems (Daviron 2002). Thus lint traded on international markets was differentiated according to national origin, grade (by colour, trash content and gin preparation) and length. Generally, classification by *visual* and fairly simple assessments of fibre properties took place prior to sales on domestic or export markets, and public institutions (e.g., marketing boards in Africa) assured the quality of lint according to national grades. The variety of lint 'products' traded on the market was narrow and reflected the relatively low and undifferentiated quality requirements of the user industry at that time.

Since the late 1970s, however, spinners have searched continuously for an improved level of consistency in fibre measurement and imposed new demands relating to quality and accuracy in assessing fibre properties. This has followed from two (distinct but interrelated) developments. The first relates to technological developments in spinning, for example, the automation of spinning processes. For instance, recent developments in high-speed yarn-spinning technology make detailed measurement of the strength of fibres much more important, because the inherent breaking strength of individual cotton fibres is now considered to be the most important factor in determining the strength of the yarn spun from these fibres (Bradow and Davidonis 2000). The second is related to increased competition in spinning and textile markets and follows a move away from the scale of relatively homogenous commodities to product differentiation (and more sophisticated textiles) as a basis for competition.

Against this background, the 'old' classification system provided only very limited information about the industry-relevant characteristics of fibre properties (Daviron 2002: 178). Manually operated instruments to measure strength and micronaire began to penetrate the commercial arena and were used for some contractual pricing arrangements in certain markets during the 1960s and 1970s. This laid the foundation for the development of a new system of mechanical classification, the so-called High Volume Instrument (HVI).[1] The latter is able to measure virtually all main fibre characteristics – fibre length, micronaire, strength, trash content and colour – using a single automatic operation and in a very short time, giving users more exact descriptions of the relevant properties of the lint. Since 1993, samples from all cotton bales produced in the US have been HVI calibrated and classified prior to sale. More recently, the entire Australian, Brazilian and Israeli cotton crop has been HVI calibrated, while HVI machines have been installed in several (African) developing countries.

Thus to some extent the assessment of fibre properties has changed from the subjective visual inspection of 'search' characteristics to the objective (technical and measurable) calibration of each bale of cotton. Apart from the availability of accurate and detailed information on traditional fibre properties (grade and length), the number of measured properties has increased significantly, providing greater scope for differentiation of the cotton product traded on the market. As a result, batches of cotton can now be separated and sold to spinners on a more customized basis. This seems to suggest that the classification of fibre properties is moving towards a more technical calibration of the industry-relevant properties of fibres. It also indicates the demise of the former classification system, whereby differentiation occurred mainly according to national origin and correspondence to a category defined by national (public) classification systems.

Thus two tendencies are envisaged: first, a trend towards 'privatizing' the arbitration of quality, where trade agreements are based on arrangements between individual companies and lint is supplied according to HVI specifications, using the universal (US) standard as a point of reference (Daviron and Gibbon 2002). In this case, producers/ginners are able to bypass or leap-frog international traders by selling directly to spinners and offering a detailed HVI assessment of the quality of lint based on the spinners' de-

---

1. The mechanical classification system was designed and promoted by the US Department of Agriculture during the 1980s.

mands for specific qualities. Some ginners/exporters, notably in the northern hemisphere, have taken on this function. Second, there is a tendency towards reducing the role of quality management and control upstream in the chain now that, to use Daviron's words, 'quality management can be based on *ex post* selection, that is, after agricultural production' (Daviron 2002: 181). For instance, lint contaminated by stickiness or neps, which have traditionally caused major problems in the spinning process (and traditionally downgraded cotton with these properties on the world market), can in theory be blended into a mix which will be harmless for the spinning process, as long as the spinner knows the exact level of stickiness in the bale of lint (Mor 2001).

Mechanical calibration systems, in combination with improvements in spinning technology, have to some extent facilitated a higher degree of substitution of different lint qualities at the spinning level, thus increasing flexibility and the scope to blend bales of different average fibre properties. As such, spinners may not only be able to reduce the costs of lint but tend also to be less vulnerable to shortages of particular national origins. In this case, the ability to substitute higher with lower quality lint may support the argument touched upon in the introduction, namely that declining quality in cotton-producing countries is the result of what spinners are willing to pay for the lint. However, the degree of inter-substitution and flexibility in blend formulas is apparently lower relative to, for instance, coffee or cocoa blends, where processors have become decreasingly dependent on national origins and/or associated traditional quality standards.[1] Part of the reason for this is associated with difficulties in measuring types and degrees of contamination. Control of contamination has become more important for spinners because downstream yarn-processing is increasingly performed by machines, which are not able to detect contamination or foreign matter, let alone eliminate it. Among the most serious problems affecting the spinning industry worldwide appear to be stickiness (still) caused by insect honeydew deposits[2] and the presence of different kinds of foreign matter. For example, damage from strings of polypropylene only becomes visible after dyeing

---

1. According to Ponte (2002), new processing techniques have allowed roasters to substitute some types of coffee with others more easily, as a result of which 'roasters seem to be decreasingly committed to particular origins' (and less vulnerable to shortages of them) (Ponte 2002:260). As already indicated, the same tendency is observable in the cocoa-chocolate chain (Fold 2002).
2. Insect droppings become randomly distributed on the lint in heavy droplets, cause costly disruption in yarn-spinning processes and may actually damage the processing machinery itself (Ethridge 1998; Bradow and Davidonis 2000).

or at the time the fabric leaves the final finishing process. In this case it is too late to apply any remedy. Although HVI machines are able to measure average trash content (at the bale level), the accuracy is limited and measuring contamination is still done by visual inspection or by a combination of mechanical assessment and visual inspection (LCA, pers. comm. 2003). In all cases, the assessment of contamination is based on samples that may not adequately represent or quantify the magnitude and distribution of trash in each bale of lint (Hunter and Barkhuysen 1999). In addition, HVI machines provide spinners with only imperfect information, as there are frequent reliability problems with HVI readings and concerns about the degree of accuracy in test results for fibre properties such as colour, which rather depends on the seed cotton variety (Larsen 2003b). Thus certain kinds of fibre properties remain 'experience' attributes, in particular degrees and types of contamination. As a result, international traders are more reluctant to source lint in countries that have a reputation for high levels of contamination (see Larsen 2003b for an elaboration).

According to international traders, some spinners are able to compensate for variations and/or substitution in quality and fibre properties, but most normally favour specific blends of different national origins in order to obtain the desired yarn properties. This is frequently referred to by international traders in terms of 'spinners are conservative – they don't want to change their blend' (pers. comm. 2003). This 'rigidity' in substitution implies that there has not been any significant reduction in entry barriers in different spinning end-markets. At the same time, it also signifies that producers of seed cotton and lint may experience difficulties in regaining or re-entering a specific market segment once the reputation of a 'national crop' has suffered and former customers have changed their blend. Thus, while the HVI system provides a potential means to calibrate strictly industry-relevant fibre properties, the reputation of national origins and preservation of quality upstream in the chain is still a source of differentiation in end markets. Since some forms of contamination are most easily checked at the first point of sale, while others can be best minimized by insistence on the use of specific packing materials at the first point of sale, quality control at farm level would appear to remain critical.

Against the background of these considerations, the next section moves on to the African context. It starts with an outline of recent changes in the organization of marketing systems in Francophone and Anglophone cotton-producing countries following the implementation of SAPs. In particular, the focus is on quality control procedures and the organization of input provision to smallholders, these being two of the key issues involved in maintaining high lint quality.

Sector organization in anglophone and francophone cotton-producing countries

Historically, cotton production was promoted in Africa through state monopolies, in Francophone West Africa by the French government-owned Compagnie Française pour le Développement des Fibres Textiles (CFDT), and in the Anglophone countries of East and South Africa by parastatal marketing boards and/or cooperative unions. After independence in West Africa, the CFDT remained a shareholder in each 'cotton-to-textile' parastatal, each of which benefited from a monopsony for purchasing seed cotton, while most had a monopoly in ginning and marketing too. The parastatals were responsible for organizing virtually all services associated with cotton production and marketing, from research and extension to sale of the fibre.

As in the case of the Francophone region, the state-dominated single-channel marketing system was sustained after independence in the Anglophone region. Farmers were guaranteed fixed producer prices and output markets, prices were set in advance of each planting season on a pan-territorial and pan-seasonal basis and parastatal cotton boards or cooperatives had effective monopolies in primary purchase and ginning. In both regulatory regimes, governments attempted to overcome widespread credit market failure either by interlocked transaction – where input credits were repaid by deducting their costs from the value of the seed cotton delivered to the ginnery – or through offering various soft credit facilities. Through the parastatals or marketing boards, governments performed and managed the quality control system from primary marketing to ginning, as well as coordinating sales of lint on the domestic and export markets. As the parastatals had predictable volumes and qualities of seed cotton, they were able to sell on a forward basis or via tender sales, thus capturing additional margins on the world market.

During the 1990s, public monopolies have been progressively abolished through privatization and liberalization, although in varying degree. To a large extent, the Anglophone countries' cotton sectors have been fully liberalized and private companies now dominate input supply, primary purchase, ginning and marketing activities. The Francophone countries represent a contrast to their Anglophone counterparts because the cotton sector continues to be dominated by state agencies (or managed coexistence between public and private companies), due mainly to vigorous resistance from governments in the region and from the French state-owned CFDT to liberalizing the sectors. Nevertheless, the Francophone region is under increasing pressure to liberalize its cotton sectors as part of the World Bank-launched SAP, and some recent changes have emerged as several countries have opened themselves up to private participation at the ginning level and in the marketing of lint on export markets.

Market structures in francophone cotton-producing countries

There are currently two different kinds of market structure observable in the Francophone region: monopolies and concentrated local monopolies. Mali is the only country where the parastatal Compagnie Malienne pour le Développement Textile (CMDT) still operates a monopoly and SAPs have not yet affected the production-marketing chain for cotton, except in a few marginal aspects. The CMDT still manages input distribution and credit recovery, but private companies are allowed to bid on import inputs and supply CMDT with them. Producer prices are still set by CMDT within the framework of a policy of price stabilization. As a result, gains from increases in the world market price go to CMDT, but when prices fall the CMDT absorbs the losses, thus protecting farmers from sudden drops in income. However, the system in Mali has imposed heavy subsidy costs on the government, and in recent years, with decreasing world lint prices, the CMDT's deficits have piled up (Goreux and Macrae 2003).

In the other major Francophone cotton-producing and -exporting countries, Côte d'Ivoire, Benin and Burkina Faso, the sectors are characterized by concentrated local monopolies, where the sector has been 'privatized' but not fully liberalized. In general, the former parastatals' monopsonistic positions have been broken up by privatizing some of the ginning companies and/or allowing private companies to enter the ginning market. In Burkina Faso, one producers' association acquired a 30 per cent share in the parastatal SOFITEX, and it was recently decided to break up SOFITEX's monopsonistic position by putting up two gins for sale. In Côte d'Ivoire, the CIDT was broken up into three companies in 1998. One is still jointly owned by the CIDT and the state (CIDT Nouvelle), but the two other companies were sold to private international trading companies and granted geographical monopolies in the primary purchase of seed cotton. Thus the quantity of seed cotton that a company receives is in principle determined by the level of production within its assigned geographic area (Levin 1999).

In Benin, several private ginning companies exist together with the former (and somewhat reformed) parastatal, and ginning companies are allocated seed cotton market shares proportional to their installed capacity. Thus, in these countries the administrative allocation of seed cotton takes different forms. The sectors remain heavily regulated in all cases and producer prices are still set centrally: they are announced before the start of either the planting or marketing of seed cotton, following negotiations between the government and the private sector.

The export segment has, nevertheless, become somewhat more competitive, due to the entry of private (domestic and international) ginning and trading companies. Nearly all cotton lint produced in the region is exported, and a large share of exports is still marketed by the CFDT's affiliated trading arm, COPACO (the 10th largest international trading company). Yet COPACO has recently lost substantial market share to new private trading companies, notably L'Aiglon (a Swiss-registered but Malian-owned company founded in 1994). The latter is currently involved in cotton lint trading in Mali, Benin, Togo and the Côte d'Ivoire, as well as ginning operations in the latter country (ICAC, 2002). In addition, several European- and Asian-based trading companies have expanded trade operations in West Africa, including Reinhart, Plexus, Baumann Hinde and Olam International, in addition to smaller and less well-known trading companies.

Input provision and quality-control procedures in the Francophone countries

The increase in cotton production in the Francophone region has been associated with comprehensive national schemes that enable the efficient provision of quality-inducing inputs (fertilizers and pesticides in particular) on favourable credit terms to smallholders. Despite recent changes at the ginning and export levels, input credit systems have been maintained in all but one country (Benin, see below). Ginning companies, public or private, are expected to provide input credit to all cotton farmers in their respective concession areas. Credit in the form of physical inputs (seed fertilizer and chemicals) is extended to farmer groups, and the ginning companies recover it by making deductions at the point of sale (Badiane et al. 2002). This system can be preserved mainly because effective competition in seed cotton market shares among ginning companies does not yet exist.

The farthest-reaching reforms have been implemented in Benin. Until 1999, private companies could obtain licences to import inputs but the parastatal SONAPRA remained responsible for distribution and credit recovery (as the parastatal continued to collect seed cotton and allocated agreed volumes among the ginning companies). Apparently, in order to reduce problems of rent-seeking, responsibilities for bid selection and the distribution of inputs were transferred from SONAPRA to CAGIA (a cooperative of producers) in 1999. But the 'de-linking' of the provision of inputs from seed cotton purchase and ginning created a major problem in respect of credit recovery. The problem of side-selling was solved in 2000 when the CSPR (Centrale de Sécurisation des Paiements et des Recouvrements) became the sole agency responsible for the recovery of credit. On the input side, the CSPR has to register every input sale from input providers to producer groups and every credit extended for purchasing these inputs. On the output side, it is mandated to register sales of seed cotton from each farmer group to each ginning company. Although there are several thousand village groups to monitor, the problem remains manageable because the data required can be collected from a small number of financial institutions, input suppliers and cotton ginning companies (Minot and Daniels 2002; Goreux and Macrae 2003). The system is based on the ginneries' geographical monopolies, and cotton farmers are not allowed to sell seed cotton outside the specified zones or to purchase inputs from suppliers of their own choice. Recovery of credit is carried out through a series of contracts between the private sector operators that are involved (via comprehensive regulation imposed on the players) and does not exclusively involve the ginning companies in credit recovery.

So far, at least, the past practice of the (parastatal) ginning companies in imposing publicly determined grades and in controlling quality along the chain persists in all the Francophone countries, although private companies have entered the market in some of them. The assessment and classification of seed-cotton quality is carried out prior to ginning according to three distinctive categories of grades and staple length. When the parastatals still had a monopolistic position, cotton lint was tested and classified by a single ginnery in each country. According to Goreux and Macrae (2003), this particular ginnery has remained responsible for testing fibre quality for all ginning companies in at least Benin and Côte d'Ivoire. However, in contrast to the grading system prevailing in the Anglophone countries prior to liberalization, grading is carried out when the seed cotton is delivered to the ginnery and not at the primary marketing level (see below).

Market structures in anglophone cotton-producing countries

In the major Anglophone cotton-producing countries considered here – Zimbabwe, Zambia, Tanzania and Uganda – privatization and liberalization of the cotton sector have been completed. Two distinct market structures are observable within the cotton systems: concentrated, market-based sectors (Zambia and Zimbabwe), and multiple small players (Tanzania and Uganda).[1] In all four countries, private companies are allowed to compete for a share of the seed cotton market and of ginning, prices being determined by prevailing market conditions.

Since liberalization in the mid-1990s, the Zambian and Zimbabwean cotton markets have been dominated by a few large private companies. In Zambia, international companies entered the market in ginning and marketing when the former cotton parastatal was sold in two parts, one to the international trading company Lonrho Cotton (which subsequently sold out to one of the largest international trading companies, Dunavant), and the other to Clark Cotton of South Africa. In the first few years of liberalization, competition in cotton-purchasing was minimal, as the companies operated in different parts of the country. Since 1997, the expansion of national cotton production has attracted several other ginning companies and seed cotton traders, but the two companies still dominate the sector with a combined market share of 90 per cent (Zulu and Tschirley 2002). In Zimbabwe, the former Cotton Board (privatized in 1997 and renamed Cottco) remained the major player after liberalization. Two other ginning companies entered the market, the international trading company Cargill and Cotpro (formed by a consortium of large-scale cotton growers and two French-based cotton trading companies). Cottco subsequently took over Cotpro in 2000 when the latter ran into liquidity problems (Larsen, 2002). Cottco and Cargill continue to dominate the seed cotton market with a combined share of 90 per cent in 2000–01, but the sector has recently become less concentrated as several new companies have entered the market in primary purchase and invested in ginneries (Hanyani-Mlambo et al. 2002).

Uganda and Tanzania are the only national sectors where a large number of private companies have entered the market in primary purchase, ginning

---

1. Apart from the author's own research in Zimbabwe and Tanzania, this section draws heavily on work from a DFID-funded research project, 'Competition and Coordination in Cotton Market Systems', which is seeking to monitor and analyze the performance of cotton systems in southern and eastern Africa (see Poulton et al. 2004).

and sales of cotton lint (multiple small players). In Tanzania, over twenty new private ginneries had been built by 2002 and the number is still increasing (Maro and Poulton 2002; Larsen 2003a). One of the results of this development is that total ginning capacity has now expanded to around three times the level of the highest seed cotton crop since liberalization. The sector is characterized by a large number of small and under-capitalized ginning companies, with average market shares of less than one per cent (Gibbon 1998). Only one ginnery has been established in Uganda since 1994, but twenty-three ginneries that were formerly in cooperative hands have been rehabilitated or otherwise upgraded by new private owners (Poulton et al. 2004). Apparently, only a few international trading companies are engaged in ginning in Tanzania and Uganda, but several international trading companies are involved in the cotton trade in both countries, including Cargill, Dunavant, Reinhart, Plexus, Baumann Hinde and Olam International.

Input provision and quality-control procedures in the anglophone countries

The liberalized cotton sectors in the Anglophone region have contrasting experiences in the areas of quality control and the provision of inputs. Again, a distinction between less concentrated (Uganda and Tanzania) and more concentrated (Zambia and Zimbabwe) sectors can be made.

On paper, the former system of quality control has been preserved in Tanzania and Uganda, where buyers and ginners are obliged to purchase seed cotton on the basis of two grades, AR and BR. In practice, quality control at the primary level has broken down. High levels of ginning over-capacity have created a scramble for cotton among a large number of traders, and ginning companies in the sector and a large number of buyers purchase seed cotton regardless of quality, forcing others to use the same strategy. In both countries, grading has disappeared at first point of purchase and different grades are purchased and ginned together. In Tanzania, at least, the proportion of lower grade seed cotton is almost certainly increasing due to declining input use and the mixing of cotton seed varieties since liberalization.[1]

In addition, competition in the seed cotton market has undermined the links between input supply on credit and output marketing by increasing

---

1. Historically, seed varieties were developed to suit different sub-zones, but as cotton buyers moved across former distinct ginning zones in order to increase market share, different seed varieties suitable only for specific agronomic zones were mixed, as were diseased and non-diseased seed.

the scope for side-marketing by farmers. After a failed attempt to launch an input credit scheme by one of the largest private ginning companies in Uganda, the Uganda Ginners and Exporters Association (UGEA) collectively initiated such a scheme in the 1998–99 season: the UGEA financed the procurement of chemicals through a Bank of Uganda loan, while the Cotton Development Organization (a parastatal formed when the sector was liberalized) coordinated the distribution of cotton seed and chemicals on credit to smallholders. Ginning companies were responsible for loan repayment and each company paid a levy to the UGEA based on the volume of seed cotton ginned. Ginning companies were free to compete on seed cotton market shares, while average unit input costs were deducted from the price paid to farmers. In this way, the problem of side-marketing was formally avoided (Gordon and Goodland 1999). However, the scheme was abandoned after two seasons because it did not yield the desired results. In the 2000–01 season, ginning companies provided inputs only on cash terms (Poulton et al. 2004).

In Tanzania, the regional cooperative unions stopped providing inputs on credit to farmers a few years after liberalization, due to very low credit recovery rates. As the regional unions also reduced their input procurement levels at a time when only a few private input traders were entering the market, the availability of inputs was severely reduced. Gibbon (1998) estimated that insecticide use had probably fallen by two-thirds between 1994–95 and 1997–98. Recently, several new measures were taken by the Tanzanian Cotton Board to address prevailing problems in the sector. With effect from 2000, the enforcement of statutory quality regulations at ginnery level was contracted out to private companies. Meanwhile, chemicals were imported by the Cotton Board and distributed through district and village authorities at a heavily subsidized price, at least in the first two seasons of operation (1999–2002). Both initiatives are financed by levies imposed on the private sector, including the regional unions. The availability of chemicals has increased significantly as a result of this intervention, but probably at the expense of developing private sector supply. Although the measures taken to enforce quality regulations may result in improved quality practices at the ginnery level, there is no evidence that this has lead to tighter quality control at the primary marketing level. Thus, the enforcement of quality regulations is still therefore afflicted by numerous problems (see Larsen 2003a; Poulton et al. 2004).

The two concentrated sectors have performed better as a result of their greater ability to achieve coordination between private ginners. In

Zimbabwe, a very elaborate grading system imposed by the Cotton Board prior to liberalization was continued afterwards by the dominant companies in the sector (Cargill and Cottco). The National Cotton Council, a policy discussion forum representing all stakeholders in the sector, has played a vital role in coordinating quality control and grading procedures. The existing companies have committed themselves to following common grading procedures whereby the classification and purchase of seed cotton is based on four different grades and a price premium attaches to higher quality seed cotton. In Zambia, the largest ginner (Dunavant) has recently added a superior grade (A+) to the official three grades (A to C). In both countries, the problem of seed cotton being contaminated by plastic fibres has to a large extent been eliminated. In Zimbabwe, all companies agreed to discount seed cotton contaminated by plastic fibres by the same amount, and polypropylene-free bags were distributed for rent at every depot and buying post, regardless of ownership. The dominant ginning company in Zambia, Dunavant, refused to purchase any seed cotton that did not arrive at their buying posts in specified bags, and the company has established cleaning stations at the entrance of the gins in order to remove polypropylene fibres (Zulu and Tschirley 2002).

Despite the entry of other ginning companies into the Zimbabwean sector, Cottco has continued to provide inputs on credit to smallholder farmers since liberalization, and its recovery rates have been remarkably high (above 95 per cent over a number of years). Cottco's scheme has expanded significantly during the decade, covering approximately 70,000 farmers (around 28 per cent of all cotton farmers) in the 1999–2000 season. The other major player, Cargill, operated an input voucher scheme until 2002–03, when the company decided to launch its own input credit scheme (covering 10,000 farmers), apparently for the first time in the company's long history of cotton trading and ginning worldwide. At least two new entrants have also initiated their own credit schemes, but emerging side-marketing has resulted in lower repayment rates (Hanyani-Mlambo et al. 2003). Apparently, just before the beginning of the 2003–04 production season, several companies (including Cottco) announced that they would not provide inputs on credit as a result of very low repayment rates in 2002–03. Nevertheless, until recently these interventions had resulted in record levels of the production of good quality cotton and rising yields for smallholder producers.

After the entry of several smaller buyers into the Zambian cotton market, Lonrho abandoned its input credit scheme due to increased loan default rates. Instead, Lonrho (and subsequently Dunavant) launched a 'distributor system' whereby the company lent inputs to independent agents, who then lent them on to selected farmers. According to Zulu and Tshirley (2002), Dunavant had nearly 1,400 distributors during the 2001–02 season, each working with an average of forty farmers. The credit repayment rate has improved considerably from around 65 per cent to 85 per cent. With the exception of Clark Cotton (which continues to operate a 'traditional' input credit scheme), other ginning companies have followed an approach similar to Dunavant's.

This brief examination of these case studies shows that on the one hand, although liberalization has taken place in most producing countries, the results have not been uniform. Reforms went further in the Anglophone countries, but the examples of Zimbabwe and Zambia show that this has not necessarily led to high levels of competition between private companies, although here too several new players have entered the sectors. On the other hand, different kinds of market organization have different consequences for the provision of inputs to smallholders and the preservation of quality upstream in the chain to farm level. As will be discussed in more detail in the next section, this has significant repercussions for the reputation of the national crop in the world market, and thus for the premiums (and discounts) attached to exported lint.

Reputation of national crops and premiums attached to exported lint

As shown elsewhere (Larsen, 2003b), premiums and discounts above or below the A Index are triggered in relation to various 'components' of quality, as well as by other factors. With respect to the latter, price premiums can be obtained according to a number of quality-neutral criteria, including forms of sale (forward, tender) and the timing of sale, which is primarily in relation to the first new crops appearing on the international market in a given season (see footnote 2 on page 158). Thus it is difficult to distinguish the precise balance between purely quality components and other quality-neutral components of prices at any one time. This is mainly because of the supply-demand balance positions of national origins during and between marketing season(s). In respect of purely quality components, higher or lower grades (and hence premiums/discounts) originate from different aspects of lint preparation – from crop management practices and agro-climatic conditions to types of gin technology (i.e., saw or roller gin) – whereas other premiums are obtained as a result of the inherited characteristics of the fibre (e.g., seed variety).

The majority of the world's cotton production and cotton produced in sub-Saharan Africa tends to fall into the category of medium cotton quality as defined by colour grade and staple length.[1] As such, national origins compete not only with each other, but also with cotton originating from developed countries in end markets. Hence, apart from the timing of sales, specific 'national advantages' (e.g., seed variety, gin preparation), as well as degrees and types of contamination, are important competitive aspects in end markets. In general terms, however, a quality premium is attached to lint from African cotton-producing countries because it is hand-picked. This is because hand-picking theoretically reduces the incidence of, for instance, stain compared with machine-picked cotton from Australia and the US. The latter generally contains more trash than hand-picked cotton, and the subsequent pre-ginning cleaning processes required adversely affect the incidence of short fibres. In addition, as the African ginning process is relatively slow compared with its US and Australian counterparts, there is less stress on the fibre and the frequency of neps is reduced significantly (whether saw or roller gins are used).

Besides these general advantages of 'African lint' in the world market, Uganda and Tanzania have traditionally occupied a unique position as two of only a few countries exporting roller-ginned lint globally.[2] Turkey and India, the other major roller ginners, consume a majority of the roller-ginned cotton domestically. Roller gins, as opposed to saw gins, are superior in terms of maintaining fibre length during the ginning process, an attribute spinners have been inclined to pay a premium for. Until the cotton sector was liberalized in the mid-1990s, Tanzanian lint qualified for a premium of 5–7 US cents/lb by virtue of being roller ginned. After liberalization, however, Tanzania has lost this unique position on the world market. At least half of the new private ginneries installed in Tanzania are saw gins, which conventionally produce lower cotton quality – or rather, cotton to which no premium is attached *per se*. Thus, as a rising proportion of Tanzanian lint is saw-ginned, Tanzania has lost part of its 'original' roller-ginned premium (Larsen 2003a; Gibbon 1998).

---

1. Different national origins can be categorized as belonging to one of four distinct quality 'classes' as defined by colour grades and length: extra fine cotton, fine and high-medium cotton, medium cotton (the A Index) and coarse count cotton (the B Index). See Larsen (2003b) for an elaboration of the hierarchy of the various national origins.
2. More than 80 per cent of internationally traded lint is saw-ginned.

Perhaps more seriously, the former grading system at the first point of purchase disappeared in the mid-1990s, and an absence of price differentiation between grades removed important price-based incentives for farmers to improve seed cotton quality and to grade properly before selling their produce. This is reflected in lint quality and influences the broader reputation of Tanzanian lint and the premiums and discounts with which it is associated. According to the latest International Textile Manufacturers Federation (ITMF) survey (2001), only certain cotton types from, for instance, Nigeria, India and Pakistan were found to be more contaminated than Tanzanian lint, out of a total of 72 national origins reported. When a percentage of a country's output is of recognisably poor quality (as in Tanzania's case), this tends to drag down the prices paid for the rest, even if this is of good quality, because of the risk that spinners and international trading companies feel they are taking (Shepherd and Farolfi 1999). In other words, the reputation of Tanzanian lint has suffered, and export has shifted to a lower market segment, as one international trader explained:

> Tanzania has a reputation for very contaminated lint. The most serious problems are polypropylene and all sorts of foreign matters. The amount of trash has increased tremendously. Some of the spinners who traditionally used and required roller-ginned lint from Tanzania have changed their blend – they have just experienced too many problems. So, demand for Tanzanian lint has declined (and hence with it the premium they used to get) and even though we are able to offer 'high' quality roller lint to our customers, they are more reluctant to purchase it now … Tanzania has lost its reputation (pers. comm. 2003).

As indicated above, it is difficult to distinguish the different components of prices (quality and quality-neutral factors) attached to national origins, but interviews with ginning companies in Tanzania and international trading companies revealed that some roller ginners obtain 1–2 US cents/lb above the A Index, while others (both roller and saw ginneries) are discounted by 1–5 US cents/lb on the traditional quality premium, due to the high level of contamination (see Larsen 2003a). At least one of the largest international trading companies (Cargill) has recently lost interest in Tanzania. This company entered the market after liberalization and built two large ginneries. It withdrew in 1998 because of the low quantity and quality of the national crop, returned in 2001 (against a background of very high crop volume expectations and improved quality due to new initiatives by the state as mentioned above), only to withdraw again in 2002.

Uganda still occupies a special niche-market position by supplying mainly roller-ginned lint (Lundbæk 2002), but the problem of contaminated lint is severe here too (ITMF 2001), although according to international trading companies the quality is still considered comparatively high *vis-à-vis* Tanzanian lint. In addition, due to the relatively low (albeit increasing) production of lint and a large number of ginning companies, it has become increasingly difficult for international traders to obtain significant quantities of lint. Under these circumstances, more spinners are likely to exclude Tanzanian and Ugandan lint from their blends.

During the last decade, Zimbabwean lint has commanded a premium of around 10 per cent above the A Index, while some international traders suggest that Zambian lint has obtained a significant premium above the A Index[1] in recent years, because spinners now regard the problem of polypropylene-contamination as having been resolved (see also Zulu and Tschirley 2002). Historically, the quality premium attached to Zimbabwean lint derives partly from the detailed grading of seed cotton before ginning, which results in a strongly standardized and homogeneous lint quality. As mentioned above, the elaborate grading system (laid down by the now defunct Cotton Marketing Board) continued after liberalization, and most ginning companies impose uniform grading procedures at the primary purchase stage. Price differentials between grades provide important incentives to farmers to aim at producing high quality seed cotton. At the same time, the dominant ginners have taken a leading role in controlling or eliminating the problem of lint contaminated with polypropylene in both countries. These initiatives would have been much more difficult to implement for a small company facing fierce competition to secure sufficient volumes of seed cotton in order to fulfil contacts with international traders. Besides, obtaining agreements on uniform quality-control procedures (as in Zimbabwe) is generally easier where fewer agents are involved and where they have a greater chance of capturing the returns from investment through such measures. In both countries, the dominant ginning companies have made huge fixed investments in ginneries and/or developed input credit schemes in order to obtain a sufficient supply of high quality seed cotton. Thus they have a sunk cost in maintaining volume levels and grading procedures that will safeguard the reputation of the national origin (see Larsen 2003b on other factors behind the sector's ability to maintain higher quality cotton lint).

---

1. Zambian lint is not included in the selection of national origins quoted in the A Index.

Against this background, Zambia and Zimbabwe have the most secure position in relation to the reputation of their cotton crop in the Anglophone region. Ginning companies are able to offer significant volumes of a range of standardized and homogeneous lint quality endowed with traditional quality parameters, and the risk of contaminated lint is significantly reduced. However, the reputation of Zimbabwean lint as contamination-free has recently been questioned by some Asian and South African spinners and apparently the premium has declined slightly. As argued elsewhere (Larsen 2003b; Hanyani-Mlambo et al. 2003), this may point towards emerging difficulties in sustaining uniform quality procedures in a context where competition over market share is increasing.

Traditionally, cotton lint from the Francophone region has been of either high-medium or medium quality. One of the key questions raised in relation to complete liberalization of cotton sectors in this region has been whether unrestrained competition in seed cotton market shares and ginning may undermine quality-control procedures and input provision on credit terms, leading to deteriorating quality and declining production. At present, lint from Francophone countries is still seen as being of relatively high quality and paid for accordingly. As Goreux and Macrae note (2003), neither grading procedures nor quality have yet been affected by the reforms. On average, Francophone cotton lint commanded an 8.6 per cent quality premium above the Cotlook A Index between 1990–91 and 2001–02 (Cotton Outlook, various years; Baffes 2002). However, it is worth noting that there are significant inter-seasonal variations (e.g., the premium averaged 3.8 per cent in 2000–01 and 10 per cent in 2001–02), as well as significant differences between lint from different Francophone countries, which accordingly obtain different prices on the world market. The A Index, however, only reports a 'West Africa' price. Part of the premium derives from a very low neps count and short fibre content (Levin, 1999). Furthermore, the region's lint has a reputation for (relatively) low levels of contamination. Obviously, to a large extent this can be ascribed to the fact that the former quality-control system in this region is still being preserved, despite recent initiatives towards liberalization.[1]

At the same time, although the ginning and export segment is more competitive now, international traders and spinners are still largely able to

---

1. However, as Goreux and Macrae point out (2003), the current delivery system, in which cotton lots are often mixed together in the same truck, does not induce growers to harvest cotton with greater care, as the farmer who has produced clean cotton receives the same grade as one who has produced dirty cotton if the two lots are carried in the same truck.

obtain significant volumes of lint, as described by one trader sourcing lint from Uganda, Tanzania and West Africa:

> We have to distinguish between West and East Africa. It is much easier to purchase and trade lint from West Africa. In most countries – except for Ivory Coast, because of the conflict at the moment – we are sure we get the right volume and we can rely on the quality standards [i.e., fewer claims over quality] so we can fulfil our contracts with spinners. We don't have to deal with a lot of smaller ginning companies, and we don't have the same kind of risk associated with lint trade(pers. comm. 2003).

A wish to preserve quality, combined with West Africa's still unchallenged position as the major cotton-producing region in Africa, seems to be a strong incentive for international traders and spinners alike to increase sourcing in this region, and probably also to rely less on lint from Tanzania, at any rate until the country regains its former position in end markets.

In broader terms, tighter quality requirements in end markets and the continued emphasis on specific national origins (and quality characteristics) are transmitted upstream to African producer countries. So far, at least, the concentrated market systems in the Anglophone region and the privatized but regulated sectors in the Francophone region seem to have an advantage over markets composed of numerous small or medium-sized companies in complying with quality requirements.

Concluding remarks

Because of technological developments (e.g., automation of the spinning process) and increased competition, the management of lint quality has become increasingly important for spinners. Despite recent developments in the mechanical calibration of fibre properties, crucial fibre properties are still tested on an 'experience' basis because calibration is based on samples from each bale of lint, and some properties – notably contamination – need to be tested more generically. In addition, there are uncertainties about the reliability of test results. In any case, international traders and spinners are reluctant to source lint from countries that have a reputation for high levels of contamination, even if quicker and cheaper ways have been found to segregate more from less contaminated product. At the same time, producing countries command reputations for higher or lower export crop quality, and quality premiums and discounts in end-markets remain (partly) attached to national origins. Most spinners are still dependent on the use of national origins and associated traditional quality standards, as they tend to define desired yarn properties in terms of specific national origins. This implies that once the reputation of a national crop has suffered and former customers have changed the composition of their blends, it becomes difficult to regain a specific market segment. Thus, as tighter quality requirements in end markets and the continued emphasis on specific national origins are transmitted upstream to African producing countries, there are significant benefits for collective action in producing countries to maintain compliance with processing requirements at the spinning level and to preserve the national reputation.

Meanwhile, most public monopolies in sub-Saharan Africa have been progressively abolished through privatization and liberalization. Although the Anglophone countries' cotton sectors have been fully liberalized, those in the Francophone region continue to be dominated by state agencies, although here too private companies have entered the market in ginning and export. However, so far at least, public input supply schemes and quality-control systems have been preserved in the Francophone region, despite recent initiatives towards liberalization. As such, the region still occupies a position in the world market as a producer of significant quantities of medium and high-medium quality cotton. Nevertheless, the region remains under pressure to liberalize its cotton systems as part of SAPs launched by the World Bank.

The experiences of the Anglophone countries examined in this paper suggest that the ability to maintain quality control and to provide quality-inducing inputs on credit terms to smallholder farmers give concentrated market systems significant advantages over markets composed of numerous small or medium-sized players. In the concentrated market systems in Zimbabwe and Zambia, the dominant ginning companies operate input credit schemes as a means of securing a sufficient supply of good quality seed cotton. In addition, the major ginning companies impose uniform grading procedures (with price premiums attached to higher quality seed cotton) and have taken coordinated initiatives to control the problem of lint contaminated with polypropylene. These initiatives would have been more difficult to implement in a highly competitive environment consisting of numerous small-sized companies, as in the case of the Ugandan and Tanzanian cotton sectors, where each company's chance to capture the returns from investment in such measures is (relatively) lower. Thus Zimbabwe and Zambia seem to have the most secure position in relation to crop reputation in the Anglophone region, and lint from these two countries still commands a quality premium in the world market.

By contrast, the quality-control and input systems collapsed in both Uganda and Tanzania after liberalization as a result of the 'scramble for cotton' among a large number of small private ginning companies. At least for Tanzanian lint, its national reputation has suffered and prices now reflect a lower market segment, while in the Ugandan cotton sector, it has become increasingly difficult for international traders and spinners to obtain significant quantities of lint due to relatively low lint production and the latter's dispersal among a large number of ginning companies. In both cases, spinners are more reluctant to buy lint from Tanzania and Uganda, at least until the countries have restored their international reputation.

Indirectly, the case studies examined in this paper also indicate that although market liberalization has taken place in most cotton sectors in sub-Saharan Africa, the results have not been uniform and the dismantling of parastatal marketing boards has not in itself led to higher levels of competition in ginning and marketing activities. More directly, experiences in the Anglophone and Francophone regions indicate that different kinds of market organization have different consequences for the provision of inputs to smallholder farmers and for the preservation of quality upstream in the chain at farm level. They also indicate that different kinds of liberalized market systems demand different kinds of state support and/or private-sector coordination and collaboration. The case studies reviewed here suggest that the implications of the further liberalization of cotton sectors (especially in the Francophone region) have to be considered thoroughly prior to any additional opening up of markets. In particular, as preservation of quality is a key parameter in end markets, this needs to be transmitted all the way down the marketing chain to the farmers, as the average quality of seed cotton determines the maximum level of final quality product that can be achieved and hence the premium or discount obtained on export markets (Poulton 2002: 8). The experience of Tanzania especially, but also to some extent of Uganda, suggests that liberalization should be preceded by the establishment of an effective regulatory framework and/or a strong (private) coordinating institution. Some recent steps have been taken to re-regulate the cotton sector in Tanzania and there are similar initiatives planned in Uganda and Zambia. As the Tanzanian case illustrates (see Larsen 2003a), it is clearly more difficult to re-regulate a sector after several years of unrestricted competition characterized by a high number of undercapitalized small ginning companies than it is to establish an effective regulatory framework prior to liberalization. Thus it seems that the efforts made in Zambia in this regard stand a higher chance of success.

References

Badiane, O., D. Ghura, L. Goreux, and P. Masson (2002) *Cotton Sector Strategies in West and Central Africa*. Policy Research Working Paper 2867. Washington DC: World Bank.

Baffes, J. (2002) *Tanzania's Cotton Sector: Constraints and Challenges in a Global Environment*. Africa Region Working Paper Series no. 42. Washington DC: World Bank.

Bradow, J.M. and G.H. Davidonis (2000) 'Quantitation of Fiber Quality and the Cotton Production-Processing Interface: A Physiologist's Perspective', *Journal of Cotton Science*, 4:34–64.

Cotton Outlook (various years) 'Week in Brief'.

Daviron, B. (2002) 'Small Farm Production and the Standardization of Tropical Products', *Journal of Agrarian Change*, 2(2):162–84.

Daviron, B. and P. Gibbon (2002) 'Global Commodity Chains and African Export Agriculture', *Journal of Agrarian Change*, 2(2):137–61.

Ethridge, M.D. (1998) *Status of Research on the Meaning and Measurement of Cotton Stickiness*, Cotton Gin and Oil Mill Press, 20 June 1998. Online. Available HTTP: <http://www.utexas.edu/depts/bbr/natfiber/natnews/1998/Aug.1998.nat.htm>

Fold, N. (2002) 'Lead Firms and Competition in 'Bi-polar' Commodity Chains: Grinders and Branders in the Global Cocoa–Chocolate Industry', *Journal of Agrarian Change*, 2(2):228–47.

Gibbon, P. (1998) *King Cotton Under Market Sovereignty: The Private Marketing Chain for Cotton in Western Tanzania, 1997/98*. Copenhagen: CDR Working Paper, 98.17.

Gilbert, C.L. and E. Tollens (2002) *Does Market Liberalization Jeopardize Export Quality? Cameroonian Cocoa, 1995–2000*. Discussion Paper 3224. London: Centre for Economic Policy Research.

Gordon, A. and A. Goodland (1999) 'Credit Provision for Small-holders Growing Cotton: Uganda Case Study', in A. Gordon and A. Goodland (eds) *The Use of Purchased Inputs by Communal Farmers in Zimbabwe*. Proceedings of a workshop organized by the Natural Resource Institute.

Goreux, L. (2003) *Prejudice Caused by Industrialized Countries Subsidies to Cotton Sectors in Western and Central Africa*. Report to the Ministers of Agriculture of Western and Central Africa.

Goreux, L. and J. Macrae (2003) *Reforming the Cotton Sector in sub-Saharan Africa*. Africa Region Working Paper Series no. 47. Washington: World Bank.

Hanyani-Mlambo, B., C. Poulton and M.N. Larsen (2002) *An Overview Report of the Cotton Sub-sector in Zimbabwe*, prepared as part of the DFID-funded project Competition and Coordination in Liberalized African Cotton Market Systems.

Online. Available HTTP: <http://www.wye.ic.ac.uk/AgEcon/ADU/research/projects/cottonE/compcord>.

—— (2003) *Zimbabwe Country Report*, prepared as part of the DFID-funded project "Competition and Coordination in Liberalized African Cotton Market Systems". Online. Available HTTP: <http://www.wye.ic.ac.uk/AgEcon/ADU/research/projects/cottonE/compcord>.

Heijbroek, A. and H. Husken (1996) *The International Cotton Complex: Changing Competitiveness between Seed and Consumer.* Rabobank Commodity Studies. HG Utrecht: Rabobank International.

Hunter, L. and F.A. Barkhuysen (1999) *Developments in the Instrument Measurement of the Quality of National Fibres.* Online. Available HTTP: <http://www.sympotex.co.za/fab130-3%20Lawrence%20Hunter>.

ICAC [International Cotton Advisory Committee] (various years) *Cotton: Review of the World Situation.* Washington DC: ICAC.

ITMF [International Textile Manufacturers Federation] (2001) *Cotton Contamination Survey.* Zurich: ITMF.

Larsen, M.N. (2002) 'Is Oligopoly a Precondition for Successful Privatization? The Case of Cotton in Zimbabwe', *Journal of Agrarian Change*, 2(2):185–205.

—— (2003a) 'Re-regulating a Failed Market: The Tanzanian Cotton Sector 1999–2002', *Working Paper*, 03.2. Copenhagen: Danish Institute for International Studies/Gl. Kongevej.

—— (2003b) 'Quality Standard-setting in the Global Cotton Chain and Cotton Sector Reforms in sub-Saharan Africa', *Working Paper*, 03.13. Danish Institute for International Studies /Gl. Kongevej.

Levin, A. (1999) 'Developments and Outlook for Cotton in Francophone West Africa', paper presented at the Beltwide Cotton Conference, Orlando 1999.

Lundbæk, J. (2002) 'Privatization of the Cotton Sub-Sector in Uganda: Market Failures and Institutional Mechanisms to Overcome These', unpublished Master's thesis, Copenhagen: Royal Veterinary and Agricultural University.

Maro, W. and C. Poulton (2002) *System Overview Report for Tanzania*, prepared as part of the DFID-funded project "Competition and Coordination in Liberalized African Cotton Market Systems". Online. Available HTTP: <http://www.wye.ic.ac.uk/AgEcon/ADU/research/projects/cottonE/compcord>.

Minot, N. and L. Daniels (2002) 'Impact of Global Cotton Markets on Rural Poverty in Benin', *Discussion Paper* 48. International Food Policy Research Institute, MSSD.

Mor, U. (2001) 'Fibre Testing Machinery Plays a Major Role in Marketing', *Cotton International,* 68th Annual Edition.

Ponte, S. (2002) 'Brewing a Bitter Cup? Deregulation, Quality and the Re-organization of Coffee Marketing in East Africa', *Journal of Agrarian Change*, 2(2):248–72.

Poulton, C. (2002) 'Competition and Coordination in Liberalized African Cash Crop Systems', paper presented at the workshop *African – Value Chains – Globalisation,* Copenhagen, November.

Poulton, C., P. Gibbon, B. Hanyani-Mlambo, J. Kydd, M.N. Larsen, W. Maro,
    A. Osorio, D. Tschirley and B. Zulu (2004) 'Competition and Coordination
    in Liberalized African Cotton Market Systems', *World Development*, 32(3):
    519–36.

Shepherd, A. and S. Farolfi (1999) 'Export Crop Liberalisation in Africa: A Review',
    FAO Agricultural Services Bulletin 135.

Zulu, B. and D. Tschirley (2002) *An Overview of the Cotton Sub-Sector in Zambia*,
    prepared as part of the DFID-funded project "Competition and Coordination
    in Liberalized African Cotton Market Systems". Online. Available HTTP:
    <http://www.wye.ic.ac.uk/AgEcon/ADU/research/projects/cottonE/
    compcord>.

8. Segmentation, Governance and Upgrading in Global Clothing Chains
A Mauritian Case Study

Peter Gibbon

Introduction

Global Commodity Chain (GCC) analysis has become an increasingly influential methodological entry point into debates within political economy, ranging from the nature of present-day capitalism in Northern countries to the effects of market liberalization in least developed ones. Most recently, it has been used as a way into the exploration of industrial upgrading in developing countries.

This chapter seeks to engage – critically but constructively – with some of the central elements of GCC analysis in relation to a consideration of the GCC for clothing emanating from the Indian Ocean island of Mauritius. Mauritius is a relatively minor, but nonetheless mature player in the global clothing industry. Clothing production there is linked to both the world's two main markets, and recent developments in these links raise important questions for GCC analysis. Furthermore, because of the relatively comprehensive nature of survey, official and corporate data on the Mauritian industry, it is possible to use this case to suggest provisional answers to some of these questions.

The chapter first sketches the recent development of GCC analysis and sets out current debates within it. It then introduces the Mauritian case material before examining in turn the main issues this raises. These concern the identity of chains; the content of chain governance structures; the relationship between these structures and the distribution of opportunities for industrial upgrading; and the rationality of upgrading (as opposed to other business strategies), in the context of different kinds of chain structures.

Two phases in GCC analysis

Two phases in the evolution of GCC analysis during the 1990s can be identified. The first, lasting until around 1999, saw the elaboration of the main outlines of the analysis. The second, beginning around 1999 and still continuing, has seen the opening up of a series of important methodological issues.

1992–99

For most of the 1990s, the main components of a commodity chain were defined by its principal author as comprising an input-output structure or configuration; a specific geography; and an internal governance structure (e.g., Gereffi 1994). It was the emphasis on the last of these three which, at this stage, differentiated GCC analysis from other analyses of international commodity trade. The notion of 'internal governance structure' was elaborated in relation to the distinction between 'buyer-driven' and 'producer-driven' commodity chains, with the implication that it was the nature of specific categories of lead agent that determined both input-output structures and chain geographies. The category of 'buyer-driven' chains was the second key innovation in the analysis and – up to now – its most enduring contribution to political economy. It introduced both recognition of the heightened significance of the phenomenon of branded marketing and of the previously unrecognized link between its rise on the one hand, and the emergence of arm's-length global production networks on the other. Many GCC case studies in this period deal with apparel, an exemplary 'buyer-driven' chain.

A third key innovation in the original GCC analytical framework was embodied in Gereffi's account of the mechanisms of internal governance within 'buyer-driven' chains, or at least of the outcomes of these mechanisms. Two inter-related (buyer-driven) 'governance effects' were identified: first, the attainment by lead agents of greater organizational flexibility, and second, the triggering by lead agents of a redistribution of functional activities between agents at different links or nodes within the chain. A specific outcome of 'buyer-driven-ness' was that branded marketers and retailers were able to externalize their lower-profit functions to those 'upstream' of them. So for example, in the GCC for clothing, branded marketers operated global networks of independent manufacturer-suppliers, organized according to a division of labour whereby 'buyers' could optimize the comparative advantage of different production locations (with regard to costs, delivery times, Multifibre Arrangement [MFA] quota availability, etc.). At the same time, they managed to pass several 'post-finishing' functions to these manufacturers.

In papers written by Gereffi in the later part of this period (e.g., 1999), a shift in emphasis occurs from the exercise of power by lead agents to the possibilities for upgrading by subordinate ones. A fourth component of GCCs is introduced, or at least stressed more forcefully, namely their institutional frameworks. These are treated mainly in terms of structures/processes for lead agents' transmission of information upstream to suppliers, and suppliers' opportunities for organizational learning. On the basis of examples from the Hong Kong clothing sector, it is argued that organizational learning opportunities are provided both by participation as such in global production networks and by being obliged to absorb an increasing range of functions externalized by Northern customers. Along with certain other preconditions, this could allow certain suppliers to move up the hierarchy of organizational functions, from assembly to own equipment manufacture (OEM), through own design manufacture (ODM) to own brand manufacture (OBM).

1999–present

Since 1999, a wide-ranging methodological and substantive discussion has opened up around GCC analysis. This has arisen partly on the basis of researchers sympathetic to the approach applying it to a qualitatively different range of commodities from those to which it was originally applied, and partly on the basis of its more extensive confrontation with other traditions, as its appeal has broadened. In particular, it has been subject to qualifications arising from its comparison with established frameworks for analysing production and trade of agro-commodities (cf., Raikes et al. 2000; Gibbon 2001) and for analysing industrial upgrading (cf., Humphrey and Schmitz 2000; Sturgeon 2002). Subsequent critical discussion of GCC analysis has focused on methodological and substantive issues arising in relation to each of the main components of commodity chains referred to above.[1]

Geographic and economic boundaries

Methodological questions have been raised concerning whether 'GCCs' refer to the input-output and geographical structures for entire commodities, in which case difficulties of coherence may be entailed, or whether they

---

1. The remainder of this section draws on minutes of workshops on value-chain theory (Bellagio, September 2000) and on industrial upgrading (San Jose, October 2000), organized by the Rockefeller Foundation and SSRC respectively. Contributions to the Bellagio workshop can be found at www.ids.ac.uk/ids/global/bella.html.

refer also to the input-output and geographical structures concentrated on production and trade for/by certain groups of lead agents, or even certain individual lead firms. This relates to an underlying issue of the identity criteria for commodity chains, which is posed most acutely when the production and trade for the same commodity appears to take quite different forms in different contexts. Can one speak of a 'GCC for coffee', for example, as opposed to two distinct GCCs for Arabica and Robusta coffees, or/as well as distinct coffee GCCs emanating from Brazil, Vietnam, etc. or/as well as ending with Nestlé or Sara Lee? While this is a question of chain breadth, related boundary questions have been raised in relation to chain length (can one speak of a chain for clothing, as opposed to a chain stretching from clothing raw materials and textiles to retail?) and to convergence and divergence between chains (almost all chains generate by-products or absorb inputs which are part of other chains).

Internal governance

Two perhaps more substantive issues (or groups of issues) have been raised about internal governance. One concerns the proposition that chains are 'driven'. In the first place, the question has been posed of whether chains may differ not only with respect to who 'drives' them and how, but also whether all chains are driven to the same extent. Some (but not all) agro-commodity chains appear to function more according to a 'market' than a 'hierarchy' model, for example. Others have suggested that hierarchy and market are the ends of a continuum, with different degrees of 'driving' lying in between.

The other issue related to internal governance concerns the relation between governance processes/structures internal to chains and those which, to one extent or another, are exogenous to them. In their work on the global fresh produce chain serving British supermarkets, Dolan and Humphrey (2000) note buyers' drive towards greater organizational flexibility and also the externalization to developing country exporters of a wide range of lower-profit functions formerly carried out by supermarkets and importers. However, they note that exporters' 'forced upgrading' was also made necessary because of recent British health and food safety legislation, which requires traceability. A complementary point is made by Jensen (2000, 2002) in his discussion of the effects of the promulgation of new standards with respect to crop pesticide residues, food hygiene and traceability. These require that growers adopt a specific process technology consistent with the Hazard Analysis Critical Control Point (HACCP) concept. Furthermore, it is not only such public, private (or public-private) 'quality conventions' that play a key regulative role in (re-)structuring commodity chains, but also international trade agreements such as MFA and the Lomé Convention.

The issue of the relation of these different forms of external regulation to internal forms of chain governance has two aspects, which are both empirical questions – although not necessarily easy to answer empirically. The first is that of their respective contributions to chain governance in particular cases, and the second whether their mutual inter-relationship might include a causal dimension. It could be argued, for example, that Northern fresh produce importers have a clear interest in promulgating HACCP-consistent process technology as a global standard, since this removes from them costs and risks which would be implied by a simple product-based standard (e.g., costs of carrying out tests at port of entry and risks of disruptions to supply chains).

Upgrading

The issue of upgrading is one of those most recently introduced into GCC analysis and its treatment is perhaps least developed. The issues raised by its treatment to date are wide-ranging. They include whether, assuming that the functional re-bundling of activities corresponding to OBM is accepted as an adequate definition of upgrading, its preconditions correspond to those Gereffi suggests. For example, what role is played by structures of chain governance (e.g., hierarchy vs. market, types of hierarchy, etc.), degrees of codification of knowledge and the nature of the broader industrial structures of particular sectors in the distribution of opportunities for learning?

Second, there is the question of whether the definition of upgrading in terms of movement towards OBM, with its normative suggestion of a hierarchy of forms of firm-level industrial organization, is adequate or appropriate. Earlier accounts of industrial upgrading focused more on product or process upgrading, for example. While OBM does correspond to an internalization of higher-value functions, it may also embody 'competency traps' – represented by design and branding in highly product-specific forms that cannot be generalized. This leads on to the broader question of whether, at least for new or subordinate players such as developing country suppliers, there are not equally or more profitable positions available within commodity chains – and other forms of upgrading associated with them. The recent work of Sturgeon (2002) suggests that, at least in the computer sector, there are currently both easier conditions of entry and higher levels of profits to be found in the role of 'contract manufacture' than in that of branding/marketing. By defining themselves as specialized manufacturers, improving product quality, rationalizing their own sourcing and adding new 'producer services', 'turnkey manufacturers' can develop a highly profitable core competence. If developed properly, this competence can both be used across a diversified customer base within its sub-sector of origin and also extended across sub-sectors. Manufacturers of one kind of electronic equipment, for example, have often developed competencies that can be used to manufacture others.

The Mauritius clothing case study

Background

The results reported are based upon a survey of a stratified sample of fifty Mauritian clothing manufacturer-exporters, corresponding to approx. 20 per cent of the total population in this category, conducted by the author in the first half of 2000. This was complemented by interviews with nine of the twelve-to-fifteen clothing sourcing and Quality Control (QC) agencies based on the island, by archival work covering the period 1989–99 at Companies House in Port Louis on the company annual reports and accounts of the sample, and by employment data from the Government of Mauritius (GoM) ministry of industry and commerce. Interviews were obtained with thirty-eight of the fifty enterprises, including twenty-four with a turnover of more than 100 million Mauritian rupees (approx. US$ 4 million) per year. Discussion in the remainder of this paper will concern enterprises in this category.[1]

In relation to key issues in GCC analysis, and particularly those in the analysis of the GCC for clothing, it was expected that the Mauritian clothing sector's relatively mature character (see below) and its economic and geographical 'outer-ring' status[2] would enable a clarification of some of the following points:

---

1. For a discussion of smaller enterprises in the sector, see Gibbon (2000:23 and 39–41).
2. According to GCC analysis, world clothing suppliers are distributed in a series of concentric rings around the main end-markets, corresponding to a combination of functional role, market-segment/share and degree of geographical proximity to end markets. 'Outer ring' countries are mostly remote ones with relatively restricted functional roles and low market shares.

- Current processes of geographical reconfiguration in the clothing GCC (specifically, the predicted (re-)location of outer-ring production to countries nearer to main end-markets, following customers' demands for shorter lead/delivery times)
- opportunities/trends towards new forms of functional re-bundling in the outer ring, including towards ODM/OBM
- opportunities for/constraints on organizational learning for outer ring suppliers

As the case study proceeded, however, two issues arose that confirmed the relevance of certain of the emergent critical discussions around GCC analysis. The first of these was the Mauritian sector's apparently extreme degree of end-market segmentation, coupled with an almost equally great segmentation with respect to suppliers' orientations to future markets. The second was the clear presence of *delocalization* rather than functional upgrading as the dominant strategy for coping with increased competitive pressures.

A thumbnail sketch of the sector to the mid-1990s

At the time of fieldwork, the Mauritian clothing sector comprised around two hundred and fifty enterprises, employing in all 77,000 persons (approx. 15 per cent of the national workforce) and with annual exports worth about US$ 1 billion. Upstream was a textile sector employing a further 5,000. The sector was characterized by a high degree of concentration, with the largest eight groups accounting jointly for around half of all employment and output. Ownership was by now predominantly Mauritian, although a significant number of the Hong Kong-owned firms, which were the backbone of the sector during the 1970s and 1980s, were still present. The industry was initially an assembly one, but in the early 1980s several large Mauritian-owned enterprises integrated backwards into knitting and – in a few cases – dyeing and (wool) spinning. Until the 1990s, production was of labour-intensive garments (shirts, shorts, woollen sweaters) in basic materials for lower market segments in the EU and US. At the end of the 1980s, the US accounted for around 20 per cent of Mauritian clothing exports by value and the EU virtually all the rest. Mauritius's competitiveness at this time rested upon cheap labour, US quota status and the provisions of the Yaoundé and Lomé conventions concerning privileged access to the EU market.[1]

---

1. For a summary of the literature on the Mauritian clothing industry prior to 1990, see Gibbon (2000). Discussion of the early 1990s is based on the author's interviews and on official statistics.

The first years of the 1990s were marked by crisis, based on an exhaustion of cheap labour supplies. Unsuccessful attempts to move into garments with higher margins initially followed. Structurally, an adjustment during ca. 1992–94 took the form of almost 30 per cent of all enterprises (mostly local sub-contractors for exporters) disappearing, and of most remaining larger enterprises undertaking improvements in quality assurance, reducing lead times, shifting towards less labour-intensive garments such as t-shirts and polo shirts and replacing domestic with foreign contract labour. The proportion of foreign contract workers in the sector's labour force increased from 1.8 per cent in 1992 to 8.8 per cent in 1994. On this basis, and as mid-market retail chains and brands steadily came to increase their market shares in both the EU and US, suppliers were able to add them to their portfolios of customers. Exports to the US increased to around 25 per cent by value of the total. The leading twenty or so enterprises also undertook a mostly piecemeal technological upgrading: the most frequently introduced automated equipment were numerically-controlled large circular knitting machines, computerized pattern markers and overhead conveyors.

Market segmentation and differentiated governance structures

As noted, the author's fieldwork uncovered an unexpectedly high level of end-market segmentation. The great majority of enterprises produced very largely – in some cases exclusively – either for the EU or the US markets. Underlying this was not a preference for single, exclusive markets as such, since those producing for the EU typically had customers in two or more distinct national markets within the EU (normally Britain and France). Rather, it was enterprises' conceptions about their compatibility with the (imputed) characteristics of 'European' and 'American' customers. Second – and consequently – very few enterprises producing largely for the EU market had intentions of switching to a great extent to the US market, despite the increasing incentives to do so during 2000. From 1999 onwards, while still slowly depreciating against the US$, the Mauritian rupee began to steadily appreciate against the Euro-zone basket of currencies. From the 1980s until 1999 it had slowly depreciated against both, and Mauritian exporters had used this to offset local cost increases. Greater interest in the US market might also have been expected as a result of Congress's ratification of the Africa Trade and Development Act, which gave Mauritian exporters using Mauritian-produced cloth or fabric[1] quota-free and duty-free access to the US market.

This suggests the existence of two distinct global commodity chains for clothing, or at least two quite distinct 'thick' filaments of a single chain, differentiated according to 'export channel'. Furthermore, the apparently entrenched nature of this differentiation could be regarded as signalling a more fundamental type of segmentation than those associated with certain apparently more fluid divisions, such as those between types of lead agent (retailer, branded marketer, branded manufacturer) or types of garment (basic/standardized or fancy/fashion). Indeed, at least in Mauritius, there was no great difference in fashion content between garments produced for the EU and US markets.

On the other hand, GCCs comprise not just geographically and economically bounded input-output structures, but also governance structures and institutional frameworks. If enterprises' self-perceived exclusive compatibility with a particular export channel could be shown to be linked to the presence of different governance structures, then the hypothesis of distinct chains would be considerably strengthened. During interviews, the issue of enterprises' experience of chain governance and of 'governance effects' was raised by the author only in relation to lead agents' levels of externalization of specific functions: what functions were enterprises expected to carry out in 2000 that lead agents would themselves have carried out before? It was anticipated that all suppliers would be increasingly expected to take on a broader range of functions, although those producing for 'branded manufacturers' (if there were any) would be expected to take on considerably fewer than those producing for retailers or branded marketers. This anticipation proved to be an over-simplification, since interviewees described a much broader set of governance-related structures in the course of answering this question. These related to criteria for supplier certification, procedures for product specification, required quality control levels and mechanisms, procedures for reporting on work done and procedures for resolution of contractual differences. In addition, they referred to customers' demands for shares of capacity, which they regarded as having important power dimensions.

The clothing export trades to the US and EU were of course governed by distinct public regulative frameworks, the MFA quota system and the

---

1. Or cloth or fabric manufactured in the US or in another African country. Under this Bill, most African low income countries also gained quota-free and duty-free access to the US market for clothing manufactured from cloth or fabric originating anywhere, for a period of four years. Mauritius was excluded from the latter provision.

Lomé Convention respectively. Under the MFA system, fixed volumes of imports from Mauritius of specific clothing categories could qualify for concessionary entry in to the US market, provided they met US rules of origin requirements. These required that both assembly and finishing operations take place in Mauritius. Under the Lomé Convention, quota- and duty-free entry to the EU market required that imports had to have been subject to a 'double transformation', i.e., assembly plus at least one pre-assembly operation (spinning and/or weaving/knitting) in the exporting country. To conform to this requirement without being dependent on other local enterprises, almost all Mauritian-based exporters producing for the EU market had undertaken the backward integration referred to earlier. On the other hand, it was not a demand of EU *customers* that their Mauritian suppliers undertake backward integration.

It was clear that EU customers had a much more extensive set of expectations than US ones concerning what non-production functions could be demanded of exporters. Most suppliers to the US market were expected to do their own sourcing of fabrics and components, albeit only from suppliers designated by customers, and were expected to be able to provide samples in specified materials to a full range of fittings,[1] as well as to assemble and finish. In addition to this, suppliers to the EU market were expected to source completely independently (including in-house if preferred), provided that certain quality requirements were met. They were also expected to have a considerable input into styling, and to take care of the organization of consolidation, clearing and forwarding (instead of depending on nominated agents, as in the case of the US market). Core suppliers, even in locations such as Mauritius, were also expected to be able to participate in product development.

The different combinations of functional roles identified here do not exactly correspond to those depicted by classifications such as assembly, OEM and ODM. There were only a handful of assemblers on Mauritius, most companies producing for the US market were OEMers, while the role of most of those producing for the EU market lay somewhere between OEM and ODM. On the other hand, most of the largest operations producing in Mauritius for the US market were branch plants of Hong Kong-owned companies that were also playing a role in between OEM and ODM in their global operations as a whole, but outside Mauritius. In both cases, the nature of functional specializations reflected the fact that the OEM role,

---

1. The range of fittings for the US market is greater than for the EU one.

Figure 8.1. US and EU clothing chain governance structures

	US-Destined	EU-destined
Level of externalisation of functions to suppliers	Lower	Higher
Basis of supplier certification	Process + product	Functional + product
Nature of product specification an of QC system	Detailed, specified unilaterally; QC by customers' outstationed employees.	Les detailed, negotiated QC contracted-out to third party.
Nature of critical path reporting	Frequent, detailed	Less frequent, less detailed
Prodcedure for resolving contractual differences	Bureaucratic	Informal
Level of suppliers' capacity typically occupied.	30–100%	10–15%

or role of 'full package supplier' (FPSer)[1] as Gereffi calls it, had become a 'moving target', subject to a continuous process of expansion as retailers/branders shed an increasing range of functions. In the EU market, this target seemed simply to have moved a little further than in the US one.

The development and enforcement of supplier certification criteria by buyers is an important element of clothing chain governance structures, in that it controls entry to the chain in the same way that 'quality conventions' do for agro-commodity chains. Interviewees usually had some experience of both US and EU buyers and were therefore in a position to compare them, even though they largely ended up producing for only one of these markets. According to them, US customers generally had more demanding certification criteria and procedures, even though the variety of roles that suppliers were expected to play for US buyers was narrower. US buyers were interested first in whether suppliers could produce a given garment to a given standard, itself defined in a detailed way covering a very wide variety of garment properties. Furthermore, they were interested in the suppliers' technological, managerial and physical capacity to produce large volumes of such garments without problems. Lastly, but much more in the case of some buyers than others, they were interested in suppliers' labour standards. This last concern was shared by some European customers also. But in general, the latter were less process-oriented and more product- and function-oriented in their certification priorities. Suppliers had to be able to

---

1. For Gereffi, the FPS role includes sourcing (and holding inventories) of fabric/cloth, producing a wide range of types of clothing and providing a limited range of production-related services.

produce garments conforming to the customer's quality requirements and, in the case of more important suppliers, had to demonstrate flexibility and versatility with regard to garment types and materials. Yet how they did so, was up to them.

US buyers' product specifications were not only defined in a much more detailed way than those of EU buyers, but they were laid down unilaterally. According to Mauritian suppliers, EU buyers came with less detailed specifications and expected that important suppliers would be able to elaborate them independently, or even suggest slight modifications to them. Similar differences existed with regard to QC. US buyers had comprehensive QC regimes, which were often implemented by out-stationed employees of the US buyer themselves. EU buyers had narrower QC regimes whose implementation was typically contracted-out to third parties, such as international inspection services (SGS, Bureau Veritas, etc.). The use of out-stationed employees was explained in terms of costs by some interviewees: once volumes exceeded a certain level, it became cheaper to use this method than to contract out QC.

In addition to laying down more detailed, non-negotiable, product specifications and insisting upon more 'hands-on' forms of quality assurance, US buyers were also said to have stricter demands for reporting on progress of orders. Together with their suppliers, customers from all markets performed 'critical path analyses' for particular products when entering into agreements regarding them, covering coordination of necessary input and raw material supplies, production schedules, methods and timing of deliveries, etc. Supplier reporting to US customers was normally required at frequent intervals and to a high level of detail. That to EU customers was somewhat more flexible in scheduling and tended to cover more basic information.

Mauritian suppliers who had worked over a long period with EU customers saw the differences described above as significant, but not as influencing their choice of export channel. Two other governance-related perceived differences were more important. The first was differences in procedures for resolving contractual differences. Suppliers to the EU market commonly reported that, when difficulties arose for them in meeting a given volume level at a given quality by a given point in time, it was usually possible to reach a 'reasonable solution', such as prices being discounted for the relevant part of an order but not for that part for which there was no problem. US buyers, on the other hand, were considered likely to reject whole consignments if there were problems with part of them and to resort to litigation if agreement could not be reached on their terms. Stories of large claims by US customers against reputable Mauritian producers abounded, and relations with US customers were commonly characterized as 'au niveau de sang froid'.

Secondly, there were large differences – and not just perceived ones – concerning the shares of suppliers' capacity that US and EU customers demanded, and therefore in the latters' subsequent degrees of bargaining power in relation to any specific supplier. Primarily, this reflected differences in the nature of the US and EU markets. US customers, such as Gap, Target, etc. had huge volume demands that they could only manage economically if individual suppliers (including those who were large by Mauritian standards, but smaller by global ones) dedicated at least 30 per cent of their total volume to them. Suppliers who usually worked for the EU market tended to seek a broader and more diversified customer base, not only in order to offset risk but also to provide them with a blend of different types of work peaking in different seasons. A customer who took 30 per cent plus of their capacity simply obtained too much power. If, at the same time, this customer was insisting upon their own dedicated suppliers, consolidators and clearers and forwarders, this power would be near-total: 'Not only would you have serious under-capacity in your knitting department, but they'd have complete control over all your margins'.

Governance structures and suppliers' learning opportunities in US and EU clothing chains

Mauritian suppliers were questioned concerning the relative importance of customers as sources of knowledge, and which types of customer-generated learning opportunities were most important to them. The discussion below considers the nature of the replies received, particularly in relation to the distinct 'governance structures' characterizing the US- and EU-destined clothing chains.

In relation to the first part of the question, suppliers responded widely that customers were not their main external source of learning. Two other sources were mentioned more frequently, namely machinery suppliers and consultants. Machinery suppliers, usually providing a 'turnkey' service to manufacturers, were Mauritian producers' main external source of technical knowledge, not only concerning machine technology but also concerning production engineering and sometimes materials. The latter was pos-

Figure 8.2. Distribution of suppliers' learning opportunities, US and EU clothing chains

	US-destined	EU-destined
Stimulus to undertake new functions	—	X
Exposure to improved process solutions	X	—
Exposure to more exacting quality demands	XX	—
Exposure to wider variety of customer quality demands	—	X
Graduation to more complex materials/ products with same customer	—	XX
Graduation to higher volume production with same customer	XX	X

sible because of the ever-closer links between manufacturers of textile and clothing machinery and textile producers. Consultants were Mauritian producers' main external source of knowledge concerning improving quality assurance and business organization. Customers were important as a source of knowledge concerning diagnosis of quality problems, but were less important in solving them. They came behind machinery manufacturers as a source of technical knowledge (except in the case of materials) and made almost no contribution as regards business organization. As a result, few suppliers expressed a preference for participation in one chain or another as a result of the learning opportunities that they presented.

On the other hand, insofar as relations with customers did provide opportunities for learning, these were clearly related to the nature of chain governance structures. At the same time, variations in the availability of opportunities could not be reduced to a simple association between low levels of hierarchy and greater chances to learn. Although chains where governance was more egalitarian and negotiated presented a wider range of learning opportunities than hierarchical ones, participation in the latter also offered certain learning experiences.

Figure 8.2 sums up the different kinds of opportunities for learning from customers that suppliers mentioned in relation to participation in the two chains, and attempts to summarize the extent to which each learning opportunity was stressed (two crosses indicate more extensive opportunities than a single one). Whereas participation in the US-destined chain appeared to give rise to learning opportunities relating to efficiency/technical improvements within existing processes, participation in the EU-destined chain seemed to be associated with opportunities related to improving and enhancing versatility. These were less focused on processes, and also less process-specific. Given that versatility is normally thought of as creating capacities for autonomous development, participation in the EU clothing chain could be considered more likely to provide the basis for a transition to OBM than participation in the US one.

Mauritian producers' strategies 1994–2002 and their outcomes

This section considers Mauritian-based producers' business strategies after the adjustment of the mid-1990s, and the outcomes of these strategies.

Strategies of Mauritian-based producers 1994–2002

Exporters to the US

Mauritian-based companies producing mainly or exclusively for the US market were mostly large (1,000–8,000 employees) branch plants of Hong Kong- or Singapore-based corporations. These usually owned plants in other regions, and mostly followed strategies devised outside Mauritius. These strategies centred on the maximization of the comparative advantages of the different outposts of the corporation. In Mauritius, these advantages were considered to be the presence of US quota for key product categories and a reasonably good quality reputation. In addition, the GoM had a permissive policy towards the importation of foreign contract workers, a facility prized highly by these corporations wherever they located themselves.

Even for some more labour-intensive garments, the enjoyment of quota rents seems to have compensated for Mauritius's relatively high labour costs.[1] Against the general trend of declining Mauritian exports of woollen sweaters and skirts, for example, figures for these items reported by Kwai Pun (1999) indicate very large increases in quota utilization between 1994 and 1998. Meanwhile quota utilization for cotton shorts and trousers and cotton knit (including t-) shirts and blouses remained at around 100 per cent. In all, utilization of quota allocation exceeded 90 per cent for six categories of clothing in 1998, as opposed to only three for most of the 1990s (Kwai Pun 1999).

Complementing maximization of quota rents, exporters to the US market broadly followed three sub-strategies: maximization of the use of foreign contract labour, internalization of a number of previously outsourced

---

1. Including those for foreign labour, who had to be employed under broadly similar contractual conditions as local labour.

functions and investment in new finishing processes. Of these, the first was considered the most important.

Maximization of foreign contract labour was thought by managers to offer an important means of offsetting local labour shortages and to provide enhanced levels of flexibility generally. Near-full employment and rising living standards had reduced the desirability of clothing sector employment for Mauritian women and had increased the bargaining power of those remaining in the industry. It had become impossible for employers to enforce the mandatory ten hours per week overtime requirement, which technically they could insist upon under Mauritius's EPZ labour legislation. Foreign contract workers (mostly Chinese women) were perceived as willing to work 'all the hours that God could send'. Hence, having a large complement restored employers' ability to respond instantly to changes in demand.[1]

Foreign contract workers were also thought to have higher individual levels of productivity than Mauritian ones: for sewing departments, a figure commonly mentioned by interviewees was 30 per cent higher. On factory floors, these workers were typically organized in separate 'fast track' production lines, which often were also those where technological change had been concentrated. Factory managers and locally-based US-company sourcing and QC agents regarded this as an important contribution to what was seen as the superior level of general efficiency of 'the Hong Kong-US part of the industry' in Mauritius. On the other hand, they also believed that this 'part of the industry' had acquired superior production engineering and organization skills.

According to official data, by 1999 foreign contract workers accounted for 8.1 per cent of all those mainly producing sweaters and 18.6 per cent of all those mainly producing 'other garments' in Mauritius. In most of the big plants producing mainly for the US market, they comprised 25 per cent of the workforce.

As indicated, a number of enterprises producing for the US market had since the mid-1990s also internalized certain previously outsourced functions and invested in finishing plant. The first of these sub-strategies, which referred mostly to embroidery and printing but in some instances also to manufacture of labels, polybags and cartons, was designed to enable quicker response. Even though most manufacture for the US markets was of branded goods, which were pre-sold, customers were still said to be increasingly

---

1. 'L'expertise étrangère ainsi que son support stratégique nous aident à réagir bien plus vite à la demande ... we use them to respond very fast and (to) keep on adjusting' (interview).

delaying decisions on size and colour breakdowns, thus making it necessary for the first delivery (say of 50,000 pieces on an order of 200,000) to be on a quick-response basis.

Investment in finishing plant – although giving suppliers greater value-added – was essentially customer-led, and followed from the global trend towards greater differentiation of mid-market basics. For jeanswear, for example, most plants had been obliged to invest in plant for new (wet) treatments in order to 'stay in the game' by satisfying customers' demand for products with stone enzyme or stone enzyme bleach finishes.

Exporters to the EU

Two clearly distinct strategic paths emerged among exporters to the EU market during the period 1994–99, but by 2000 one of these paths had been generally abandoned. Instead, the dominant remaining path now could be found in two main versions.

Between 1994 and 1999, exporters to the EU market either attempted to functionally upgrade into OBM, or they consciously decided to remain OEMers. About five of the largest Mauritian-owned enterprises chose the OBM path. The largest Mauritian-owned company bought an existing French brand while the remainder launched their own. In general, the ambition was to attain own brand/private label sales for about 20 per cent of turnover. This was complemented by larger planned increases in shares of turnover from own-designed collections. Becoming successful in OBM was not only seen as leading to higher margins on branded products, but also as a bait to catch new customers on the basis of an enterprise's demonstrated design capability, and as a platform from which to appeal to existing customers to outsource more design work. Furthermore, there was a general emphasis on increasing proportions of fancy garments within total production.

Enterprises striking out on this path invested considerably in augmented design departments and marketing and in new plant. Indeed, during the main period in which they were developing brands and labels (1994–97), their average investment in new plant exceeded that of other categories of enterprises (Table 8.1). In their case, most investments in plant were upstream in improved fabric production, dyeing and computer aided design (CAD)-related applications rather than finishing. This strategy did not exclude recruiting increasing proportions of foreign contract labour, a trend that was common to all categories of clothing enterprise in Mauritius except the smallest (cf., Nababsing et al. 1999).

Table 8.1. Investment level by market and strategy of exporter, 1994–97

Category of exporter	Investment turnover (%) 1994–97[a]
US-oriented (N=5)	4.5 (st. dev. 4.8)
EU-oriented OBMers (N=5)	7.1 (st. dev. 6.8)
EU-oriented OEMers (N=13)	2.9 (st. dev. 2.3)
All above (N=23)[b]	4.2 (st. dev. 4.3)

[a] Investment used is measured as net additions to plant and machinery, less depreciation. Data is for cumulative investment and turnover for the three consecutive financial years 1994–95 to 1996–77.
[b] One of the twenty-four enterprises with a turnover of over US$ 4 million has been excluded from subsequent analysis, as it proved to be mainly a textile producer.

Source: Company financial records, Companies House, Port Louis.

As will be seen in a moment, all the enterprises that had embarked on the OBM strategy had retreated from it by 2000 in favour of an OEM-type one.

Those EU market-oriented enterprises not embarking on OBM continued during the period 1994–97 along the lines of the adjustment of the mid-1990s already described. They strove to improve quality (many of them acquiring ISO 9000 certification), concentrated on less labour-intensive garments, recruited increasing proportions of foreign contract labour (though not on the scale of US-oriented firms) and – often successfully – strove to attract new mid-market customers[1] while keeping abreast of any movements up-market by older ones.[2]

However, also from around 1996 or 1997, a new emphasis emerged among a significant minority of EU market-oriented OEMers. This emphasis entailed refocusing on long runs of basics, rather than shorter runs of fancier products, usually on the grounds that 'fancy means more changes of set-up, more labour on follow-up and more expenditure on meeting shorter lead times' (interview). In some cases, the basics in question were intrinsically labour-intensive garments like cotton shirts, in others they were garments that could be produced in either more or less labour-intensive ways.

These enterprises did not seek to go 'back to the basics' in Mauritius itself. Rather, their strategy was to delocalize long runs of basics to neighbouring Madagascar, where labour costs were only 18–25 per cent of those in Mauritius. Madagascar had the additional advantages that it was only one and a half hours away by air, that it was Francophone, that it already

---

1. Such as the chain stores Célio (France), Next (Britain), Hennes & Mauritz (Sweden) and Zara (Spain).
2. Such as in the case of the mail order company La Redoute (France).

possessed a textile industry of reasonable quality and that it had a locally available Asian workforce.[1] Furthermore, it was quota-free for both EU and US markets, so that if enterprises wished to experiment by adding US customers to their portfolio, they could do so. The related direct investment was small, as in most cases Mauritian companies simply transferred equipment that was two or three generations old. Although the official figures may under-represent real levels of Mauritian outward FDI, they appear to bear this out. Up to the end of 1998, less than an equivalent of US$ 3 million was invested in Madagascar (Bank of Mauritius, 2000).

By 2000, the movement to Madagascar and beyond[2] appeared irreversible. Of eighteen enterprises exporting mainly to the EU market with 1998–99 turnovers in excess of US$ 4 million, eleven had delocalized part of their production to levels equivalent to between 8.5 per cent and 89.6 per cent of their total employment (median 34.2 per cent) (source: own interviews). This group planned to delocalize substantially more, and three of the seven companies that had so far not delocalized had plans to do so. Among the six companies that by 2000 had delocalized at levels at or above the median were two that in 1994–97 had been leading OBMers.

It is worth underlining that none of the US market-oriented companies had followed the move to Madagascar by 2000. The manager of one stated that the brands his plant was producing for were doubtful about Madagascan quality levels. Managers of the remainder stated their parent company was awaiting the fate of the Africa Growth and Opportunity Bill before taking decisions concerning expansion into mainland Africa.[3]

Outcomes of strategies
OBM vs. OEM; productivity

Measuring the outcomes of the strategies followed by different categories of Mauritian producers is difficult. Most of the strategies described above are of fairly recent origin, meaning that it may be too soon to draw conclusions, while some conventional measures of business outcomes may have low reli-

---

1. Mauritian and overseas Chinese employers in Mauritius had clear preferences for employing persons of Asian rather than African descent. The latter comprised approx. 27 per cent of the Mauritian population but only a handful of workers in a large majority of clothing factories. This was justified in terms of ideologies concerning the racial distribution of 'nimble fingers'.
2. Mauritian-based enterprises producing for the EU market had also set up plants in Mozambique, South Africa and India by this time.
3. Shortly after the Bill was approved, one set up a new plant in (the now quota-free) Kenya.

Table 8.2. Profitability and labour productivity by market and strategy of exporter

Category of exporter	Profit/Turnover 1994–97 (%)[a]	Labour productivity, 1998[b]
US-oriented (N=5)	1.7 (st. dev. 8.2)	400 (st. dev. 100)
EU-oriented OBMers (N=5)	0.1 (st. dev. 8.6)	360 (st. dev. 130)
EU-oriented OEMers N=13	4.1 (st. dev. 5.2)	398 (st. dev. 151)
All above (N=23)	2.7 (st. dev. 6.7)	370 (st. dev. 134)

[a] Cumulative pre-tax profit and turnover for the three consecutive financial years 1994–95 to 1996–97
[b] Labour productivity is measured as 1998 turnover in current 1,000 Mauritius Rupees divided by number of employees.

Sources: as Table 8.1; employment data from GoM Ministry of Industry and Commerce

ability because of companies' financial reporting practices. The discussion below is based on financial data extracted from company records and from interviews. Measuring the profitability of US exporters, who were apparently all following a common strategy of maximizing quota availability, is particularly problematic as all of the companies concerned were transnationals with opportunities to engage in transfer pricing. Table 8.2 compares, inter alia, the profitability of this group of companies during 1994–97 with those in the two other categories most visible during this period.

Table 8.2 shows the absence of a clear link between levels of profitability and either end-market destination or (among exporters to the EU) choice of OBM or OEM strategy. Although EU market-oriented OBMers were on average the least profitable category of enterprises and EU market-oriented OEMers were the most profitable, profitability within each category exhibited a level of variance higher than the magnitude of the average profitability of the category.

On the other hand, given the somewhat more meaningful differences reported in Table 8.1 between the investment behaviour of different enterprise categories, the performance of EU-market OBMers can be considered more disappointing than that of other groups. Certainly, this is how the five OBMers interviewed saw things. According to their own accounts, none managed to attain company turnover shares in excess of 10 per cent for their own brands or labels and a more common figure was 5 per cent. On this basis, all described themselves as 'getting (their) fingers burnt'.

Looking back, interviewees identified three principal problems. First, there had been an underestimation (and consequent under-budgeting) of the costs of effective branding. In particular, although all of the companies concerned had been exporting to more than one EU national end-market, there was a surprising lack of recognition of the difficulty (and consequent costs) of marketing a single brand across EU countries. Second, there had been an underestimation of the specificity of the skills necessary to undertake marketing/retailing and their qualitative difference from those specific to manufacturing. Third, it had not been recognized that OBM would entail a need for greater flexibility in planning the distribution of manufacturing capacity: 'We thought we could go on as we had before, but with a given per cent now reserved for OBM. We never appreciated that demand for the brand would go up and down like a yoyo from week to week. We couldn't cope with it'.

Table 8.2 also describes differences in levels of labour productivity between categories of exporter distinguished by market and strategy. Levels of variance in labour productivity within categories were low, suggesting that some confidence can be attributed to comparisons between them can be viewed with some confidence. The category expected to show the highest levels of productivity, US-oriented exporters, had an average level above that of the sample as a whole, but not significantly higher than that for EU market-oriented OEMers. The low level of labour productivity of EU market-oriented OBMers is worth noting. This category included two large and famous groups of Mauritian-owned companies that proved to have among the lowest levels of labour productivity in the whole sample.[1]

Delocalization

An attempt was also made to examine the consequences of delocalization for the profitability of enterprises producing for the EU market. Table 8.3 presents the results of a comparison between the six enterprises delocalizing at or above the median level and all EU market-oriented enterprises. For the purposes of comparison, data are also presented on profitability for the period 1994–97, before delocalization really took root.

The comparison gives no grounds for considering that the delocalization strategy led to significant increases in profitability, at least in the short term. Delocalizers were less profitable than EU market-oriented exporters generally in 1997–99. This may have reflected one-off dislocation effects, although it is difficult to draw firm conclusions as the 'great migration' ran into major and totally unforeseen political problems in 2002. Acute con-

---

1. Three of the companies in this group were forced into receivership in 2002.

Table 8.3. Delocalization and profitability

Category of exporter	Profit/turnover 1994–97 (%)[a]	Profit/turnover 1997–99 (%)[b]
Leading delocalizers (N=6)	3.9 (st. dev. 3.2)	4.1 (st. dev. 1.7)
All EU market-oriented (N=18)	3.7 (st. dev. 5.5)	6.7 (st. dev. 4.6)

[a] Cumulative pre-tax profit and turnover for the three consecutive financial years 1994–95 to 1996–97.

[b] Cumulative pre-tax profit and turnover for 1997–98 and 1998–99, or for 1997–98 alone where figures for 1998–99 are not available.

Source: as Table 8.1.

flict over the results of a general election in Madagascar led to the closure of many factories and of the main port, and to a major fall in exports.[1]

Conclusion

On the basis of the evidence presented here, there are strong grounds to consider that – in formal GCC analysis terms – the 'buyer-driven' global chain for clothing destined for EU markets is quite separate from that destined for the US market. In Mauritius at least, companies producing for the EU market represented a sub-sector with a distinct input-output structure (sourcing largely through backward vertical integration) that was subject to unique forms of governance and had access to unique kinds of learning opportunities. Of course, Mauritius may be exceptional and it will be necessary to examine other locations before arriving at a final conclusion.

On the basis of information obtained through interviews, it was possible to arrive at an elaboration of the main elements of clothing chain governance structures more precise than those formulated hitherto. Differences between the two chains with respect to each of these elements were striking. The US-destined chain was hierarchical and embodied a series of impersonal structures or practices that were lead-agent imposed. The governance structure of the EU-destined chain was more egalitarian and embodied more personally negotiated practices. These differences were linked to the fact that suppliers' bargaining power within the EU-destined chain was considerably higher than in the US-destined one, due to the US buyers' insistence on a very large share of suppliers' capacity.

While suppliers saw opportunities for learning as arising only to a limited extent from customers, differences in the nature of the governance

---

1. For a brief review of developments in Mauritius and Madagascar in 2002–03, see Gibbon (2003).

structures of the two chains were nevertheless associated with quite different kinds of learning opportunities for suppliers. The experience of working within the US-destined chain appeared to give rise to certain narrow but highly structured learning experiences, centred on process-related competencies. On the other hand, the experience of working within the EU-destined chain allowed for broader but probably also more diffuse learning experiences, centred on competencies related to functional versatility.

If learning opportunities within chains are considered an important precondition of industrial upgrading, then upgrading in the form of the transition from OEM to OBM should be fairly easy within the EU-destined chain. The movement from OEM to OBM implies an application of the capacity for functional versatility, with which exporters to the EU should have been equipped. Certain EU market-oriented OEMers were indeed the only actors in Mauritius who attempted this transition. Even so, a large majority of Mauritian-owned OEMers made no such attempt. To this extent, building on chain-based learning opportunities cannot be considered to have played a major role in the business strategies of this group. A similar conclusion can be drawn concerning enterprises producing for the US market. While these were widely considered to have better capability in production than other enterprises engineering, their main strategic emphases lay elsewhere.

From around 1994 until around 1997, EU market OEMers predominantly followed business strategies mainly centred on upgrading portfolios of customers, as opposed to shifting to OBM. US market OEMers mainly aimed at intensifying quota utilization. Alongside importing larger numbers of foreign contract workers, this was to remain the main strategy of suppliers to the US down to 2000. But from 1997 onwards, both EU market OEMers and (former) OBMers changed emphasis to increasing the proportion of their output accounted for by long runs of basics. This was premised on large-scale delocalization of production to the nearest available low-cost location, Madagascar.

The OBM experiment was associated with high levels of investment by Mauritius standards, but generated very mixed results. Functional versatility as such did not appear to represent an adequate set of competencies for making a successful transition to OBM. Fairly specific branding, marketing and production planning-related competencies would have been more relevant, but did not arise spontaneously from the experience of working within the EU-destined chain. In addition, even if these competencies could have been acquired, it is not clear that Mauritian enterprises had the financial resources to realize benefits from them.

On the other hand, it is far from clear that the strategies adopted at this point or later by US- or EU-oriented OEMers were any more successful. In most cases, where enterprises are grouped by strategy, internal variation in their range of performances is a clearer trend than differences based on variations in strategy. Even if the corporate financial data presented here are considered valid and reliable, the only really clear trends to emerge are that OBM was associated with higher costs than other strategies, and that delocalization was associated with lower profits – at least during 1997–99.

Returning to some of GCC analysis's unresolved methodological and substantive issues, the following provisional conclusions can be suggested. First, GCC analysis to date has placed insufficient weight on the role of external public regulation, as opposed to that of 'lead agents', in the shaping of commodity chains. The existence of (at least) two distinct sets of rules governing international trade in clothing, MFA and Lomé, has meant that chains have systematically diverged not merely in their geography but in every other respect.

Second, the 'chain-based organizational learning' interpretation of the sources of successful functional upgrading is not an adequate one. Different kinds of chain-based organizational learning are indeed associated with different kinds of chain governance structure. But participation alone, even in chains whose structure enhances suppliers' functional versatility, is not a sufficient condition for functional upgrading. Steep escarpments seem to demarcate certain kinds of functional competence from others, and external resources are needed to surmount them.

Third, the rationale for considering OBM as the optimal form of industrial upgrading is doubtful. Of course, there are examples of clothing OEMers becoming successful OBMers. Among the Hong Kong OEMers of two decades ago, Tiger Manufacturing made the transition to Giordano, Fang Brothers Knitting made it to Toppy, Episode and now Pringle, while – most spectacularly of all – Novel Enterprises made it to Tommy Hilfiger. However, there are both much longer lists of failures and other examples of highly successful clothing enterprises that did not embark on branding. These include Esquel, a Hong Kong-based group with clothing assembly plants around the world, and which is vertically integrated in the Far East as far back up the chain as cotton production. Esquel is not only a clothing sector example of Sturgeon's category of 'contract manufacturer', but it also manages to capture multiple margins by persuading its branded customers to nominate it as an (sometimes the sole) approved supplier of fabrics and cloth to all the brand's other manufacturers.[1]

Finally – although this goes somewhat beyond GCC-related discussion – there is a good case for supplementing the normatively biased literature on 'paths to industrial upgrading' with more sociological and microeconomic investigations of the basis on which enterprises follow specific business strategies. In a whole series of locations, including several developing countries, [2]a majority of medium- and large-scale clothing sector enterprises have at some stage stampeded into delocalization. In contrast, upgrading strategies – whether they take an OBM form or a completely different one – mainly seem to have been embarked upon where the delocalization option was blocked or impractical. Which rationales, economic and otherwise, guide these trends, and why are they so prevalent?

References

Bank of Mauritius (2000) 'Mauritian Outward Direct Investment by Host Country, 1988–98', print-out issued at request of author.

Berger, S. (1997) 'Textiles and Clothing in Hong Kong', in S. Berger and R. Lester (eds) *Made by Hong Kong*. Hong Kong: Oxford University Press.

Dolan, C. and J. Humphrey (2000) 'Governance and Trade in Fresh Vegetables: The Impact of UK Supermarkets on the African Horticulture Industry', *Journal of Development Studies*, 37(2).

Gee, S. and W.-J. Kuo (1998) 'Export Success and Technological Capability: Textiles and Electronics in Taiwan Province of China', in D. Ernst, T. Ganiatsos and L. Mytelka (eds) *Technological Capabilities and Export Success in Asia*. London: Routledge.

Gereffi, G. (1994) 'The Organization of Buyer-driven Global Commodity Chains: How US Eetailers Shape Overseas Production Networks', in G. Gereffi and M. Korzeniewicz (eds) *Commodity Chains and Global Capitalism*. Westport: Praeger.

—— (1999) 'International Trade and Industrial Upgrading in the Apparel Commodity Chain', *Journal of International Economics*, 48:37–70.

Gibbon, P. (2000) 'Back to the Basics Through Delocalization: The Mauritian Garment Industry at the End of the Twentieth Century', *Working Paper* 00.7. Copenhagen: Centre for Development Research.

—— (2001) 'Upgrading Primary Production: A Global Commodity Chain Approach', *World Development*, 29(2).

---

1. This is also a way in which brands make additional margins – by claiming commissions from approved suppliers.
2. Cf Berger (1997:158–59, 182) on Hong Kong; Gee and Kuo (1998:54 et seq.) on Taiwan; and Mytelka and Ernst (1998:106) on Korea.

—— (2003) 'The Africa Growth & Opportunity Act and the Global Commodity Chain for Clothing', *World Development*, 31(11).

Humphrey, J. and H. Schmitz (2000) 'Governance and Upgrading: Linking Industrial Cluster and Global Value Chain Research', *Working Paper* 120. Brighton: University of Sussex, Institute of Development Studies.

Jensen, M.F. (2000) 'Standards and Smallholders: A Case Study from Kenyan Export Horticulture', Royal Danish Agricultural University, Department of Economics, mimeo.

—— (2002) 'African Exports and the Organizational Challenges Arising from Food Safety Requirements: What can be Expected from Changes in EU Food Safety Regulations?', Royal Danish Agricultural University, Department of Economics, mimeo.

Kwai Pun, M. (1999) 'Developing Exports for the US: Scope for the Future', *Industry Focus no.* 45 (Port-Louis).

Mytelka, L. and D. Ernst (1998) 'Catching Up, Keeping Up and Getting Ahead: The Korean Model under Pressure', in D. Ernst, T. Ganiatsos and L. Mytelka (eds) *Technological Capabilities and Export Success in Asia*. London: Routledge.

Nababsing, V., S. Kalasopatan and U. Kothari (1999) 'New Industrial Strategies: A Study of Gender, Migrant Labour and the EPZ in Mauritius (final report)', Rose-Hill, Mauritius Research Council, mimeo.

Raikes, P., M. Jensen and S. Ponte (2000) 'Global Commodity Chain Analysis and the French Filière Approach: Comparison and Critique', *Economy and Society*, 29(3):390–417.

Sturgeon, T. (2002) 'Modular Manufacturing Networks: A New American Model of Industrial Organization', *Industrial & Corporate Change*, 11(3).

9. The Logistical Revolution and the Changing Structure of Agriculturally Based Commodity Chains in Africa

Poul Ove Pedersen

The logistical revolution and the changing structure of agricultural marketing

During the 1970s, transport almost disappeared as a topic from theories in economic geography and development studies because the internationalization of production seemed to show that transport costs were no longer an important constraint on the location of economic activities. Transport was also generally invisible in studies of global commodity chains or value chains carried out during the 1990s. However, since the 1970s, transport has changed character as a result of the so-called logistical revolution and become much more integrated into production processes (Pedersen 2001a; Stabenau 1996). In the new production technologies, such as just-in-time and lean production, internal transport and storage have through outsourcing increasingly been replaced by external transport. As a result, enterprises no longer minimize their external transport costs, but seek to control instead the much larger logistical costs consisting of external transport costs and the costs of internal transport and storage. Simultaneously, transport time has often become as important as economic costs, if not more so. The focus has shifted from the individual mode of transport (port-to-port) to integrated multi-modal transport (door-to-door) and led to processes of the vertical coordination or integration of the transport sector similar to those described for production sectors in network and commodity chain analysis (Henderson et al. 2001; Dicken and Malmberg 2002; Raikes et al. 2000). Rapid containerization and the development of a multinational forwarding industry have played important roles in this process, in part by increasing the significance of large, often highly capital-intensive transport terminals, with high departure frequencies and efficient trans-shipment between different modes of transport.

As a result of the logistical revolution, transport has come to be seen as more closely integrated into the organization of trade and production than ever before. Logistics and supply chain management have become new areas of specialization in enterprise management, and, like other parts of the production process, transport has become subject to strategic decisions about integration and outsourcing (Schary and Skjøtt-Larsen 1995).

Although this development has been slow to materialize in sub-Saharan Africa (Mwikisa 1993), it is now under way. In the highly state-regulated trade and production regimes that predominated in African countries before the introduction of structural adjustment policies, such changes in coordination were generally not possible. However, the liberalization of trade and production is now resulting in processes of reorganization and coordination that are also influencing the transport sector. The aim of this chapter is to see how this process of coordination between logistics, trade and production has played itself out in agriculture-based commodity chains in Africa.

First, the following section examines the institutional structures that have long hindered the integration and coordination of transport and production in Africa. Then the third section describes how the new trends in increased integration or coordination resulting from structural adjustment policies in Africa have influenced three agriculture-based commodity chains, namely cocoa in Ghana, coffee in Tanzania and cotton in Zimbabwe. Sections four, five and six discuss the changes taking place in the three sections of the respective transport chains as a result of both national and global structural adjustment, namely the shipping and forwarding industry, inland transport by rail and road and rural transport, mostly head-loading and intermediate means of transport such as bicycles and ox-carts. The seventh section compares the transport costs in each of the three parts of these transport chains, before some conclusions are offered in the final section.

Disintegration of trade and transport chains in Africa after independence

At the start of the twentieth century, investments in infrastructure and in production were closely coordinated, even integrated. In Ghana, for instance, railways were built directly to the mines, feeder roads were built from the cocoa-growing areas to the railways and the opening of Takoradi harbour in 1928 reduced loading and unloading times from weeks to days (Gould 1960). European mining and trading companies controlled the whole flow, from resource exploitation to export to the industrialized countries, and collaborated closely with the harbours and railways, which were also operated as one company. The negative side of this development was a domestic transport system that was not integrated and little developed (Taaffe et al. 1963).

Especially in Eastern and Southern Africa, where there were many white farmers, agricultural marketing was often taken over by parastatal companies during the last phase of the colonial period in order for white farmers to control the trade in the main export and food crops. In most African countries, the parastatals were retained and developed further after independence. Large monopolistic parastatals took over agricultural marketing, partly in order to improve service delivery to the small African farmers. A further reason, which over time became increasingly important, was that the new states wanted to control the trade both in export crops, which became their main source of taxation, and in the main food crops, in order to feed the growing urban population and rural areas that had a grain deficit. In the latter context, main food crops became a major source of political control. In many countries, the distribution of industrial goods was also taken over, partly or wholly, by parastatals.

In order to control marketing systems, parastatals also often controlled a large part of the transport system. Especially in the case of export crops, parastatals became responsible for the national leg of the marketing and transport chain between the rural buying points and the port. Goods were customarily exported FOB (free-on-board) but imported CIF (cost, insurance and freight paid), which means that goods changed hands at the African port: foreign buyers therefore had no possibilities and little interest in integrating backward into the African transport system. Motorized land transport, therefore, became solely the responsibility of the parastatal. Similarly, the marketing parastatals bought the produce at rural buying points and left the least efficient and most expensive rural transport link to the small farmers. This tended to result in large under-estimates of transport costs, because overseas buyers only looked at the shipping costs, while the marketing parastatals usually did not take rural transport costs into account at all, because they were hidden in the payments made to farmers.

As a result of the dominance or monopoly of parastatal organizations in the marketing of African export crops, transport chains have tended to fall apart into three separate sections, between which there has been little or no coordination or integration:

- shipping to Europe or other overseas markets controlled by overseas buyers and large, mostly foreign, shipping companies and forwarders;
- transport from rural collection points, usually via one or more depots, to the port of shipment, controlled by parastatals and mainly carried in trucks, but sometimes by railway or inland shipping; and
- rural transport of produce from the field to the village and from the village to the collection point, the responsibility of the farmer and mostly head-loaded, but sometimes carried by intermediate means of transport or even on trucks.

This disintegration of often highly specialized export-oriented transport chains was defended at the time as necessary in order to create a more integrated, multipurpose transport system serving the developing domestic economy (Taaffe et al. 1963). However, in most countries in sub-Saharan Africa, such integrated transport systems never developed, because they continued to be dependent on one or a few export commodities (Pedersen 2001a).

A lack of infrastructure is one reason for both the disintegration of the transport chains and the failure to develop an integrated domestic transport system. However, the lack of infrastructure does not explain why twenty years of development between 1970 and 1990 has done so little to improve the transport infrastructure and bridge the gaps between the three sections of the transport chains.

There are at least two reasons for this, both related to changes in the international economy. First, the lack of investment in infrastructure was to a large extent due to the downgrading of the role of transport in economic geography and economic development theory during the early 1970s. In Africa, this resulted in a dramatic reduction in both state and donor investments in transport infrastructure during the 1970s and early 1980s (see, for example, Pedersen 2001b, 2001c).

Second, the nationalization and centralization of agricultural marketing in the parastatals and the resulting disintegration of the transport chain were partly based on the development of Fordist-type large-scale markets in the industrialized buyer countries. Thus, Ponte (2001) finds that the coffee marketing system developed in Tanzania in the post-independence period can to a large extent be seen as an adaptation to the requirements of the International Coffee Agreement of 1962, which treated the producer countries as market units in which national governments controlled exports. Although there were national differences in taste, the coffee produced and sold in the industrialized countries was highly standardized and often consisted of branded products sold in large amounts. The standardized qualities were produced through the roasting and blending of green coffee from different sources. Therefore, there was little need for the industry to control quality in the coffee-producing countries (they just paid less for lower quality or shifted to another country).

The nationalized parastatals created a three-tier division in the trade and transport of coffee, with a clear division of labour and responsibilities between the farmers, the state and the exporters (i.e., the importers in the industrialized countries). The exporters bought the coffee at the national coffee auction and did not need to be concerned with coffee production or collection. The state in the coffee-producing country could control and tax coffee production and export, and push the most costly and labour-intensive activities down to the peasant farmers. It might have been in the interest of the state to increase the quality of the coffee produced, but for a number of reasons, some of which were related to the poor transport system, this did not happen in Tanzania. The quality of Tanzanian coffee has generally declined since independence, a trend that has increased further since privatization.

Similar nation-based three-tier systems developed for cocoa in Ghana and cotton in Zimbabwe, although the details differ. Thus, where coffee in Tanzania was sold at a national coffee auction, cocoa and cotton were sold through agents to large buyers in Europe, where for both cocoa and cotton it was possible to obtain quality premiums above the world market price based on quality grading systems maintained by the parastatals (Fold 2002; Larsen 2002).

The three-part division of the export-crop trading system introduced around independence in most African countries was institutionalized and frozen into the import-substitution policy framework developed during the 1970s. Formal taxation of the crop export became a major source of income for the new states, and informal access to the resources of the parastatals became a major source of payment to governments' clients.

This has had serious consequences for both the farmers and their production. Farmers received a very small share of the world market price, due partly to heavy taxation and partly to parastatal inefficiency. During a large part of the post-independence period, cocoa-farmers in Ghana (Amoah 1998) and coffee-farmers in Tanzania received less than 30 per cent of the world market price. Cotton-farmers in Zimbabwe received a larger share (in 1990–95 on average 42 per cent of the world market price), because taxation was lower and the parastatal more efficient.

The parastatal trading system generally also resulted in low incentives for farmers to increase the quality of their production. In international trade in agricultural produce, the price is often based on complex grading systems. Thus, cotton is categorized according to length, grade, strength and 'micronaire' (fibre maturity), resulting in a large number of quality categories. Similarly, the coffee trade operates with seventeen quality categories. Such complex grading systems, which are often based on laboratory tests, are clearly not usable at rural buying posts. Here, simplified grading systems are used, based on visual inspection and typically with only about four grades: three acceptable quality grades with limited price differentiation plus one grade for sub-standard crop, which is either rejected or taken at a very low price. Such grading systems correspond to standardized production in a Fordist mass production system, which specifies a minimum acceptable standard but does not pay extra for high standards, because all the produce is bulked into the same transport and production chain.

The difference in the farmer's price for the main grading categories is often small in comparison with price spread between the grades of the international grading system. Although part of the quality at the international trade level is created by post-farm processing, it seems questionable whether farmers producing high qualities are paid a fair share of the quality premiums (on cotton, see the discussion in Government of Zimbabwe (1991)), and also whether this actually covers the extra cost of work and input necessary to produce the higher grade. Therefore, the farmer has often had only a limited incentive to raise the overall quality level. This is even more the case for Tanzanian coffee, where the premium was paid to the cooperative on the basis of the average quality delivered by all farmers, not the quality delivered by individual farmers.

Effect of structural adjustment in African countries on agricultural marketing chains

Because of their dependence on the heavy taxation of export crops, African governments have found it difficult to adapt to the processes of internationalization that have been taking place in the rest of the world. However, since the early 1980s, the introduction of structural adjustment policies has gradually encouraged adaptation through

- liberalization of the domestic trade;

- privatization or at least commercialization of the crop parastatals; and usually as the last step

- liberalization of the export trade.

This process has not, of course, been the same for all crops and in all countries. Because of the many vested interests in the crop parastatals, the process has often been long and tortuous. Crop exports have in many cases still not been fully liberalized, and in a number of countries the process of market liberalization has even been reversed (Cooksey 2003; Jayne et al. 2002). However, the liberalization and deregulation of the domestic sector of the commodity chains have generally reduced the marketing margin between farm and export prices and created new opportunities to bridge the gaps in the three-part division of the commodity chains. Below I summarize some of these changes primarily on the basis of the experience of the three commodity chains on which this chapter is based. First, I look at changes in crop trading and marketing margins, then in crop collection and processing and finally in the export process.

Liberalization of crop trading and reduction in marketing margins

With liberalization of the domestic trade, new traders, both national and international, have made their entry into the market for crop buying. Many of the large transport firms that earlier worked on a contract basis for the crop parastatals have ventured into the crop-buying business, often in partnership with domestic trading companies, in order not to lose their lucrative transport contracts. However, to be profitable, crop buying requires a lot of capital, not only to buy crops, but also to establish a network of buying posts and often also to finance input supplies for the crop growers. Few domestic traders have been able to access this capital. Therefore, the privatized parastatals have often also remained the most important traders in the liberalized market, and the most important new actors tend to be large multinational trading companies. This is especially true where crop exports have also been liberalized. It has generally been easier for national trading firms to enter the large-farm market, where collection costs tend to be lower. In some cases, large farmers have established their own trading firms or have sold directly on the international market as individuals.

The main argument for trade liberalization has been that the entry of new traders into the crop market would in principle open up increased competition, leading to falling marketing margins and higher farm prices. Liberalization has also generally led to a large reduction in marketing margins. Winter-Nelson and Temu (2002) show that after 1995 the marketing margin on coffee from northern Tanzania fell from more than 40 per cent to only 6–10 per cent of the export price. For cocoa in Ghana, the marketing margin dropped from more than 50 per cent in 1996–97 to only 15 per-

Table 9.1. Development in the producer price, export price and marketing margin for cocoa in Ghana

	Producer price 1,000 cedis/ton	Exchange rate cedis/US$[a]	Producer price US$/ton	JCCO price (January) US$/ton	Producer price % of JCCO price[c]	Marketing margin US$/ton
1996–97	1,200	1,754	684	1,427	48%	743
1997–98	1,800	2,272	792	1,320	60%	528
1998–99	2,250	2,526	967	1,454	47%	487
1999–2000	2,750[b]	3,535	778	917	85%	139
2000–01	3,250	7,048	461	966	48%	505
2001–02	4,384	7,190	610	1,383	44%	773

[a] Per 31.12
[b] Estimated by extrapolation.
[c] As Ghana receives a premium above the JCCO price (Fold (2001) says £60 per ton or 5–10 per cent of the JCCO price), the producer actually receives a smaller share than indicated here and the marketing margin is correspondingly greater.

cent in 1999–2000, and for cotton in Zimbabwe it fell from an average of 58 per cent in the period 1990–2000 to 47 per cent in the late 1990s, but with very large annual swings (in 2000 it was only 25 per cent).

For both coffee in Tanzania and cotton in Zimbabwe, this has led to a considerable increase in the farm price, while the rapid drop in the world market price for cocoa has meant that farm prices for cocoa in Ghana actually decreased in real terms (though not in Ghanaian cedis, due to rapid devaluation in 1999–2000).

Winter-Nelson's and Temu's figures indicate that the marketing margin for coffee has decreased to a level that is only marginally higher than the inland transport costs borne by the trader. This will hardly be sustainable for an independent domestic trader, but may be sustainable for an international trader distributing costs over a longer chain or for a domestic trader-cum-transporter, because high truck-transport rates indicate that there are still large profits in the long-distance trucking industry (Pedersen 2001c).

For Zimbabwe's cotton, the marketing margin has also been reduced to very little. In 1999–2000, the farm price was about Z$18 per kg seed cotton. As it requires about 2½ kg of seed cotton to produce one kilogram of lint, the farm price corresponding to 1 kg of lint was Z$45 or US$1.18 or about the same as the world market price, which in 1999–2000 was on average US$1.16. Although Zimbabwe receives a premium of about 10 per cent above the world market price, this indicates that the marketing margin in 2000 was much lower than the transport costs and therefore hardly sustainable.

For cocoa, the farmer's share of the export price increased from 48 per cent in 1996–97 to 85 per cent in 1999–2000 (see Table 9.1). However, due to a dramatic drop in the world market price, this still resulted in almost a halving of the producer price between 1998–99 and 2000–01, though due to a large devaluation of the Ghanaian cedi the producer price in that currency continued to increase. When the marketing margin reached its low point in 1999–2000, it was still about twice the transport costs, which may not be sustainable because of the high costs of storage and quality control. However, when the producer price reached its low point in 2000–01, this was due to a drop in the world market price: the marketing margin continued to increase to more than 50 per cent as in the early 1990s or to more than six times the transport costs. And when the export price increased again by more than 40 per cent in 2000–01, the marketing margin remained at more than 50 per cent and thus increased dramatically in dollar terms.

Changes in the crop collection process

However, in practice liberalization has generally led to very limited price competition at the farm gate. In most cases, the new traders closely follow the price set by the largest trader, usually the former parastatal. Instead, traders compete on services: cash on delivery (where the parastatals often took weeks or months to pay), input supply schemes, credit and better access to buying points (Ponte 2002; Winter-Nielsen and Temu 2002; Larsen 2002). As the new traders in the market have access to different sets of resources to provide such services, this has resulted in a degree of market segmentation.

Although the buying points of different traders often tend to cluster, the increased number of traders has probably led to a larger geographic spread of buying points, which has tended to reduce the distance from farm to buying point. Liberalization has also generally made it lawful for mobile buyers to fetch the crop directly from farmers. However, mobile buyers often pay very low prices and in Tanzania mobile coffee-trading is prohibited in order to protect farmers. Whether such a prohibition is reasonable is an open question because it is often very difficult for a very small-scale farmer to pay her own crop-transportation costs, and it may be a better option to try to improve farmers' access to transport.

In a number of cases, the increased competition appears to have resulted in decreasing crop qualities: traders may accept low quality crops because they are seeking a larger market share or because they lack experience of the grading system. Traders who buy little may also have practical difficulties in separating the different grades and therefore prefer to operate with only one (lower) grade. Experience seems to show that it requires either government control or collaboration between traders to maintain the quality control system. The problem here is that voluntary collaboration between traders is only possible if their numbers are small (Larsen 2002; Gibbon 2001).

Restructuring the export trade

Most agricultural export crops have traditionally been sold directly to large processing firms in Europe or other industrialized countries, through either direct sales or auction. However, in the 1990s markets tended to change. The large processors increasingly outsourced their raw material procurement and storage to large international traders in order to be able to concentrate on their own core functions, namely processing and their own markets. The international trading firms have become supply managers for the processors by supplying them with raw materials of specified quality, often at a short notice of days or even hours. In order to supply the specified qualities at the lowest cost, the large multinational trading firms often buy, store and mix raw materials from different countries. This shift in marketing organization from parastatal to international trader is illustrated in Figure 9.1 (the associated changes in the transport chain are discussed in section four).

At the same time, the markets for standard product qualities have become increasingly concentrated. Low-production countries have increasing difficulties in obtaining the full world market price for their produce, as has been the case with Tanzanian coffee (Ponte 2001). On the other hand, as a result of increased market segmentation in the industrialized countries, new small market niches have developed for specialized high-value produce, such as ecological and fair-trade products and high-quality estate coffee. Although this market segmentation is due to increasing incomes in the industrialized world, it has generally benefited from containerization, which allows a degree of differentiation in the transport chain that was often not economically feasible previously. At the same time, containerization and reductions in transport time have reduced quality deterioration during transport.

As a result of these changes in the market, those international traders who have a global presence have taken over an increasing share of the world market for agricultural raw materials. Few national firms in developing countries are able to provide the services of a supply manager. Large trading firms or former parastatals, like Cottco in Zimbabwe and Cocobod in

Figure 9.1. Structure of commodity and transport chains operated by parastatals and international traders, respectively

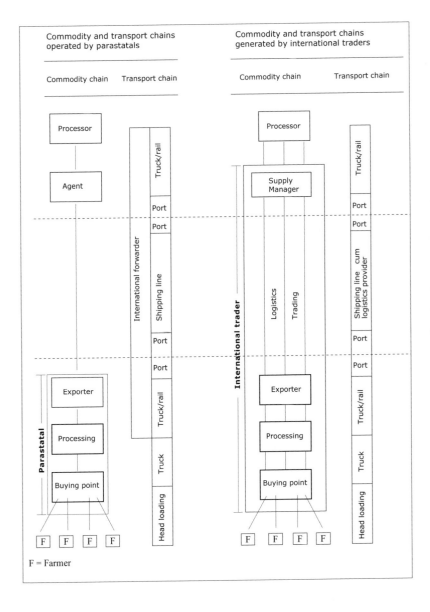

Ghana, may still be able to sell high-quality produce directly to large processors because they sell via trading agents, who are able to provide some of the services. Small trading firms may find a place in niche markets but will have increasing difficulties operating in the market for standard qualities.

The increasing importance of international traders has led to an increased use of forward sales and futures markets in order both to reduce the trader's risk and to obtain a more rapid circulation of capital, and the produce may now be traded several times before it actually materializes. Thus, the futures market for cotton is more than three times larger than the total world production of cotton, while for coffee and cocoa the futures markets are respectively eight and fourteen times larger than world production (Morgan 2001).

Zimbabwe's cotton and Ghana's cocoa were also sold forward by the parastatals when it was collected or even earlier. However, coffee in Tanzania was not sold before the coffee auction. This was at least partly because of the long and unpredictable inland travel time (often several months). Now, however, international traders buying coffee in rural areas tend to sell it forward as soon as they have bought it. Improved transportation makes this easier. As a result of forward-selling, the coffee auction no longer plays the same role as a price-setter that it did before. As the coffee has already been sold, the trading companies have to buy their own coffee at the auction no matter what the price, and as the companies at the auction are buying from themselves the price is not important (Temu et al. 2001). The auction now only plays its traditional role for estate coffee.

Many of the changes that have taken place in the commodity chains rely on changes that have taken place in the transport system. On the other hand, there is no narrow one-to-one link between trade and transport because in most cases the transport system and transport infrastructure are developed as multi-purpose systems serving many different commodity chains, often with more focus on the internal circulation of the national market than on the transport of export crops.

Development of overseas shipping and forwarding

Development of African shipping lines

At independence, African shipping was completely dominated by European shipping companies organized in shipping conferences, which controlled the freight rates. At the same time, most of what developing countries exported was sold FOB, while their imports were bought CIF, which meant that transport was usually controlled by the overseas trade partner. There was, therefore, a general feeling in the new African countries that the conference rates were unreasonably high, and during the first decade after independence the new countries attempted to capture at least some control over shipping links.

Many of the new African states established their own shipping companies in order to earn some transport income. Many of the large parastatals were also able to export CIF advantageously, partly because their transport flows were big enough to secure relatively cheap rates and partly in order to utilize their national shipping, forwarding and insurance companies. Thus, cocoa in Ghana and cotton in Zimbabwe were exported CIF, while coffee in Tanzania was sold at auction before it reached the port and therefore exported FOB. However, in terms of packaging and the conditions of transport, the flows continued to be controlled largely by the overseas buyers.

The new African shipping companies were supported by the UNCTAD Code of Liner Conduct, which from the early 1970s secured 40 per cent of the import-export trade for the new national shipping companies, 40 per cent for the shipping lines of the trade partner and only 20 per cent for third-party countries. Many countries without a shipping industry of their own set up shipping agencies that chartered slots from foreign shipping companies for their 40 per cent national share of the import-export market. However, the domestic shipping companies became a mixed blessing. They were integrated into the conference system, but as they were not very efficient by international standards, they soon became hostages to maintaining high shipping rates.

During the 1980s, the shipping conferences were met with increasing competition from shipping companies outside them (especially Maersk and some of the Far Eastern shipping lines) undercutting conference rates, and when in 1992 the EU made the conferences illegal in Europe, their role as rate-setters in African shipping came to an end. As a result, shipping rates have been decreasing since the late 1980s, which led to a number of structural changes in the shipping industry during the 1990s.

The decreasing rates led to rapidly increasing deficits for most of the African shipping lines because they were operating with too high costs. As a result, most of them have been forced to sell their ships and close down. Some have attempted to survive as shipping companies without ships by chartering slots from other shipping companies for their 40 per cent national share of the import-export market. During the 1990s, the South African shipping company Safmarine attempted to expand on the West African shipping market by supplying such slots (Iheduru 1996).

Containerization

Containerization has probably been the most important change in international transport since 1970 (Pedersen 2001a). In the industrialized countries, containerization reduced the cost of trans-shipment and opened the way to integrated door-to-door transport. Containerization of high-value goods also increased the security of transport, while containerization of high-value bulk goods increased the flexibility of transport, since it now became possible to ship a container when it was full instead of waiting until a whole shipload had been collected. For this reason, it has also allowed greater product differentiation than before. Containerization has resulted in a rapid rationalization and restructuring of liner shipping, and led to the development of a highly profitable and rapidly growing information-based sector of international freight forwarders organizing and controlling door-to-door transport.

However, in African countries door-to-door transport has been slow to materialize due to low wages and a lack of infrastructure. When containerization was introduced in Africa during the 1970s, it was mainly high-value industrial imports that were containerized by European exporters for security reasons. Therefore, only imports were containerized. In order to avoid returning empty containers, during the 1980s the shipping companies offered to containerize African exports at reduced rates, and since the late 1980s a large share of the agricultural crops that were traditionally transported in bags or in bulk has been containerized. However, the present trend towards the containerization of agricultural produce may not prove stable in the future. Already, the rebates on export containers from South Africa disappeared in 1999, when imports into South Africa declined and the excess of empty containers disappeared: similarly cocoa exports from Francophone West Africa are now increasingly being shipped in bulk again, like grain (Fold 2002).

Moreover, most containers to the domestic market are emptied at the port of entry (see Pedersen 2001a, 2001b, 2002). It is mainly transit containers to landlocked countries or multinational companies that continue inland. Therefore, most exports are containerized at the port. This is due partly to customs regulations, which often require that every container be opened and checked, and partly to low labour costs, which make the loading and unloading of containers and trucks much less costly than in the industrialized countries. At the same time, the truck often can carry more goods without the container. Therefore, African countries have generally benefited less from containerization than industrialized countries, and there have been few attempts to integrate shipping and inland transport.

Most African countries have attempted to set up their own forwarding industries in order to reap their share of the profits from the industry. This has resulted in a large number of small forwarding firms. However, most of them only function as customs clearing agents and they often have a poor reputation for corruption. They have neither the resources to organize efficient inland transport nor the global presence necessary to control the international freight flow. Therefore, only local agents who have been accepted as agents for large international forwarders have been able to develop into fully fledged forwarding companies.

Restructuring of the African shipping network

Africa has traditionally been served by shipping routes directly to Western Europe, but during the 1990s container shipping was rapidly reorganized and concentrated. Globally, container shipping has been reorganized into hub-and-spoke systems, in order to be able to provide high frequency services using large container ships on the main shipping routes. Maersk, which became one of the dominant shipping companies in Africa during the 1990s, has established a hub-and-spoke system based on an around-the-world route from the North American east coast via the Mediterranean Sea, Singapore and Hong Kong to the North American west coast. This main route is served with high frequency by very large, high-speed container ships (6600 TEU, with plans to increase to almost 10,000 TEU) connecting just a small number of large and efficient hub-ports. Two of these hub-ports, located in southern Spain (Algeciras) and Oman (Salala), have become centres for feeder lines serving the ports of West and East Africa respectively. This has reduced the number of direct connections to Western Europe, while increasing frequencies between Africa, the Far East and North America, where connections have traditionally been poor. This has given Maersk an increased share of the growing non-European transport market. However, for connections to Europe this has meant longer travel times, and many companies, including Maersk's subsidiary Safmarine, still serve Europe directly.

The shipping companies have made similar, but less successful, attempts to create hub-and-spokes networks within Africa. The best example is Durban, but Abidjan and Dakar in West Africa also function to a limited extent as hub-ports. However, in general the capacity, efficiency and inland traffic connections of the African ports are not sufficient for them to function as hub-ports. On the contrary, the ports are often major bottlenecks in the transport chains. Many African governments have been reluctant to privatize their ports because, in spite of their inefficiency, they are often important income-earners for the state, not to mention politically favoured individuals. African states have also been hesitant in developing hub-and-spoke systems because they are expected to favour hub-ports at the cost of non-hubs (Pálson 1998). However, in spite of their scepticism towards hub-and-spoke systems, many countries have plans to develop their own major port into a hub.

The restructuring of the shipping industry also led to a rapid concentration of container traffic during the 1990s. Thus, after two large mergers in 2000, only two shipping companies and their subsidiaries (the Danish Maersk and the French Delmas) controlled 80 per cent of Ghana's container traffic. And in Zimbabwe, Maersk (together with its subsidiary Safmarine) was alone responsible for more than 40 per cent of container traffic. In East Africa, the traffic remains less concentrated, with Maersk/Safmarine having only 27 per cent and P&O Nedlloyd and Mediterranean having 14.6 per cent and 13.6 per cent respectively. While the increased competition and rationalization during the 1990s led to decreasing shipping rates, there are now fears that the strong concentration will lead to new rate increases. Rate increases since 2001 seem to support that fear.

During the late 1990s, some of the large shipping companies also attempted to go inland in order to conquer part of the market for door-to-door transport from the international forwarders by offering their services directly to the shippers. As a result, the forwarders are losing market share, especially in the transport of full containers. This is possible because, for the international trader, logistics is a core function on which he is able to focus in a way that a processor cannot. Therefore, the international trader can supply part of the logistics in-house. This shift in logistics and transport coordination from the freight forwarder to a combination of the international trader and the shipping company-cum-logistics provider is illustrated in Figure 9.1.

In order to satisfy the narrow quality specifications and time windows of a supply manager without having large storage facilities, it has become crucial for international traders themselves to control the logistics and transport chain. Transport time and especially regularity have become increasingly important. The increased regularity of the shipping lines makes it possible to some extent to treat shipping time as free storage time. This means that the irregularity of inland transport in Africa has become an increasing problem because it makes it impossible to plan the transport flow in advance. The narrow time windows often required mean that in critical situations traders may be forced to carry produce as airfreight in order to meet their supply contracts. Transport flows are, therefore, tending to become more diversified than before. Thus, in one sense transport is less of a constraint than before, though the logistical costs are probably no less, and for international traders the minimization of logistical costs is crucial for profits.

Development of inland transport: rail and road transport

During most of the colonial period, inland transport in Africa was dominated by railways built during the first decades of the twentieth century. However, though the Zimbabwean railways are an important exception (they operated at a surplus until 1947 (Pedersen 2002)), most African railway systems operated from the start at a deficit. Indeed, when road traffic increased during the 1920s and 1930s, the colonial governments in many African countries attempted to protect the railways from competition from road transport by refusing to build roads parallel to the railways, but only feeder roads to them. After the Second World War, such protection became increasingly difficult, but in both Tanzania and Ghana the last gaps in the main road systems were not filled until the 1950s on the eve of independence (Pedersen 2001a, 2001b).

Around independence, that is, during the 1950s and 1960s, there was a wave of transport investment, especially in the construction of main roads, but also of new extensions to rail systems. However, this generally stopped again during the 1970s. This was partly a result of the economic stagnation that hit many African countries at that time, and partly a result of the shift in development thinking from modernization theory to dependency theory and basic needs strategies, which took place around 1970. Where modernization theory had regarded transport infrastructure as a precondition for development, basic needs strategies focused on local rural development. To the extent that transport was considered at all, the focus shifted to the development of rural roads. This led to twenty years of deterioration of the African transport infrastructure. At the same time, import controls and a lack of foreign currency led to the deterioration of the truck fleet and the monopolization of transport capacity by the parastatals and other large companies that were mainly located in urban areas.

Transport policies continued to favour the railways, first by not giving licences to trucking routes parallel to the railways, and later by requiring the parastatals to use the railways as much as possible. However, as this was generally not followed up by investments in track maintenance and new rolling stock, the railways deteriorated as rapidly as the roads. The policy focus on the railways also meant that they were considered an all-round means of transport, and not equipped to serve specialized markets like, first of all, the growing container market, where they had a chance to compete effectively with the roads. Thus, in Ghana in 2000 the railways were still unable to carry containers, while in East Africa their capacity to do so was still far too limited.

In connection with the introduction of structural adjustment policies in the late 1980s, donor interest in supporting transport infrastructures increased again. There was now a realization of the need for an increased focus on maintenance, but at the same time the main roads had deteriorated to a degree that in many areas they had become almost impassable. The focus, therefore, shifted again from the rural roads back to the main roads.

However, there was also a new realization that roads were not enough: there was also a need to develop an independent trucking industry. In many countries after independence, truck transport had increasingly been monopolized by the parastatals and other large companies, and only a small independent trucking industry had survived. In Ghana, the import liberalization of the mid-1980s led to the private importation of trucks, and at the same time the regulation and licensing of trucks for hire was completely liberalized. This led to a rapid growth in the importation of second-hand trucks from Europe and the establishment of an open market for truck transportation. Conversely, the liberalization of the trucking industry in Tanzania and Zimbabwe only took place in the late 1990s, but it then led to the rapid development of a rural trucking industry. Thus, the number of small trucks for hire increased rapidly in the cotton-growing areas of Zimbabwe during the late 1990s (Pedersen 2002) and in the coffee-growing area of Moshi a taxi-like system of pick-ups developed (Pedersen 2001c). This indicates that the old parastatal distribution and collection system was based on over-sized vehicles. In spite of the gradual liberalization and growth of the trucking industry in many countries, price competition has been limited and transport rates have remained high compared to other parts of the world (Rizet and Hine 1993). However, recent data from Tanzania (Pedersen 2001c) indicate that trucking rates may be falling.

Most African railway systems today operate with run-down tracks and rolling stock, too many staff and large deficits. Still, they represent many vested interests, which have made privatization a generally slow process. Successful privatization will require serious rationalization, an increased focus on container and bulk transport and large investments in track rehabilitation, new rolling stock and improved communication systems. In spite of this, large multinational companies have shown considerable interest in taking over railways when they are privatized. The first railway to be privatized was the line from Abidjan to Burkina Faso, which since 1996 has been operated by a private French-dominated consortium (Mitchell and Budin 1998). In Eastern and Southern Africa especially, South African railway companies have obtained contracts to rehabilitate or operate trains on a number of national railway systems, and they are now operating container trains between South Africa and Tanzania and Uganda, though still with only limited capacity. However, a real breakthrough in the development of the African railways is still to come. Railway container traffic is likely to be an important element in the development of new or improved inland ports in land-locked countries and inland cities.

Development of rural transport: Head-loading and intermediate non-motorized means of transport

In spite of the increased focus on rural roads in basic needs strategies, motorized transport in many rural areas almost disappeared during the 1970s. This was partly due to a lack of capital in rural areas, but it was as much a result of conscious policies to prevent parallel crop-trading bypassing the parastatal monopolies. Thus, in both Tanzania and Zimbabwe few rural traders were given foreign currency allocations to import vehicles, and licences to operate trucks for hire were seldom given to trucks based in rural areas. For instance, in Zimbabwe in the early 1990s there was still only one truck for hire in each of the two district service centres of Gutu and Gokwe, which are the main centres in districts with 3–400,000 inhabitants.

The crop parastatals, which were responsible for collecting the crops, were often unable to do so without long delays because the roads were poor and their truck fleets too small and often poorly managed. In any case, the parastatals usually only collected the crop at centralized depots or collection points, leaving the farmers to transport the crops from their farm to the depot or collection point, where the roads were often in a very poor condition, so that the crop had to be head-loaded or carried by non-motorized transport. Even where the roads would have permitted the use of non-motorized means of transport, the payment made to farmers was often so low that they were unable to invest even in those.

Poor rural transport may be decisive in the location of primary processing, which leads to large weight reductions. Thus, Arabica coffee in Tanzania is de-pulped and fermented at the farm because the central pulperies – which from a quality perspective would probably be preferable – would require four times the current transport costs, even if there was a pulpery at each of the buying points. Without motorized transport, this would hardly be feasible. In the case of Robusta coffee, by contrast, which is only dried at the farm, central pulperies are feasible because the weight has already been reduced to a third in the drying process (Pedersen 2001d). From a rural resources perspective, de-pulping at the farm is also important because the pulp, which can be used as fertilizer, stays there.

The liberalization of the trucking industry in both Zimbabwe and Tanzania has led to a rapidly improving level of rural transport in areas that have benefited from the liberalization of agricultural trade. For instance, at Gokwe district service centre in Zimbabwe the number of trucks for hire increased from only one in the early 1990s to about 50 in 2000. Many of these trucks are new to the centre, but others belong to traders, who, before the liberalization of the trucking industry, were only allowed to transport their own goods (which meant that the farmers were forced to sell their crops to them before it could be transported out). And in the coffee district of Moshi in northern Tanzania, a large number of pick-ups have been operating as taxis since the 1990s.

In addition to the increased access to motorized transport in Gokwe, the number of oxcarts has also increased rapidly. In the early 1990s there was only one maker of oxcarts in Gokwe, producing less than twenty a year. In 2000 there were between fifty and a hundred makers producing at least 2,000 a year, and a large number of cotton farmers were said to have their own oxcarts. A survey of 65 cotton farmers in Gokwe district carried out in 2000–01 indicated that 55–60 per cent had oxcarts compared to 32 per cent of small-scale farmers in a national survey from 1989 (Sunga et al. 1990) and 13–17 per cent in an ILO (1997) study reporting data from 1992. This improved access to transport in rural areas has been important for the success of the liberalized cotton market, because it has provided farmers with a greater choice of market outlets. Similar increases in the use of oxcarts (see Madulu 1998; Gibbon 1998), bicycles and other intermediate means of transport have been observed elsewhere in Africa. However, the trend is far from uniform, but depends on actual increases in farmers' incomes (Porter 2002).

Cost of transport in the three sections of the transport chain

In order to compare the importance of the three sections of the transport chain, Table 9.2 presents a rough estimate of the costs of each of the three sections for the cocoa export chain in Ghana, the coffee export chain in Tanzania and the cotton export chain in Zimbabwe, respectively. The value of the rural transport section is particularly difficult to estimate, because it often is not paid for in money but rather represents a drain on labour resources, which during the harvest period are often scarce. It should also be remembered that the figures presented are averages and that the actual figures vary a lot from farmer to farmer, depending on distance to the buying point.

Although in distance terms the three sections of the transport system are very different, the estimates show that in economic terms they are of the same order of magnitude, because unit costs of shipping are much lower than unit costs of rural transport, which is often head-loaded or carried on non-motorized transport, or if carried by truck is mostly transported over poor roads.

In total , the transport costs of Ghana's cocoa amounts to US$100 per ton, corresponding to 11 per cent of the world market price, which by the end of 1999 was US$911. However, the transport share of Ghana's production costs after taxation is considerably larger (up to double, although it is difficult to say how much this is due to the marketing margin in 1999 being unusually low – see Table 9.1). The cost of transporting Tanzania's coffee is much greater and amounts to between US$300 and 400 per ton, mostly because inland transport is more expensive. However, this only corresponds to 10–14 per cent of the auction price (or almost the same as in Ghana), because the value of coffee is three times higher than the value of cocoa. Finally, for cotton in Zimbabwe transport costs are even higher, namely about US$440 per ton of lint, corresponding to a third of the world market price (which in 1999–2000 was on average US$1,160 per ton of lint) plus the 10 per cent premium which Zimbabwe generally achieves.

Motorized inland transport makes up the largest share of total transport costs, although there are large variations between the different transport chains (from 30 per cent for cocoa in Ghana to 71 per cent for coffee from Tanzania's southern highlands). The large variation in inland transport costs is due partly to the large variation in transport distance and partly to dif-

Table 9.2. Cost of transport in US$ per ton in different agricultural export-crop market systems

	Shipping		Inland transport		Rural transport		Total	Total transport costs as % of export price
Cocoa in Ghana (1999)	53US$	(53%)	17US$	(17%)	30US$	(30%)	100US$	11%
Coffee in Tanzania (1997) Southern highlands	73US$	(19%)	280US$	(71%)	38US$	(10%)	391US$	14%
Northern highlands	73US$	(25%)	178US$	(62%)	38US$	(13%)	289US$	10%
Cotton (lint) in Zimbabwe (via Beira) (1999/00)	174US$	(40%)	207US$	(47%)	59US$	(13%)	440US$	34%

For the detailed assumptions made in computing the transport costs, see the appendix.

ferences in the weight removed through processing at inland depots. However, the large inland costs in Tanzania are due to high ton-km rates caused by poor infrastructure and inefficient transport organization (Pedersen 2001c).

The variation in shipping costs is partly due to the differences between commodities in the number of tons that can be loaded into a container, but it also mirrors the difference in shipping distances between Europe and Ghana, Tanzania and Zimbabwe, respectively.

Considering the large degree of uncertainty in estimating rural transport costs, they do not appear to vary very much in absolute terms. However, in terms of the farm price, transport costs are much more important for cocoa- (about 3–6 per cent) and cotton-farmers (3–10 per cent) than for coffee-farmers (only 1.5 per cent), due to the higher farm price per kg for coffee. As a share of farm prices, farmers' transport costs appear to be fairly modest. However, this is partly because labour costs are set very low (at US$1 per day). Poor transport is, therefore, still a major constraint on rural development.

The average transport cost estimates used also hide a large variation in farmers' transport costs depending on their distance to crop-buying points, and high rural transport costs are clearly a hindrance to the expansion of crop production in areas away from the main transport infrastructure. This is most clearly seen in the cocoa belt in Ghana. To the extent that large swings in the world market price are reflected in the payments made to farmers, declining world market prices will therefore tend to contract the areas where production is profitable.

The quality of the crop tends to decrease during transportation. According to Agrisystems (1998), the quality of coffee falls one to two grades (in the

17-grade international grading system) during the often one-month train journey through Tanzania to the port, corresponding to about 15 per cent of the export value of each grade. Similarly, Danida-ASSP (2001) reports that cotton waiting for transport at the roadside for hours or days may lose both weight and grading, resulting possibly in a reduction in the payment made to the farmer of over 10 per cent. Improved transport, therefore, has an importance far beyond mere transport costs.

Conclusion

Since the 1970s, the logistical revolution in the industrialized world has changed the global transport system. Transport time is now often more important than transport costs. The importance of efficient and very capital-intensive transport terminals, such as ports and airports, has increased. This has led to a hierarchization of the transport system, which generally has left Africa at the bottom of the hierarchy (although transport costs and time have often improved in absolute terms). The logistical revolution has also increased the need for closer integration between production, trade and transport, as well as between the different modes of transport along the transport chains.

However, so far the logistical revolution has had only a limited impact on African transport systems. This is at least partly because the parastatal organization of the agricultural export trade, which developed in African countries during the import-substitution era, tended to insulate them from the effects of the logistical revolution. However, the structural adjustment policies introduced in both trade and transport organization since the late 1980s gradually changed this during the 1990s, leading to mutual adaptation and coordination between the commodity and transport chains.

On the supply side, the containerization of transport chains and increased regularity of shipping lines have opened up new opportunities to speed up the flow of goods and take advantage of forward sales and seasonal and other price variations. They have also opened new opportunities to respond to the market segmentation and product differentiation that is under way in some of the commodity chains (e.g., Arabica coffee and cotton, but not cocoa).

On the demand side, containerization has made it possible for processing industries in the industrialized countries to increase their requirements to suppliers and transform them into supply managers responsible for the supply of raw materials within narrow quality specifications and time windows. By doing so, processors save costs and management resources earlier used for procurement and logistics. Thus, transport, or rather logistics, has come to play a much larger role in the organization of production than was assumed for it when it was dismissed as unimportant for economic geography in the early 1970s.

However, the potential to exploit these new opportunities is greatly constrained by slow and inefficient ports, inland transport and domestic marketing. The international traders who now function as supply managers therefore have a direct interest in going inland, improving land transport and integrating the domestic and international parts of the marketing and transport chains. Because these chains were formally broken at the port in the days before structural adjustment, neither the parastatals nor the European processors had any such interest.

At the same time, the structure of rural transport is changing. Previously, the centralized parastatal organization was expected to be able to plan and exploit its own transport and storage capacity efficiently. However, parastatal transport planning was unable to draw effectively on the diverse transport capacity of farmers and rural traders. Because of the low payments made to farmers, many parastatals came to compete with a growing parallel market and therefore even had an interest in reducing still further the transport capacity of farmers and rural traders, which is often mirrored in the administration of transport licensing. The diversity of modes of transport necessary to serve rural areas efficiently therefore never developed.

However, with deregulation and privatization, the power to constrain rural transport and the interest in doing so have both disappeared. As a result, the availability of both motorized and non-motorized intermediate means of transport has increased rapidly in many rural areas, especially where market liberalization has led to increased farm prices. The liberalization of the marketing system has also tended to increase the interest of buyers in linking up directly with farmers to increase their market share. This has often increased the number of buying points, although since these have a tendency to cluster, the distance between farms and buying points has been reduced only to a limited extent. However, farmers' market accessibility has generally improved, and the sharp break in the transport chain that occurred at parastatal buying points has become less pronounced.

References

Agrisystems (Overseas) Ltd. (1998) 'Coffee Sector Strategy Study –Tanzania. Final Report and Appendices', prepared for the Government of Tanzania and the European Commission. Aylesbury, UK.

Amoah, J.E.K. (1998) *Marketing of Ghana Cocoa 1885–1992*, Cocoa Outline Series. Accra: Jemre Enterprises.

Arhin, K. (1985) *The Expansion of Cocoa Production: The Working Conditions of Migrant Cocoa Farmers in the Central and Western Regions*. Legon: Institute of African Studies.

Cooksey, B. (2003) 'Marketing Reform? The Rise and Fall of Agricultural Liberalisation in Tanzania', *Development Policy Review*, 21(1):67–91.

Danida-ASSP (2001) 'HASP Marketing Study', Harare.

Dicken, P. and A. Malmberg (2002) 'Firms in Territories: A Relational Perspective', *Economic Geography*, 78:345–63.

Fold, N. (2000) 'A Matter of Good Taste? Quality and the Construction of Standards for Chocolate Products in the European Union', *Cahier d'economie et sociologie rurales*, 55–56:92–110.

—— (2001) 'Restructuring of the European Chocolate Industry and the Impact on Cocoa Production in West Africa', *Journal of Economic Geography*, 77(1): 405–20.

—— (2002) 'Lead Firms and Competition in Bipolar Commodity Chains: Grinders and Branders in the Global Cocoa -Chocolate Industry', *Journal of Agrarian Change*, 2(2):228–47.

—— (2004) 'Spilling the Beans of a Tough Nut: Liberalisation and Local Supply Systems Changes in Ghana's Cocoa and Shea Chains', in A. Hughes and S. Reimer (eds) *Geographies of Commodity Chains*. London: Routledge.

Gibbon, P. (1998) *Peasant Cotton Cultivation and Marketing Behaviour in Tanzania Since Liberalisation*, CDR Working Paper 98.16. Copenhagen: Centre for Development Research.

—— (2001) 'Agro-commodity chains: an introduction', *IDS Bulletin*, 32(3):60–8.

Gould, P.R. (1960) *Transportation in Ghana*. Evanston, IL: Department of Geography, Northwestern University.

Government of Zimbabwe (1991) *Cotton Sub-sector Study*, Main report, Harare: Ministry of Lands Agriculture and Rural Settlement (and Hemel Hempstead, UK: Hunting Technical Services).

Henderson, J., P. Dicken, M. Hess, N. Coe and H.W.-C.Yeung (2001) 'Global Production Networks and the Analysis of Economic Development', unpubl. paper, Manchester: Manchester Business School, University of Manchester.

Hine, J. (1998) 'Transport and Marketing Priorities to Improve Food Security in Ghana and the Rest of Africa', paper presented at seminar on 'The Managing of Rural Transport', 12–23 October. Crowthorne, Berkshire, UK: Transport Research Laboratory.

Iheduru, O.C. (1996) 'Post-apartheid South Africa and its Neighbours: A Maritime Transport Perspective', *Journal of Modern African Studies*, 34(1):1–26.

ILO (1997) *Rural Transport Study in Three Districts of Zimbabwe*, vol. 1–3. Harare: ILO, Zimbabwe Ministry of Transport and Energy & SIDA.

Jayne, T.S., A. Chapoto, J. Nyoro, A. Mwanaumo and J. Govereh (2002) 'False Promise or False Premise? The Experience of Food and Input Market Reform in Eastern and Southern Africa', *World Development*, 30(11):1967–85.

Larsen, M.N. (2002) 'Is Oligopoly a Condition for Successful Privatisation? The Case of Cotton in Zimbabwe', *Journal of Agrarian Change*, 2(2):185–205.

Madulu, N.F. (1998) *Changing Lifestyles in Farming Societies in Sukumaland: Kwimba District, Tanzania*. Dar es Salaam: Institute of Resource Assessment & Leiden: African Studies Centre Working Paper 27.

Mitchell, B. and K.-J. Budin (1998) *The Abidjan–Ouagadougou Railway Concession*. Africa Transport Technical Note.13. Washington DC: World Bank and Economic Commission for Africa.

Morgan, C.V. (2001) 'Commodity Futures Markets in LDCs: A Review and Prospects', *Progress in Development Studies*, 1(2):139–150.

Mwikisa, C.N. (1993) *Materials Management in Developing Countries: Case Study of Zambia*, Doctor dissertation, Mannheim: Universität Mannheim.

Pálson, G. (1998) 'Multiple Ports of Call Versus Hub-and-Spoke: Containerized Maritime Trade between West Africa and Europe', Sub-Saharan Africa Transport Policy Program Working Paper 31. Washington DC: World Bank and Economic Commission for Africa.

Pedersen, P.O. (2001a) 'Freight Transport under Globalisation and its Impact on Africa', *Journal of Transport Geography*, 9:85–99.

—— (2001b) *The Freight Transport and Logistical System of Ghana*. CDR Working Paper 01.2. Copenhagen: Centre for Development Research.

—— (2001c) *The Tanga–Moshi –Arusha Corridor: Decline or Restructuring of an African Transport Corridor?* CDR Working Paper 01.6. Copenhagen: Centre for Development Research.

—— (2001d) 'Transport and Logistics of the Tanzanian Coffee Marketing Chain', unpublished appendix to Pedersen (2001c).

—— (2002) *Zimbabwe's Freight Transport and Logistical System*. CDR Working Paper 02.4. Copenhagen: Centre for Development Research.

—— (2003) 'Development of Freight Transport and Logistics in sub-Saharan Africa: Taaffe, Morrill and Gould Revisited', *Transport Reviews*, 23(3):275–97.

Ponte, S. (2001) *The 'Latte Revolution? Winners and Losers in the Restructuring of the Global Coffee Marketing Chain*. CDR Working Paper 01.3. Copenhagen: Centre for Development Research.

—— (2002) 'Brewing a Bitter Cup? Deregulation, Quality and the Re-organisation of the Coffee Marketing Chain in East Africa', *Journal of Agrarian Change*, 2(2):248–72.

Porter, G. (2002) 'Living in a Walking World: Rural Mobility and Social Equity Issues in sub-Saharan Africa', *World Development*, 30(2):285–300.

Raikes, P., M.F. Jensen and S. Ponte (2000) 'Global Commodity Chain Analysis and the French *filière* Approach: Comparison and Critique', *Economy and Society,* 29(3):390–417.

Rizet, C. and J.L. Hine (1993) 'A Comparison of the Costs and Productivity of Road Transport in Africa and Pakistan', *Transport Reviews,* 13:151–65.

Schary, P.B. and T. Skjøtt-Larsen (1995) *Managing the Global Supply Chain,* Copenhagen: Handelshøjskolens Forlag/Munksgård International Publishers.

Stabenau, H. (1996) 'New Trends in Logistics: Germany', in *New Trends in Logistics in Europe.* Report of the 104th Round Table on Transport Economics. Paris: European Conference of Ministers of Transport.

Sunga, E., E. Chabayanzara, S. Moyo, R. Mpande, P. Mutuma and H. Page (1990) 'Farm Extension Survey Results', unpublished manuscript, Department of Agriculture and Rural Development. Harare: Zimbabwe Institute of Development Studies.

Taaffe, E.J., R.L. Morrill and P.R. Gould (1963) 'Transport Expansion in Underdeveloped Countries: A Comparative Analysis', *Geographical Review,* 53:503–29.

Temu, A., A. Winter-Nelson, and P. Garcia (2001) 'Market Liberalisation, Vertical Integration and Price Behaviour in Tanzania's Coffee Auction', *Development Policy Review,* 19(2):205–22.

Winter-Nelson, A., and A. Temu (2002) 'Institutional Adjustment and Transport Costs: Product and Input Markets in the Tanzanian Coffee System', *World Development,* 30(4):561–74.

Appendix

Assumptions behind the transport-cost data in Table 9.2 for the production and marketing chains for cocoa in Ghana, coffee in Tanzania and cotton in Zimbabwe

---

Transport costs in cocoa production and marketing in Ghana, 1999

Rural transport

Head-loading costs

One ton of cocoa beans are produced on about 1.1 acres. Empirical studies indicate that the average distance from field to village is about 4 km and from village to collection point about 5 km (Hine 1998; Arhin 1985). If one head loads 20 kg at a time it will require 50 trips to move one ton. If we assume that most of the movement of the cocoa from the field to the village is done in connection with work in the field, only loading from village to buying point should be counted. One person will hardly be able to walk more than two trips or 20 km a day. It will then take 25 days or about one person-month to move one ton. There is no simple way of estimating the value of one month's work in rural areas, but we have set it to US$1 a day or US$30 per ton.

Inland transport

Trucking costs

I assume an average distance of 300 km from the collection point to the port, and a transport rate of about US cents 3 per ton-km, which amounts to US$9 per ton. In addition we assume that the cocoa is reloaded at a midway depot, at a cost of US$2 per loading and unloading, in total US$8 per ton.

Shipping costs

The transport rate for a container between Tema and Rotterdam, including handling in Tema and Rotterdam, is US$878. As a container load 267 bags of 62.5 kg, this give a transport rate of US$53 per ton. Of this, US$43 represent shipping costs and US$10 the bunker adjustment factor and terminal handling costs.

Transport, packaging and storage costs in different sectors of the coffee transport chain in Tanzania, 1997 Tsh per ton of green coffee

Sector of the chain	Farm to buying post	Buying post to mill	Mill to point of sale	Mill or other point of sale to port	Ship transport[3]	Total transport		Auction price	Total transport costs as % of auction prices	Payment to farmer 1000 Tsh	Farmers' transport costs as % of payment to farmers[1]
Responsible	Farmer	Coop. union for private buyer	Coop. union for private buyer	Exporter	Exporter						
Mode of transport	Head load or intermediate transport	Truck	Truck	Truck or railway	Ship						
	Tsh/t %	Tsh/t %	Tsh/t %	Tsh/t %	Tsh/t %	Tsh/t	US$/t %	US$/t %	%		%
Northern Highlands	22,000 (13%)	70,000 (42%)		33,000 (20%)	42,000 (25%)	167,000	288(100%)	2850	(10%)	1590	1.4%
Southern (Mbozo)	22,000 (10%)	57,000 (25%)		105,000 (46%)	42,000 (19%)	226,000	390(100%)	2850	(14%)	1470	1.5%
Southern (Mbuga)	22,000 (9%)	57,000 (24%)	27,000 (12%)	85,000 (36%)	42,000 (18%)	233,000	402(100%)	2850	(14%)	1350	1.6%
Kagera Region[2]	35,000 (15%)	55,000 (24%)	81,000 (35%)	20,000 (9%)	42,000 (18%)	233,000	402(100%)			550	6.4%

Source: Based on Agrisystems (1998, Appendix E) and Pedersen (2001d).

[1] Computed at 5 work days at 870 Tsh per ha of 200 kg green coffee.

[2] Farmers' transport costs in Kagera are higher than in the other areas because there go about 1800 kg magenda per 1000 kg robusta green coffee, but only 1200 kg parchment per 1000 kg arabica.

[3] Based on a freight rate of US$1200 per 20' container of 16.5 tons of coffee and an exchange rate of 580 Tsh per US$

Transport costs in cotton production in Zimbabwe, 2000

Rural transport

From farm to cotton depot/buying point

Transport between the farm and the cotton depot or buying point is paid by the farmer.

The transport rate in rural areas is generally a rate per cotton bale regardless of distance, though the rate per bale tends to increase at longer distances, partly because rates for hire of scotch carts are lower than for the hire of tractors and lorries, and scotch carts seldom go beyond 15 km, while tractors may go up to 40–50 km and lorries are used for longer distances.

Transport rates varied in 2000 between Z$100 and 350 per bale or between Z$400 and 1400 per ton. On average this is Z$900 per ton seed cotton or US$23.6 per ton. As the farm price in 2000 was about Z$18 per kg, the transport rate corresponds to 5 per cent of the price paid to farmers.

In the ginning process, the lint extracted is about 40 per cent of the weight of seed cotton (the new ginneries extract 43–44 per cent, while the old only extract 35–37 per cent). Therefore 2.5 tons of seed cotton is needed to produce one ton of lint. This means that the rural transport needed to produce one ton of lint costs US$59.

Inland transport

Transport between depots and ginnery

This part of the transport costs is paid by the cotton-buying organization and the transport made by truck.

On the basis of data from Cargill, I have estimated this transport cost at about Z$1000 per ton of seed cotton (US$26.2). As the farm price in 1999–2000 was about Z$18 per kg, this corresponds to about 5–6 per cent of the farm price.

Information in Danida-ASSP (2001) shows similar figures for the transport between depot and ginnery at 5 per cent of the farm price or Z$900 (US$24) per ton of seed cotton, corresponding to US$60 per ton of lint.

Transport from ginnery to railway

I do not have any information on this but I estimate it to be about the same as between the depot and the ginnery, or US$24 per ton of lint, corresponding to a distance of about 140 km.

Transport by railway from Harare to Beira

According to Maersk (June 2002), the cost of transporting one 40' container between Harare and Beira is US$2207 (rail transport: US$2092 + bill of lading release fee: US$40 + carrier merchant haulage service fee: US$75). As a 40' container contains 18 tonnes of cotton lint, this corresponds to US$123/ton of cotton lint.

Shipping costs

<u>Shipping costs from Beira to western Europe</u>

According to Maersk (June 2002), the shipping costs of transporting a 40' container from Beira to western Europe is US$3123 (sea fare incl. 9.13% bunker adjustment: US$2738 + harbour handling charges in Beira: US$140 and in Europe: US$212 + bill of lading fee: US$33). As a 40' container contains 18 tons of cotton lint, this corresponds to US$174/ton of cotton lint.

10. Singing in the Dark?
World Music and Issues of Power and Agency

Tuulikki Pietilä

Introduction

In the mid-1980s a new category of music, World Music, appeared in Western markets and the mass media. It was launched by a group of independent record labels in Britain as a marketing category for music that did not seem to fit properly into any of the existing racks in the retail outlets (*fRoots Magazine* 2003). What was originally a campaign for a couple of months in the record stores eventually grew into an institution. Today, World Music has its own section in record stores, and there are trade fairs, festivals, radio programmes, magazines and organizations dedicated solely to it. World Music has become an example of economic and cultural globalization.

The main focus in academic research into World Music has been on issues of dominance and agency in the global music market. Two main but quite opposite understandings of these themes have emerged in the literature. According to one view, World Music provides a positive basis for the creation of fluid and negotiable identities, and even for resistance from the margins to dominant systems and meanings.[1] In the other view, World Music is just another phenomenon through which the Western world is appropriating the Third World's resources, this time musical creativity.[2]

In this chapter, I argue that, in order to assess the impacts of the World Music institution, a more nuanced view of notions of power and agency, as well as of the actors involved, needs to be developed. I do this by first reviewing some of the findings of previous World Music research and then explore the possibilities of enriching it by adding two different approaches to globalization: that is, sociological studies of the structures of the global music industry on the one hand, and some of the methods of politico-economic GVC analysis on the other. Power and its distribution are central questions in each of these three branches of research, though the approaches

---

1. See, for instance, Chambers (1992:141), Frith (1989:5), Taylor (1997).
2. See, for instance, Erlmann (1994, 1996), Feld (1994a, 1994b, 2000), Meintjes (1990).

taken and units of analysis used are different in each case. Much of the literature reviewed below focuses on music of African origin, which from the very beginning has formed a very significant sub-group within the category of World Music. I supplement this literature with some of my own material gathered in London and South Africa. At the northern end of the world, the focus is on World Music markets in Europe. Rather than produce a final analysis of issues of power and agency in World Music, however, the article attempts to sharpen the relevant questions for a more precise means of approaching them.[1]

World music research

Questions of power in both its positive and negative senses have been central to research on World Music. Established views usually emphasize either the possibilities of agency and resistance or the facts of hegemony and dominance. Feld (2000:152–3) has called these views the 'celebratory' and 'anxious narratives' of World Music, respectively.

One example of a 'celebratory' reading is Frith's (1989:5), which emphasizes the 'vigour and imagination with which local musicians take over "hegemonic" pop forms for themselves'. Consequently, he sees popular music as an empowering and democratic force.[2] Similarly, Taylor (1997:197) sees World Music as a quite unprecedented system empowering both hybrid sounds and hybrid selves. While not denying the existence of Western dominance in the industry, Taylor emphasizes the new spaces of resistance that have arisen in reaction to these new forms of dominance. He shows how non-Western musicians appropriate and modify Western songs and images to address issues important to them in their music and performances, as well as in musicians' discourses about their own identities in published interviews. Taylor concludes that the possibilities for innovative resistance in World Music derive from the fact that 'new technologies and modes of musical production allow these musicians to occupy different subject positions in a kind of simultaneity never before possible' (1997:94).

Many more academic accounts express rather anxiety regarding this phenomenon, arguing that the Western music industry, musicians and me-

---

1. I thank the Danish Social Science Research Council (SSF) for providing a two-year funding for the project (in 2003–2005) and the Danish Institute for International Studies in Copenhagen for providing the academic environment and facilities for its realization.
2. For other, comparable views, see e.g., Chambers (1992:141); Goodwin and Gore (1990:77).

dia are exploiting Third World musical forms and musicians. They see in World Music another late capitalist and post- or neo-colonial system sustaining the structural inequality between the First and Third Worlds. In what follows, I discuss the economic and symbolic forms of appropriation uncovered in this literature.

Many commentators have remarked that the term World Music in itself implies a division of the world into two disparate and unequal parts. First used by academics in the early 1960s to refer to non-Western music, the phrase had a liberal and relativist ring to it, emphasizing musical plurality and contesting the Eurocentric tendency to define music as Western or European art music (Feld 1994b:266; Taylor 1997:2). In the mid-1980s, the term was adopted by the music industry as a new marketing category. Being initially associated especially with musical forms from Africa and the African diaspora, World Music has gradually come to embrace music of non-Western origin in general, as well as that of European and American minorities. Even though it is often marketed as the music of a specific ethnic group, World Music is usually fusion music accommodating a variety of musical styles and traditions, often in a single piece of music. Rather than a style or genre, the term thus connotes a social and territorial space by referring to musical styles originating outside the dominant northwestern Euro-America, those of marginal populations (Erlmann 1994:179; Feld 1994b:266; Mitchell 1993:310). The distinction between music and musicians of different origins is retained in how recordings are offered for consumption in music stores: while Western music is usually categorized according to genre or artist's name, World Music is often categorized according to its continent, country or ethnic group of origin. Even while it broadens our musical sensibilities, then, it can be remarked that the category of World Music simultaneously reminds us of and reinforces the boundary between the First and Third Worlds, that is, between 'us' and 'them'.

The most concrete forms of appropriation are discussed in terms of the meagre salaries paid to musicians and the use of their artistic and intellectual resources and property without proper acknowledgement of copyright, as well as in settings that are far-removed from the musician's original intention (e.g., Feld 1994a, 1994b, 2000; Taylor 1997:40–63). The production of World Music has also frequently involved the collaboration of Third World musicians and Western pop stars, such as Paul Simon, David Byrne, Peter Gabriel and Ry Cooder. In complex ways, these collaborations are often found to benefit mostly the Western partners. For instance, Paul Simon is acknowledged to have paid good wages for recording studio time, as well as the standard shares in royalties to his South African collaborators, Ladysmith Black Mambazo, in the *Graceland* record (1986). However, he also claims the overall ownership of the product: the record cover mentions only his name, and the inside says: 'Produced by Paul Simon', and 'All Songs Copyright by Paul Simon' (Feld 1994a:239–42).[1]

Elaborate musical, textual and performance analyses reveal other, more subtle modes of appropriation (see, e.g., Erlmann 1994:176–9; Meintjes 1990; Taylor 1997:41–50). For instance, Meintjes's analysis finds in *Graceland* a text that, while it celebrates plural authorship and constitutes a dialogue between centre and periphery, at a deeper level contains highly power-laden images of the 'other'.[2] Taylor's (1997:41–50) examination of Peter Gabriel's *Us* album shows that, while Gabriel uses a wide array of foreign musical styles and musicians, it is his own singing that is foregrounded, the singing, music and lyrics of the other musicians being distanced by mixing them into the background. This also occurs on the album's cover, which depicts Gabriel straining alone into the unknown, as well as in the video of the first track of the album, which also focuses on Gabriel. Feld (1994b) has applied the Canadian composer Schafer's term 'schizophonia' to this kind of separation, splitting and distancing of sounds from their original sources and musicians.

The issues of appropriation and copyright involved in such splitting become even more complex in the ambient and New-Age style of music, where the musicians do not perform together, but instead Western composers and musicians use recorded non-Western music as an inspirational source and treat it as oral tradition, which therefore, it is claimed, does not belong to anyone (Feld 2000). Feld (1994a:245) concludes that Western elite pop artists are in the strongest artistic and economic position to appropriate global music diversity with the full support of their record companies. Other researchers (Goodwin and Gore 1990:78) move beyond the role of specific actors to argue that 'media imperialism is not perpetuated by pop musicians, but by the Western cultural hegemony inherent in the structure of the global media'.

---

1. Conversely, Simon is acknowledged to have paid copyright fees for using the basic pattern of a Ghanaian song. Eventually, with this money a National Folkloric Board of Trustees was formed in Ghana to deal with copyright issues concerning national folklore (Collins 1994:144–5).
2. Meintjes's (1990) analysis does not, however, fall one-sidedly on the 'anxious' side, but shows how *Graceland* is a complex polysemic sign that enables many kinds of readings.

Whether on the industry or individual levels, economic appropriation often goes hand in hand with more symbolic forms of appropriation. Several studies have shown how the World Music industry is based on and reproduces primitivist images and stereotypes of non-Western peoples. The music and the way it is presented and produced emphasize exoticism, sensuality and mysticism, which all add up to images of pre-modern vitality (Erlmann 1994:179; Taylor 1997:19–27). An example of the actual processes through which such images are produced can be found in Meintjes's (2003:180) examination of how Zuluness, as an epitome of 'ageless and virile Africa', is worked into the sound of *mbaqanga* music in a South African studio. This is done in several ways and on multiple levels: for instance, drums and percussion are emphasized, the timbre of the drum is made to sound acoustic and live, the genre and lyrics of the songs are transformed and aspects of different traditional forms are combined. The overall idea is to make the music sound pre-industrial, participatory, human, unmediated, spontaneous, rural and thus more traditional and ideally more African than *mbaqanga* is or ever was: there is no actual history of acoustic *mbaqanga*, nor much connection with rural South African modes of expression (Meintjes 2003:130, 134).

Meintjes (2003) remarks that ideas of race, class and ethnicity are produced for the world market through musical sound. Indeed, many analysts (e.g., Feld 1994b:266) have criticized the essentialization and commodification of ethnicity which lie at the heart of World Music production and consumption and which, by reproducing symbolic images of less civilized others, sustain the unequal power and economic structures between the First and Third Worlds.

In live performances and on record covers, primitivist images are often produced by presenting half-naked bodies in ethnic costumes and vigorous dancing styles, which convey the sense of passionate, powerful and somewhat dangerous Africans. Images of heroic warriors, freedom fighters and political militants are also used successfully in World Music markets. Such ideas are strongly associated with Zuluness (Meintjes 2003) and with several African musicians, such as the Zimbabwean Thomas Mapfumo, the Algerian Khaled and the Nigerian Fela Kuti. Schade-Poulsen (1999:28–37) describes how, in the Western media, Algerian *raï* music and its main representatives, like Khaled, have been politicized by evoking images of youthful rebellion familiar to Westerners. With repeated references to such figures as Elvis Presley, Jim Morrison and James Dean, and to such music genres as rock, punk, reggae and rap, *raï* music was made sociologically understandable and familiar to Western audiences. The media interpreted drinking and *raï* music as part of the struggle for a liberal, modern Islam in opposition to an intolerant, archaic Islam and the totalitarian state.

Turino (2000:335) makes a similar remark concerning the production of sounds for the world market. He suggests that instrumental and musical sounds must be foreign and distinctive, yet simultaneously sufficiently accessible and familiar-sounding in order to attract a World Music audience. The interest in the world market for Zimbabwean *mbira* music, for instance, was largely due to the fact that the sound and style of that music were easy for Westerners to recognize and comment on (ibid.:340–1). The music of Thomas Mapfumo, a central figure in the popularization and politicization of *mbira*, was also made more accessible through particular modes of technical production, such as softening vocal styles, clarifying the distinct parts of a musical piece and transforming the sound of *mbira* from the dense, buzzy quality preferred by indigenous players into a light, clear, metallic sound (Turino 2000:345–6).

This paradox of 'different yet familiar enough' is entirely logical to Erlmann (1994, 1996), who sees World Music as an example of late capitalism's systemic reproduction of itself through the production of difference. In this system, homogenization and differentiation are not mutually exclusive features, but integral constituents of musical aesthetics and globalization. Analyzing the sound texture, lyrics and onstage performance of a *Graceland* song, Erlmann finds a 'post-modern space littered with semiotic debris without any referent to authenticity ... Graceland offers a sonic scenery without actors, pulverized into gazes, copies of copies' (1994:179). Thus, regardless of the celebratory rhetoric of multiculturalism, there is no space for authentic otherness or difference in the global institution: in Erlmann's (1994:470; 1996) view, everything is produced by and reduced to the all-encompassing system. Consequently, according to him, 'a serious analysis of global musics can only be written from a subject position in the West' (Erlmann 1996:470). This view of the 'absence of the other' (Erlmann 1994:468) that the late capitalist system produces in order to reproduce itself might be true on the macro level, but it is too strong an assumption to be applied to the realities on the ground. In denying any possibility of agency for the 'other', it wipes out the need even to study the 'other', and consequently the view itself abolishes the 'other'.

Erlmann's conclusion is diametrically opposed to the celebratory views of World Music that see it as offering a genuine space for musical and cultural diversity for musicians in the Third World and elsewhere. However, these extreme views on the possibilities for agency, whether optimistic or pessimistic, are too totalizing and difficult to substantiate. The core problem with them is their nurturing of dichotomies such as us/them, Third World/First World and dominance/resistance. This is because they are too far removed from the realities and experiences of actors in the real world, as well as the structures within which such actors operate. In order to obtain a better understanding of these structures, I next deal with the literature on the global music industry of which World Music is a part.

The global music industry

Existing sociological research on the music industry concentrates especially on the history of the recording industry, and that of the major companies in particular. Because this history has largely been one of concentration, issues of power have also surfaced centrally in this research, concerning especially the questions of the ability of a few transnational companies to dictate cultural production and consumption, and of the relationships between the major companies and the independents.

The origins of the music industry lay in the late nineteenth century, when the industrial production of phonograms and gramophones began (Graham 1988:11; Wallis and Malm 1984:1). The industry experienced three periods of expansion in the twentieth century. By the end of the first period, prior to the First World War, it had developed many of its present-day working structures and established itself around the world. The second period of growth was in the late 1920s and ended with the Great Depression. The third period of expansion took place between the late 1950s and the late 1970s (Gronow and Saunio 1998).[1] After a clear decline in sales in the late 1970s, the situation improved again in the 1980s, thanks to increased cassette sales and a substantial increase in compact disc sales (Burnett 1996:45). At the beginning of the twenty-first century, however, worldwide sales in the industry are decreasing again. This is due to an upsurge in downloading from the Internet and the proliferation of CD-burning, combined with competition from other entertainment sectors.

Even though concentration was the overall tendency in the music industry for much of the twentieth century, this trend became particularly strong in the 1980s as the industry responded to the downturn in sales and the recession with a flurry of takeovers and mergers. Between the end of the

---

1. For a meticulous history of the recording industry, see Gronow and Saunio (1998).

1970s and the beginning of the 2000s there were at different times five or six major companies with total market share fluctuating between 70 and 90 per cent of worldwide record sales (see Burnett 1996:50–9; Taylor 1997:198). In 2004, the 'big five' became the 'big four' as Sony and BMG merged, and in descending order of market share the largest companies now are Universal Music, Sony BMG, EMI Music and the Warner Music Group. Together, the four companies are reported to control almost 72 per cent of worldwide sales, while the independent companies' share of the markets is around 28 per cent (IFPI 2005).

In addition to mergers, the majors responded to the decline of the 1970s and 1980s by increasing the importance of international markets: by the 1990s they were reportedly deriving over half of their incomes from them (Burnett 1996:4, 48). This internationalization has been realized through subsidiaries, affiliates and non-affiliated licensees in foreign countries.

The major music industry, though large in its own right, is part of even larger global media, electronics and entertainment conglomerates. Each of the major music companies belongs to huge corporate groups, which have spread their actions to cover a range of business sectors. These sectors are subject to constant restructurings of the corporations themselves and acquisitions between them, but in addition to the record industry, several of the following areas can be found in each of the existing conglomerates: the manufacture of electronic technology; book, magazine and music publishing; and the ownership of retail outlets, film studios and video and film distribution networks, as well as television, cable and computer networks.

A major driving force in the concentration, diversification and internationalization of these corporations has been increases in their control of the market through their control of different production and distribution sections in the field of entertainment. Diversification facilitates the spreading of a creative product across as many outlets as possible. Audiences who have seen a film may buy the book, a magazine with the star on the cover, the music of the soundtrack and maybe a T-shirt. They may even rent the video or watch the film again on television, or listen to the theme song on radio or music television (Burnett 1996:17, 22).

The differences and relationships between the independents and the major companies have attracted considerable discussion in the literature. Small companies are often seen as the innovators in the industry, since they are constantly looking for and experimenting with the production of new sounds, in contrast to the majors, which aim to minimize risk and expand their market share by trying to produce mainstream hits for a global audience. The dominance in the market of the small and large companies respectively has often been described as cyclical. Smaller labels are frequently seen as the risk-takers and market-testers for new acts, which are then taken over by the majors as soon as they prove successful. The same happens easily to the successful independent labels themselves, which tend to become merged with or enter into partnerships with the major companies. Such partnerships are typically licensing or distribution deals, through which a major company distributes and markets an independent label's products and possibly helps it financially.[1] Usually the independent labels also rely on the majors to press their records. As a result of their purchases of smaller record companies and distribution deals with other companies, the major companies typically own several record labels and may also distribute several independent ones. Individual labels usually specialize in certain music genres, and acquiring such a label can thus be seen as a form of branding for a company.

As well as concentration in the industry, there has also been a discernible increase in outsourcing since the 1960s (Frith 1981:137; Hesmondhalgh 1996:479; Kealy 1982:104). This means using outside rather than in-house professionals, such as producers, sound engineers and managers. According to Hirsch (1990), outsourcing fits well with the nature of cultural industries and typifies them. The record industry relies on creative material generated outside itself. It is rational for the company to delegate on a contract basis the responsibility for finding and producing new talent to outside professionals such as record producers, rather than having them in-house, adding to its overheads. The same logic applies to the artists, who are contracted on a royalty basis. While this kind of craft administration of production is typical of cultural industries, the distribution sector is much more bureaucratically organized and is characterized by greater economic concentration than the production sector (Hirsch 1990:131). The distribution and exhibition of products are especially crucial spheres in cultural industries: sales are often significantly dependent on the extent of publicity and on availability.

Control over the distribution sector has become ever more vital in the music industry, as well as more concentrated. Indeed, one industry executive quoted by Burnett (1996:2) remarked in the 1990s, 'one of the definitions of a major record company is that you are in the distribution business.' Until the 1970s, the record industry relied largely on independent record distributors acting as intermediaries between the record manufacturers and

---

1. For the typical types of partnerships between major corporations and independents, see Hesmondhalgh (1996:475–7).

the retailers. In the 1980s, the independent distribution system began to break down, as many independent labels agreed to be distributed by a major (Burnett 1996:61). Burnett has described the development as follows: 'The 1980s saw a change from retail sales via well-stocked music shops with knowledgeable staff to rack sales via small outlets lacking knowledgeable staff [on the one hand], and a trend towards a few large record mega stores [on the other hand]' (1996:75).[1]

Also within the major record companies, distribution divisions seem to have increased their power (Negus 1999:55). Such divisions link the record company with retailers and may include market researchers, sales staff and business analysts. Negus (1999:56) relates their growing power in the US to the increasing competition between retailers, which has resulted in the strategy of the 'tight control of inventory'. In response, record companies have made their distribution services more flexible by adopting 'just in time' methods of distribution and allowing retailers to return unsold records. Distribution divisions in record companies have consequently acquired more power in that they control not only how many records should be shipped, but also how many should be manufactured by the labels in the first place. The distribution units can exert this power in relation to both the other divisions within the record company and the independent labels that the company distributes (Negus 1999:57).

Because promotion is essential in the music industry, and increasingly expensive, usually only a small selection of all the music produced is promoted. Those who decide which products to promote are thus also very influential in the industry, typically being situated in the promotion and marketing departments in a large company. According to Frith (2002), these departments have acquired a greater say even regarding what is produced in the first place, decisions that formerly used to be taken primarily by the A&R people (artists and repertoire).

Some of these changes in the global music industry accord with the much wider changes in global industrial organization that have taken place in the last twenty years. Among such wider developments are the increasing internationalization of retail activities and the concentration of their control in the countries of the North, as well as the overall increase in the power of firms specializing in retailing, branding and marketing. The strategy of the 'lead firms' in various industries has been to retain control over product

---

1. The increasing importance of Internet downloading – both legal and illegal – poses a threat to the existing distribution system and the majors' dominance of it. At the time of writing, however, the changes in the industry that might result are still too difficult to predict.

definition and marketing while outsourcing certain other functions, such as production and inventory management (Gibbon and Ponte 2005). These tendencies are also found in the global music industry, although, as already mentioned, outsourcing has been more characteristic of cultural industries than, for instance, manufacturing industries. In addition to the artists and producers that work on a contract basis, the independent companies may act as outsourced talent scouts for the music industry (Frith 1981:156).

There is no shared understanding among researchers about how the relationships between the independent and the major companies should be interpreted.[1] Perhaps most often, however, the position of the independent companies and what they represent – diversity and innovation – have been treated as precarious and under constant threat from the 'predatory' majors (e.g., Gillett 1971; Wallis and Malm 1992). The high concentration of transnational control has been related to the low diversity of musical output (Peterson and Berger 1975; Rothenbuhler and Dimmick 1982). However, other writers have described the relationship between the independents and the majors more as one of cooperation and symbiosis than of competition. According to Frith (1989:107), in experimenting with sounds, trends and artists, the independent firms play a necessary role in the industry and have achieved a permanent if subordinate position in it. According to Burnett (1996:61–2), concentration has left greater room for specialists in the form of the independent labels and has led to cooperation rather than competition in the industry. Consequently, he suggests (1996:137) that both diversity and concentration increased in the 1980s.

Hesmondhalgh (1996:480) has suggested that nowadays the independent labels can be seen as outsourced A&R departments, contracted to the major record companies in a similar way to artists. However, he does not interpret the tendency towards externalization in terms of a wider distribution of power within the recording industry. Quite the contrary, he emphasizes the continuity of patterns of power in the industry (1996:479, 483). He also suggests (1996:485) that the situation in the music industry is comparable to

---

1. Many researchers acknowledge that the distinction between the major and the independent companies is spurious because there are hardly any strictly independent companies today, given their reliance on the majors for various services. Negus (1999:28), for instance, refuses to use the distinction altogether, though it is frequently made within the industry. It can also be argued that there are important differences in mode of operation between the independents and the major companies. Using the distinction does not necessarily entail accepting the moralizing it often suggests, that is, the view of the majors as simply ruthless profit-seekers and of the independents as music enthusiasts devoted to creativity.

that in the film industry as analyzed by Aksoy and Robins (1992) – that is, the forces of oligopoly, reintegration and centralization remain strong.

This dichotomy in the attitudes of researchers into the global music industry resembles that found in the World Music research: on the one hand the view of an all-consuming transnational industry as a system that leaves little space for autonomy for minor actors, and on the other hand the view of the potential for alternative spaces for the minor actors within the system. The studies reviewed above give us some idea of the structures and nodes of power in the global music industry and of their changes. In order to probe further into questions of dominance and agency, however, more unpacking of the industry into yet finer categories of agents and forms of power and empowerment is required.

Structures or networks of power?

The economic power of the major record companies and their parent corporations and its overall concentration in Europe, the US and Japan is undeniable. The division of labour in World Music fits into the general description of the music industry offered above, in the sense that the majors become interested in artists who have become successful and who appear to have sufficient cross-over potential. These cases are, however, relatively few, because often even the most famous World Music artists do not sell enough from the major record companies' point of view. For that reason, World Music has been and remains driven largely by the efforts of the small industry actors, such as specialized independent labels, freelance producers, agents and media people. Their efforts include the release of records, arranging live performances and all kinds of publicity and promotional work for the music. This is a very important point to remember when considering the structures of power and domination in World Music and one that the 'anxious narratives' tend to miss, because they often implicitly equate the global music industry with the most dominant agents in it, that is, the major record and media companies (allied with Western stars), and apply this 'domination model' to the analysis of World Music. In doing so, the adopted 'subject position' is not only *in* the West, but also that of the most powerful in the West.

Nor is the distinction between the majors and the independent companies sufficient: a subtler understanding of the various categories of actors and their functions and networks is needed. Approaches that pay closer attention to the specific occupational groups and production processes within the music industry have been developed in the fields of organizational sociology and popular music studies. Hirsch (n.d.; 1990) first described the culture industries as pre-selection systems where each product has to pass through several filtering stages before it reaches the audience. Because at each stage there are more products available than what gets through, Hirsch calls the professionals that do the selection and filtering 'gatekeepers'. Some of those gatekeepers are within the industry, but others are situated outside it and outside its effective control, such as the mass media people who select the products that receive media coverage (Hirsch n.d.:7).

Hirsch's view directs our attention to the different occupational groups within the industry, but in Negus's opinion it does not accord enough creative power to the gatekeepers, but depicts them more as assembly-line workers shifting the product rather mechanically from one stage to the next (Negus 1996:56–7).[1] In order to emphasize the active role of these people in shaping the product, Negus (2002) uses the concept of 'cultural intermediaries' instead of gatekeepers. Additionally, rather than focusing on how the industry creates the cultural product, he shifts to considering how the industry is shaped by the wider socio-cultural context and values (Negus 1992:1999). Consequently, instead of emphasizing corporate control in music production, Negus is interested rather in the more informal webs of meaning and practice that function in popular music production, as well as the diversity of the groups of workers that mediate between the artist and the audience, that is, between production and consumption.

This kind of disaggregating of the industry into occupational groups is helpful in revealing the diversity within the industry and in directing attention to the networks that function beyond and across the company formations. In the case of World Music, the focus on networks is particularly apt: as already mentioned, much of the work is done by small industry actors, and often on a freelance or short-term contractual basis. Simultaneously, because World Music networks consist of agents of very diverse origin, the essential questions are also what is the wider socio-cultural context and who are the agents moulding the meanings and practices in them. There is also a need for a clearer differentiation between the different kinds of power, as well as of the modes of interaction, influence and control between the different categories of actor. In order to formulate more specific questions about structures and qualities of power, World Music research might benefit from utilizing some of the ideas of GVC analysis, to which I now turn.

---

1. For a review of other research that has been carried out along these lines, as well as critical studies, see Negus (1996:55–61).

GVC analysis offers a method for studying networks that are involved in the production of a commodity for consumption. The networks are envisioned as chains, and the aim is to define the agents that 'drive' or 'lead' the chain, as well as the conditions under which the subordinate participants can 'upgrade' their performance (Gereffi 1994). Rather than distinct categories of actors, the focus is thus on the connections between them, as well as the quality and the impact of the connections. Consequently, GVC analysis approaches power too as something in between the agents rather than inherent in either themselves or in the structures. Moreover, it studies power from two perspectives: as a superordinate agent's ability and means to control a subordinate agent on the one hand, and as the latter's possibility to improve his/her position and status on the other.

The heuristic significance of GVC analysis for World Music research is thus to be found in its focus on both the structuring and enabling aspects of industrial networks, rather than on rigid industry structures or on networks as escaping structures. The two latter views form the underlying understandings of the industry in the 'anxious' and 'celebratory' narratives of the World Music institution respectively. The distinction in GVC analysis between power as an ability to control others and power as empowerment avoids the tendency in World Music research to take an either/or position in relation to issues of dominance and agency.

World music and spaces of power and empowerment

World Music is a category created for markets and consumers in the West. What exactly is included in that category varies in different places, but what is categorized as World Music in the West is not generally so labelled in its home area but falls into finer, local genre categories. Thus, for instance, in South Africa, Ladysmith Black Mambazo's music would be called *Mbube* music or Vocal Harmonies.

Because the World Music markets are in the West, the key actors who define what qualifies for release in the World Music market and what that music should sound like are usually people based in or with strong connections to the West. I think it is analytically useful to distinguish between what I call the regular chains and the celebrity chains with respect to their modes of functioning and key actors. It is the latter sort of chain that existing research tends to emphasize as the examples of the World Music industry's workings and drivers: these chains are often initiated by a famous Western musician and take the form of collaboration with a non-Western musician or band. In addition to *Graceland* record, which was initiated by Paul Simon as was mentioned earlier, there have been several others, such as Ry Cooder's collaboration with Ali Farka Toure and a number of Cuban musicians (Rubén González, Compay Segundo, Ibrahim Ferrer, Omara Portuondo and others), which produced the record and film *Buena Vista Social Club*. Many of these musical collaborations have proven very successful. Another route to popularity has been through the film and advertisement industry. The film *Buena Vista Social Club* focused on the music and musicians, but World Music has also been increasingly used in feature films. The old song "Lion sleeps tonight" (originally *Mbube*) entered the charts anew in the mid-1990s through the Walt Disney film *Lion King*, and recently the music of the Ethiopian Mulatu Astatqé has attracted worldwide attention by appearing in Jim Jarmusch's film *Broken Flowers*. Earlier, Ladysmith Black Mambazo's success in the UK was boosted not only by the *Graceland* record but also by the use of their music in a TV advertisement for Heinz tomato ketchup. Western pop stars and agents in neighbouring entertainment sectors have thus occupied an important position as brokers in selecting and bringing non-Western music to the ears of Western consumers.

In contrast, by regular chains I mean the less visible but more frequent paths for non-Western music to World Music markets. In this section I focus on this aspect, and specifically on African music in European markets. The agents in the regular chains do important groundwork for bringing in and making music known in Europe. The drivers of these chains are also based in Europe, but differ somewhat between Francophone and Anglophone African music. For Francophone African music, Paris and Brussels are important centres of production, attracting musicians to move from Africa and also catering to the music and entertainment needs of the rather large immigrant population. In general, there is stronger African control in these chains in comparison to those of Anglophone African music, as many of the key actors in the Francophone chains are producers of African origin. Because of the resident immigrant audience, market-wise the Francophone chains are also relatively less dependent on attracting a white European audience, although the latter is far from being indifferent to it: indeed, Francophone African music has been very successful in appealing to a white audience.

Germany, the UK and the Netherlands form the most important European markets for Anglophone African music. I carried out a brief study of the labels that release records of African music for commercial markets in London in 2003. These were nine in number, all of which had found their own specialized niches in what was already a small niche market. There are several ways to categorize the labels. The first differentiating axis is in relation to the source of their material: there are labels that produce music and those that license music produced by others. Secondly, in the latter group, some focus on making compilation records by licensing tracks, others on licensing whole records.

Productions of African music in London were relatively few. Only one of the nine labels produced some African music, and three others had produced individual projects of African music.[1] The emphasis among the London actors was certainly on the compilation markets. Four of the London labels concentrated on making compilation records by licensing tracks from the original producers, mostly in Europe and Africa. Two labels focused on licensing whole records rather than individual tracks, one of these directly from African musicians.

Whether they produce or license music, these labels can be further categorized according to how market-oriented they are. By market-oriented I mean an actor's overall emphasis on fashioning, branding and marketing the product for the market, and its attempts to control these functions. Of the licensees, the compilation-makers tend to be more market-oriented than those who license whole records. The former make a new product by compiling tracks by diverse musicians and records under a chosen theme, while the latter's final product is very close to the original one. Of the producers, the more market-oriented ones put a rather strong imprint or sound of their own on the final production, while the less market-oriented producers place greater emphasis on preserving the 'original' sound and coherence of the music.

Although only one of the London producers can easily be categorized as belonging to the market-oriented group, that label had put out many more records than the other few labels that had produced African music on a more occasional basis. Because of the importance of this one market-oriented producer and the overall predominance of the compilation makers, one can say that there was a clear emphasis on market orientation among the London actors.[2] These actors are naturally dependent on what African

1. One of these labels' major concentrations was on releasing compilations, but it had also produced some African music.
2. In the market-oriented group, I include the one producing label and the four labels that focus on making compilation records. The group with lower market orientation consists of two producing labels and two labels that concentrate on licensing whole records. Except for the one licensee, the record volumes of the four actors in this latter group are remarkably small compared to those of the actors in the market-oriented group.

musicians produce the in the first place, but they exercise rather strong control by selecting, shaping and branding the final product. One feature of their high degree of market orientation is also that their products often employ the most stereotypical or exoticizing images of 'otherness'. Of the whole group, the compilation releasers are the most market-responsive, including in the sense that they appeal to customers by offering lower than normal record prices. This is possible because, as licensees, they do not invest money in production: they therefore take the fewest risks and are in the safest position in the market.

The current emphasis on making compilations is partly due to the general nature of the market and price pressures that are increasingly being experienced in the music industry. These pressures relate to both the wider 'crisis' and the structures of the global music industry. Increasing the supply of other entertainment products and the Internet downloading and CD burning of music lead customers to demand lower prices. Retail stores that are part of the larger chains belonging to the big business corporations put pressure on labels for lower prices and special deals. To my knowledge, all but one of the compilation releasers in London had some kind of backing from a larger company for their operations: some were part of a bigger record company, while others had secured a special licensing deal with a major record company. All but one of the five actors that I have here classified as market-oriented in fact seemed to enjoy the financial or contractual benefit of being part of a larger structure in one or more of the above-mentioned ways. Of the four less market-oriented actors, three were operating independently and only one was part of a larger record company.

Those releasing compilation records under the wings of a larger record company are in the safest position in the market: in addition to the financial or contractual security provided by the larger structure, they do not take the risk of investing in production and dealing with musicians, seldom even licensing unknown or unproven music. Although ultimately dependent on African creativity, these actors remain remote from African artists, and in selecting, compiling and marketing their music as they like, are in a rather strong position vis-à-vis the artists. The royalties for an artist from a track on a compilation record are also meagre. With regard to the other labels, the compilation makers seek a competitive edge through their records' availability and visibility in the markets, lower record prices and special deals with retailers to ensure that their products are effectively displayed in the latter's stores. Additionally, they aim to achieve accessibility through distribution via a wide variety of outlets, including such non-conventional ones as curio shops and cafeterias.

The strategies of the market-oriented actors accord with the wider developments in music and other global industries mentioned earlier in that they put their efforts into product-definition, marketing, distribution and retailing (Gibbon and Ponte 2005). The increasing pressure of the retail sector vis-à-vis the record labels can be noticed in this small case, too. Compilers especially may be in a relatively safe position in the market, but can they be called 'leaders'? Or are they more properly survivors who carve out and sustain their position in the market by attempting to withdraw from interaction with – and the influence of – other agents on the production side, instead pushing themselves strongly at the marketing and retail end?

African musicians often prefer face-to-face collaboration to the distant licensing business, even if this means their compromising initially on style and remuneration. This is partly because they do not always trust their record companies to do favourable licensing deals for them or pay them the full fees and royalties for those deals. Many South African musicians, for instance, are well aware of the potential economic and symbolic appropriation involved in the offer of an opportunity to perform or record abroad, but often prefer to take the chance rather than let it go. Is this just further proof of their weak position, or some kind of 'false consciousness'? I do not think so. Rather, they see the proffered opportunity as a chance to network and to build up their popularity and fame: that is, they feel they may eventually have more control by accepting the opportunity, especially if it involves face-to-face collaboration. An example of how this can work at its best is the South African group Ladysmith Black Mambazo. Regardless of the criticisms of the *Graceland* record, their collaboration on it paved their way to world renown, climaxing with their second own Grammy award in 2005, their third Grammy including that won by *Graceland* in 1987. Although Ladysmith Black Mambazo have been exceptionally successful, their case shows that what might seem to be – and actually be – appropriation from one perspective can indeed turn into success in the longer run.

In accepting such opportunities, musicians understand the importance of exposure and publicity for their careers and position in the industry. Rewards and negotiating power in the music industry are usually directly proportional to a musician's fame. Enhancement in the 'symbolic capital' of fame is thus a form of upgrading in the music industry. Participation in World Music chains can lead to such upgrading for African agents, not necessarily in the original chain or contract, but possibly in other music chains and through new contracts. The cost of fame and success can indeed, however, involve a compromise in style and in the possibility for renewing styles: that is, once African artists have become famous in World Music circles, they are often faced with the expectation that they reproduce the rather stereotypical, essentializing images of Africanness. Thus, ironically achieving and maintaining symbolic capital often tends to require accepting the symbolically loaded imagery of 'otherness'. Some musicians manage to break away from these musical and stylistic limitations, but others accept them, willingly or unwillingly.

However, African musicians are not always merely troubled by the essentialized and commoditified ethnicities that tend to be an inescapable part of the World Music business: sometimes they willingly enhance and make use of them. For instance, Meintjes's (2003) study shows how the most stereotypical images of 'Africanness' or 'Zuluness' are created in a South African studio by an African producer, who is well aware of the stylistic expectations of both the domestic and international markets, and who modifies the sound accordingly. It is not unusual for artists either to adapt to the situation by releasing different kinds of music for World Music markets in the West and at home. Youssou N'Dour has done this, and even customized some of his records for European and American markets separately. The whole genre of Congolese *soukous* was developed for Western markets (White 2000:37). African artists are thus not necessarily always simply victims of the appropriative images of the 'system', but can find ways to circumvent, utilize or live with it.

The ethnic or regional classification of World Music, even though it may entail stereotyping, has had some positive repercussions too. It has helped familiarize Western audiences with foreign musical styles, one success raising interest in other examples of music from the same region. For instance, the controversial *Graceland* album opened the way to a number of other international releases of South African music (Meintjes 1990:62). This is an example of a more socially inclusive form of upgrading than the enhancement of an individual musician's or group's position in the industry. Other such social forms of upgrading are the stylistic, technological and informational influences that flow back from the West to developing countries. For instance, internationally successful African stars sometimes use their resources to boost the music industry at home. In the mid-1990s, 80 per cent of recording studios in Ghana had been set up by musicians who had made money abroad (Collins 1994:146). The Senegalese Youssou N'Dour has built recording studios in Dakar and promoted other African musicians in world markets. These forms of upgrading do not necessarily take place within the global music industry, but alongside it, even though they may at some point become part of the global chains.

Participation in World Music circles can also create other kinds of value and linkages that extend beyond hegemonic centres. Hernandez (1993:64, 67) has remarked that in Colombia, for instance, World Music has expanded musical horizons by revitalizing the country's own, formerly despised, African musical heritage.[1] As a consequence, in Colombia and the Spanish Caribbean the World Music boom has enhanced transcultural musical and economic flows both within the region and with Africa. According to Guilbault (1993:39), Antillean music was only recognized in the Western media and markets after first becoming popular among West Indian and African immigrant groups in Paris. Such increases in horizontal linkages between different immigrant groups and multilateral linkages within the Third World are usually of both economic and cultural value.

The above cases are also examples of how World Music helps construct meaningful identities and communities, rather than a means of simplifying and stereotyping identities for outsiders' consumption. One African example of this sort of impact on community-building is the emergence of *mbira* as a major national and nationalist symbol in Zimbabwe after it had first become popular in World Music circles in the 1980s (Turino 2000:340–1). Cross-cultural and cross-racial collaborative productions especially enable multiple readings and identifications by diverse audiences: for instance, black and white South Africans of very different social standings and political tendencies found in *Graceland* a way to construct their claim to national identity (Meintjes 1990). Born links music's adaptability in evoking and marking various kinds of identities to the fact that, in contrast to the visual and literary arts, music lacks denotative meaning and is consequently hyperconnotative in character (Born and Hesmondhalgh 2000:32). For this reason, the symbolic imagery even of World Music is open to divergent readings and interpretations.

The point in bringing out these examples of how Third World participants can benefit from or make use of the World Music institution is not to prove that the 'anxious' narratives are simply wrong and misguided, but rather to alert us to the complexities of power and control, as well as the diversity of agents and agency. The existing arguments in World Music research tend to add up to a list of different forms and levels of domination

1. Similarly, according to Guilbault (1993:41), the international success of *zouk* (a music of the French West Indies) significantly lifted the status of Antillean music at home in the Caribbean.

and agency rather than a debate. In other words, the kinds of agency and domination that they refer to are often so disparate that they are not easily comparable to each other. One way to make the comparison more manageable is to be clear about the breadth of the context in which issues of domination and agency are being considered: that is, are we considering relationships within the industry itself, or its possible wider effects? Another issue that requires clarification and further analysis, which has only been touched on here, is the very diversity in both the industry networks and the kinds of control and agency that actors can achieve in different industry settings.

Conclusion

In my view, both the celebratory and the anxious narratives are too extreme in their respective emphases on agency and domination. Participation and success in World Music can certainly contribute to a re-creation of identities by heightening or constructing a sense of community for both those participating and their audiences abroad and at home. However, the celebratory narratives that see the liberating potential of the 'system' in enabling a new play with identities and the construction of 'fluid' identities for Third World artists over-emphasize Western influence in attributing a certain pre-contact rigidity and frozenness to Third World music and identities, and their opening out into a more post-modern way of being through the touch of the West. Often urbane and used to dealing with all kinds of people and influences, African artists, for instance, have for a long time frequently proved more cosmopolitan and flexible than many in their Western audience in their own world view. For their part, conversely, anxious narratives assume an excessive degree of domination of World Music by the Western system, and fail to analyze sufficiently the structure of the system or the diversity of the agents involved.

For this reason, a more subtle understanding is needed of the structure of the industry and the different forms of power and control within it. I have suggested utilizing GVC analysis as a heuristic tool for formulating methods and questions to that end. I presented some of the results of my own brief research into London actors in the industry who release African music in order to show the complexity of questions of control. Operating in a small and rather difficult niche market, the minor actors of what I call the regular chains have found their own very specialized market slots. Compilers are in the safest position and focus on marketing and branding their products, but they cannot be said to exert very strong proactive control vis-à-vis musicians or the other labels in the industry. With regard to these agents, control by compilers is more hands-off in quality, while their attempts to influence their customers is more intense. The compilers retain a distance, and consequently relative independence from the artists whose products they license. Their control with regard to the other labels is also indirect, and takes place by their 'pushing' themselves in the market. Through lower prices and special deals with retailers, they can succeed in securing improved space and attention in retail stores than the competing labels. The one market-oriented producer is in a stronger position vis-à-vis the artist in that he influences the final sound of the product. At the same time, however, the label gives its artists a relatively better chance to develop their networks and popularity, and ultimately the artists' possibilities for control, than do the licensees, of whom the compilers especially usually pick music that is already popular.

The kinds of control and the possibilities for assessing them against each other are more complicated in the music industry than in many other industries. Music industry chains are more volatile than many other industry chains, and music is a more complicated product than, for instance, agricultural or manufactured products generally are. Music chains have often an integral human element to them in that what moves in them are not only commodities, but people, that is, musicians. The rather short-term contracts that are common make the agents in the chains mobile and the chains themselves changing and difficult to pin down. Against this mobility, the success of the product – and any kind of profit from it – is uncertain and often proves rather slow, because it requires the building up of one's fame and popularity. Just like forms of control, the question of the proceeds or profits in the music industry is a complicated one and is partly, though not only, linked to the slow development of one's fame. Fame can be envisioned as symbolic value that in time can be turned into economic value (Bourdieu 1977). For this reason, accumulating symbolic capital even without proper initial economic rewards is often wise for an artist in the longer run.

The time lag in proving the success of a product also needs to be taken into consideration in evaluating degrees of agency and power in the industry, and is something that existing World Music research and GVC analysis do not adequately address. For analytical clarity, it is beneficial to separate the power that particular agents might have or lack within the World Music industry at one point in time or in one chain from the power that derives – sometimes indirectly and beyond the industry itself – from one's participation in the industry in the longer term. While the former includes the forms of control one agent has in relation to the other agents in the industry, the latter includes the different kinds of repercussions that the exposure of a particular style of music or an artist in the World Music industry may accrue over time. These include such issues as the strengthening of an individual musician's or a musical style's overall potential in the industry, enhancing the recording industry and musical professionalism at home, new multilateral cooperation and networks between different territories and a heightened sense of and pride in a community through music.

One might argue, against the anxious narratives, that the mere existence of the World Music institution has probably given Third World artists a level of exposure and visibility in world markets that they would otherwise have had difficulty in obtaining. Achieving such visibility through a more mainstream genre is always difficult for any musician coming from outside the dominant Anglo-American centre. This exposure has not always turned into success, but it has opened up further possibilities. Instead of seeing the 'system' in terms of domination only, as 'anxious' approaches tend to do, the system can in this sense be seen to include an empowering potential.

In providing opportunities for exposure and the building up of fame, the World Music infrastructure enables Third World artists and musical styles to win at least symbolic value, which is essential for obtaining economic value. The anxious narratives are right in pointing out that the gaining and maintaining of such symbolic and economic value often requires accepting the essentializing symbolic imagery of 'the system', at least initially, and sometimes later too.

How should we evaluate the weight of the 'symbolic appropriation' that stereotypical and simplified images entail vis-à-vis the possible symbolic and economic rewards that come from them? Is the symbolic imagery more of a problem for academic commentators than the artists? In my experience, many South African artists acknowledge this as a problem, but would rather choose to participate in the global industry than stay away from it. How widely is the 'symbolic package' of the World Music industry considered a problem by the artists, and if so, how large and inescapable a problem is it?

More research on the networks and agents and their forms of control is needed to achieve a more detailed analysis. One should consider all the different economic and symbolic rewards and costs that accrue either directly or indirectly from the existence of the World Music institution, yet also keep in mind that they constitute phenomena of different kinds that are not directly comparable or measurable against one another. The final answer is also a matter of interpretation and evaluation by the agents themselves: as a cultural commodity, music is at least as much about such issues as sociality, community, style, status and reputation as it is about markets and selling. For the participating agents, the symbolic value might not be simply equal to its convertibility to economic value: one might outweigh the other. Agents might also find diverse forms of symbolic value and different arenas for realizing them. For a more detailed understanding of the structures of power and control in the World Music industry, the challenge is to include both macro- and micro-level realities in one project. To understand the meaning of the forms of valuation and control, it is essential to drop one's 'subject position in the West' and to study the institution instead from the subject positions of the diverse agents that make it up.

References

Aksoy, A. and K. Robins (1992) 'Hollywood for the 21st Century: Global Competition for Critical Mass in Image Markets', *Cambridge Journal of Economics*, 16:1–22.

Born, G. and D. Hesmondhalgh (eds) (2000) *Western Music and Its Others: Difference, Representation, and Appropriation in Music*. Berkeley, Los Angeles and London: University of California Press.

Bourdieu, P. (1977) *Outline of a Theory of Practice*. Cambridge: Cambridge University Press.

Burnett, R. (1996) *The Global Jukebox: The International Music Industry*. London and New York: Routledge.

Chambers, I. (1992) 'Travelling Sounds: Whose Centre, Whose Periphery?' *Popular Music Perspectives*, 3.

Collins, J. (1994) 'An Interview with John Collins on Cultural Policy, Folklore and the Recording Industry in Ghana by Cynthia Schmidt', *The World of Music*, 36(2):138–47.

Erlmann, V. (1994) 'Africa Civilised, Africa Uncivilised: Local Culture, World System and South African Music', *Journal of Southern African Studies* 20(2):165–79.

—— (1996) 'The Aesthetics of the Global Imagination: Reflections on World Music in the 1990s', *Public Culture*, 8:467–87.

Feld, S. (1994a) 'Notes on "World Beat"', in K. Charles and S. Feld, *Music Grooves*. Chicago and London: University of Chicago Press.

—— (1994b) 'From Schizophonia to Schismogenesis: On the Discourses and Commodification Practices of "World Music" and "World Beat"', in K. Charles and S. Feld, *Music Grooves*. Chicago and London: University of Chicago Press.

—— (2000) 'A Sweet Lullaby for World Music', *Public Culture*, 12(1):145–71.

Frith, S. (1981) *Sound Effects: Youth, Leisure, and the Politics of Rock 'n' Roll*. New York: Pantheon.

—— (1989) *World Music, Politics and Social Change*. Manchester and New York: Manchester University Press.

—— (2002) 'Interview by Jason Gross', May 2002. Online. Available HTTP: <http://www.furious.com/perfect/simonfrith.html>

fRoots Magazine (2003) 'History of World Music', December 2003. Online. Availabe HTTP: <http://www.frootsmag.com/content/features/world_music_history/minutes>

Gereffi, G (1994) 'The Organisation of Buyer-Driven Global Commodity Chains: How US Retailers Shape Overseas Production Networks', in G. Gereffi and M. Korzeniewicz (eds), *Commodity Chains and Global Capitalism*. Westport, CT: Praeger.

Gibbon, P. and S. Ponte (2005) *Trading Down: Africa, Value Chains and the Global Economy*. Philadelphia: Temple University Press.

Gillett, C. (1971) *The Sound of the City: The Rise of Rock and Roll*. London: Sphere.

Goodwin, A. and J. Gore (1990) 'World Beat and the Cultural Imperialism Debate', *Socialist Review*, 20:63–80.

Graham, R. (1988) *Stern's Guide to Contemporary African Music*. London: Zwan Publications.

Gronow, P. and I. Saunio (1998) *An International History of the Recording Industry*. London and New York: Cassell.

Guilbault, J. (1993) 'On Redefining the "Local" Through World Music', *The World of Music*, 35(2):33–47.

Hernandez, D.P. (1993) 'A View from the South: Spanish Caribbean Perspectives on World Beat', *The World of Music*, 35(2):48–69.

Hesmondhalgh, D. (1996) 'Flexibility, Post-Fordism and the Music Industries', *Media, Culture & Society*, 18:469–88.

Hirsch, P. (n.d.) *The Structure of the Popular Music Industry: The Filtering Process by which Records are Preselected for Public Consumption*. Ann Arbor: University of Michigan, Institute for Social Research.

—— (1990) 'Processing Fads and Fashions: An Organization-set Analysis of Cultural Industry Systems', in S. Frith and A. Goodwin (eds) *On Record: Rock, Pop, and the Written Word*. New York: Pantheon.

IFPI (2005) 'The Recording Industry in Numbers 2002', International Federation of the Phonographic Industry.

Kealy, E. (1982) 'Conventions and the Production of the Popular Music Aesthetic', *Journal of Popular Culture*, 16:100–15.

Meintjes, L. (1990) 'Paul Simon's Graceland, South Africa, and the Mediation of Musical Meaning', *Ethnomusicology*, 34:37–73.

—— (2003) *Sound of Africa! Making Music Zulu in a South African Studio*. Durham and London: Duke University Press.

Mitchell, T. (1993) 'World Music and the Popular Music Industry: An Australian View', *Ethnomusicology*, 37:309–37.

Negus, K. (1992) *Producing Pop: Culture and Conflict in the Popular Music Industry*. London: Edward Arnold.

—— (1996) *Popular Music in Theory: An Introduction.* Cambridge: Polity Press.

—— (1999) *Music Genres and Corporate Cultures.* London and New York: Routledge.

—— (2002) 'The Work of Cultural Intermediaries and the Enduring Distance Between Production and Consumption', *Cultural Studies* 16(4):501–15.

Peterson, R. and D. Berger (1975) 'Cycles of Symbol Production: The Case of Popular Music', *American Sociological Review*, 40:158–73.

Rothenbuhler, E. and J. Dimmick (1982) 'Popular Music: Concentration and Diversity in the Industry, 1974–1980', *Journal of Communication*, 32:143–9.

Schade-Poulsen, M. (1999) *Men and Popular Music in Algeria: The Social Significance of Raï.* Austin: University of Texas Press.

Taylor, T. (1997) *Global Pop: World Music, World Markets.* New York and London: Routledge.

Turino, T. (2000) *Nationalism, Cosmopolitanism, and Popular Music in Zimbabwe.* Chicago and London: University of Chicago Press.

Wallis, R. and K. Malm (1984) *Big Sounds from Small Peoples: The Music Industry in Small Countries.* New York: Pendragon Press.

—— (1992) *Media Policy and Music Activity.* London: Routledge.

White, B. (2000) 'Soukouss or Sell-Out? Congolese Popular Dance Music as Cultural Commodity', in A. Haugerud, M. P. Stone and P. D. Little (eds) *Commodities and Globalization.* Lanham: Rowman & Littlefield.

Contributors

Benoit Daviron is a senior researcher at the Centre de Coopération Internationale en Recherche Agronomique pour le Développement (CIRAD) in Montpellier, France. His research has focused on issues of food policy and food trade, in particular the organisation and regulation of tropical commodity chains (coffee and cocoa). Recently he has paid special attention to the function of international commodity bodies and standards in agricultural trade.

Niels Fold is a professor at the Department of Geography and Geology, University of Copenhagen. His research has focused on the dynamics in global agro-industrial chains with relevance for perennial crops in Ghana (cocoa, oil palm, shea nuts, and pineapple) and Malaysia (oil palm). Recently he started research on livelihood aspects of smallholders in agro-industrial chains originating in the Asia-Pacific, particularly in Vietnam (coffee, fresh fruit).

Peter Gibbon is a senior researcher in the Trade and Development Research Group at the Danish Institute for International Studies, Copenhagen. Over the last decade his work has focused on global value chains (particularly issues of governance) and on trade relations between Africa and developed countries. He has worked on governance and upgrading in African clothing chains (Mauritius and South Africa). His recent research is concerned with the organic standard-setting and regulation in Europe, and export of organic produce from African countries (in particular Uganda).

Michael Friis Jensen is an economist at the International Trade Department at the World Bank. He has worked extensively on agro-food standards and trade both at an industry level as well as at the multilateral level. His major country level experience has been in Kenya (horticulture) and Vietnam (seafood). He is currently involved in a research project that looks at best practices of donor interventions to create smallholder market linkages in four African countries and he also works on how to design development friendly carbon labelling schemes.

Charles Mather is an associate professor in the School of Geography, Archaeology and Environmental Studies. His research interest lies in the field of geographical approaches to agri-food restructuring. He has been concerned with the impact of market liberalization on the transformation of the citrus export sector in South Africa. More recently his research has focused on contemporary changes in the food economies of South and Southern Africa in the context of new trade regimes, the rise of supermarkets and new patterns of intra-regional investment. In 2007 he started a project on South Africa's intensive broiler industry.

Marianne Nylandsted Larsen is an assistant professor at the Department of Geography and Geology, University of Copenhagen. Her research has concentrated on market liberalization and agricultural restructuring and on coordination challenges in post-liberalized cotton market systems (Tanzania and Zimbabwe). More recently her research has focused on the impact of quality standards on trade in tea products from developing countries (India and Tanzania).

Poul Ove Pedersen was senior researcher (now retired) at the Danish Institute for International Studies. His research has focused on urban-regional development in Eastern and Southern Africa, with special focus on small towns and small enterprise development. More recently he has been concerned with the development of the transport and logistics system in Africa and its interaction with the agriculturally based commodity chains (in particular cacao, coffee, and cotton).

Tuulikki Pietilä is lecturer in social and cultural anthropology at the University of Helsinki. A major focus in her research has been the interplay of diverse global and local structures of value and meaning. She has investigated changing livelihoods and notions of personhood, morality, and gender in the neoliberal era in Kilimanjaro, Tanzania. Her current research explores the structures and networks of the World Music industry, with a particular focus on South African music.

Stefano Ponte is a senior researcher at the Danish Institute for International Studies. He conducts research on the changing role of Africa in the global economy. His research has focused on the restructuring of the coffee marketing systems in East Africa (Ethiopia, Kenya, Tanzania and Uganda). He is currently working on the political economy of food safety standards, environmental and social labels, and corporate codes of conduct – with specific reference to the Ugandan and South African fish export industries and the South African wine industry.

Index

The suffix *n* after a page number denotes a footnote; *tab* denotes a table

Africa
  economic performance, 9, 12–15
  food exports, 44, 53*tab*, 55–6, 70–4,
    71*tab*, 72*tab*
  foreign investment, 9, 12, 49
  geographical disadvantages, 10, 11*n2*,
    12, 13
  human labour exports, 75
  marginalization, 10–11, 15
  world export share, 9
Africa Trade and Development Act
  (2000), 191–2
African Growth and Opportunity Act
  (2000), 16*n1*
agricultural labour, 54
agricultural policies, 44, 64–5
  common agricultural policy (CAP), 4
    7–8, 64–5
  self–sufficiency, 47–8, 49, 60, 61*tab*,
    74
  see also food regimes; food trade
alcoholic beverages *see* legal drugs
Algeria, raï music, 245–6
Anglophone countries
  African music in, 255–7
  cotton sector, 165, 169–73, 174–7
  see also East Africa
Antilles, music industry, 260
Argentina
  citrus exports, 82*tab*
  soya exports, 67
Arrighi, G., 14–15
Asia, food export share, 70*tab*
Asian vegetables, 107, 109, 110, 116–17,
  117*tab*
Astaqé, Mulatu, 255
Australia
  citrus exports, 82*tab*
  cotton quality, 162

avocados, 107, 109, 111, 116–17,
  117*tab*

Baumann Hinde, 167, 170
Benin, cotton sector, 159*n2*, 166, 167–8
Berg Report, 10
Brazil
  citrus exports, 82*tab*
  cocoa exports, 148
  cotton industry, 159*n2*, 162
  food exports, 67
British Empire, 48–9, 58
  imperial autarchy food regime, 51–2,
    56–8
British Retail Consortium, Food
  Technical Standard, 114
Broken Flowers, 255
BSE crisis, 115
Buena Vista Social Club, 255
Burkino Faso, cotton sector, 166
Bush, President George W., 96
buyer–driven chains, 27, 28–31, 32, 92,
  99–100, 185
Byrne, David, 243

Cameroon, cocoa trade, 143, 148
Capespan, 86–7
capital movements, 14–15
Cargill, 169, 170, 175
Caribbean, music industry, 260
cereals trade, 72*tab*
China, cotton industry, 159*n2*
chocolate manufacture, 31, 135
  see also cocoa sector
citrus chain
  buyer-driven, 92, 99–100
  effect of liberalization, 80–1, 87–8, 90
  producer–driven, 81, 82–7, 99–100
  upgrading, 92
Citrus Exchange, South Africa, 82–7
citrus sector
  brand names, 95
  citrus black spot (CBS), 96–7